WALKING IN MADEIRA

About the Author

Paddy Dillon is a prolific walker and author of over 40 guidebooks, with contributions to a further 25 books. He has written extensively for outdoor magazines and other publications and has appeared on radio and television. *Walking in Madeira* was his first full-colour guide for *Cicerone*.

Paddy is a dedicated island-hopper who has visited Madeira several times, exploring widely and enjoying a huge variety of walking routes. He has walked alongside many levadas, penetrated deep into the *laurisilva* forest, followed narrow, rugged paths through the mountains and also visited Porto Santo and the Ilhas Desertas. Paddy uses a palmtop computer to write his route descriptions while walking, noting changes to routes and the recent signposting of trails. His descriptions are therefore precise, having been written at the very point at which the reader uses them.

Paddy is an indefatigable long-distance walker who has walked all of Britain's National Trails and several major European ones. Now living on the edge of the English Lake District, he has walked, and written about walking, in every county of the British Isles and guided walking holidays and walked throughout Europe, as well as in Nepal, Tibet and the Rocky Mountains. Paddy is a member of the Outdoor Writers and Photographers Guild.

Other Cicerone guides by the author

Walking in the North Pennines
The Mountains of Ireland
Walking in the Galloway Hills
The Irish Coast to Coast Walk
Walking on the Isle of Arran
Irish Coastal Walks
Channel Island Walks
Walking in the Isles of Scilly
GR20 Corsica – High Level Route
Walking in Madeira
Walking in the Canaries: Vol 1 West

Walking in the Canaries: Vol 2 East
The South West Coast Path
Walking in Malta
Cleveland Way & Yorkshire Wolds Way
The North York Moors
The Great Glen Way
The National Trails
GR5 – Through the French Alps
Walking in County Durham

WALKING IN MADEIRA

by

Paddy Dillon

2 POLICE SQUARE, MILNTHORPE, CUMBRIA LA7 7PY
www.cicerone.co.uk

© Paddy Dillon 2002, 2009
Second edition 2009
ISBN-13: 978 1 85284 531 5
First edition 2002
ISBN-10: 1 85284 334 9
ISBN-13: 978 1 85284 334 2

Advice to Readers

Readers are advised that, while every effort is made by our authors to ensure the accuracy of our guidebooks as they go to print, changes can occur during the lifetime of a particular edition. Please check the Cicerone website for any updates before planning your trip. It is also advisable to check information on such things as transport, accommodation and shops locally. Even rights of way can be altered over time.

At Cicerone, we are always grateful to have your information about any discrepancies between a guidebook and the facts on the ground – to info@cicerone.co.uk or by post. Useful updates received will be published on the Cicerone website after checking with the author.

Front cover: View of Pico Branco on the northern part of Porto Santo

CONTENTS

MADEIRA and PORTO SANTO
Location of routes and sections

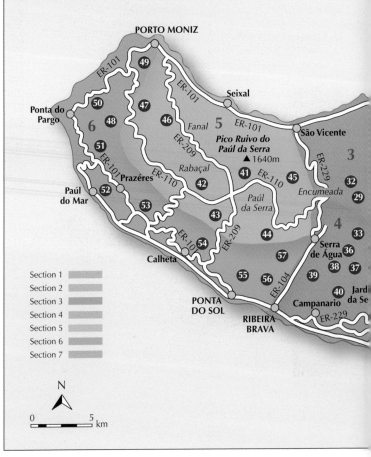

PORTO MONIZ

ER-101

49

Seixal

ER-101

Ponta do Pargo

50

47

46

Fanal 5

ER-101

São Vicente

48

6

ER-209

Pico Ruivo do Paúl da Serra
▲ 1640m

ER-229

3

51

Rabaçal

41 ER-110 45

32

29

ER-101

Prazéres

42

Encumeada

Paúl do Mar

ER-110

Paúl da Serra

52

53

43

44

4

33

Serra de Água

36

ER-101

ER-209

54

57

38

37

Calheta

55

56

39

ER-104

40 Jard da Se

PONTA DO SOL

Campanario

RIBEIRA BRAVA

ER-229

Section 1
Section 2
Section 3
Section 4
Section 5
Section 6
Section 7

N

0   5 km

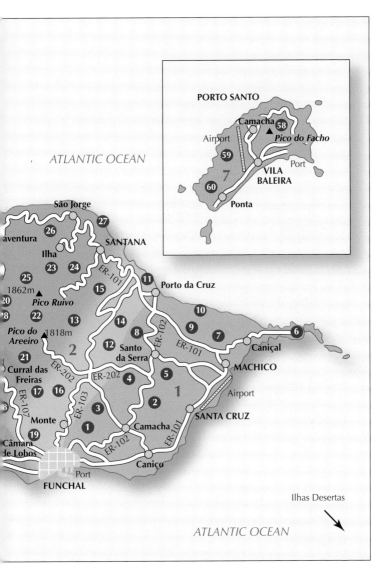

PORTO SANTO

Camacha

Airport

▲ 58
Pico do Facho

59

Port

VILA
BALEIRA

60

7

Ponta

ATLANTIC OCEAN

São Jorge

27

26

aventura

SANTANA

Ilha

23   24

25

1862m

ER-101

15

11   Porto da Cruz

20

Pico Ruivo

22

13

14

10

*Pico do
Areeiro*   1818m

8

ER-102

9

7

6

21

12   Santo
da Serra

Canical

Curral das
Freiras

ER-202

ER-202

4

5

MACHICO

17   16

ER-103

3

2

Airport

Monte

1

Camacha

SANTA CRUZ

19

Câmara
de Lobos

ER-102

ER-101

Caniço

Port

FUNCHAL

Ilhas Desertas

ATLANTIC OCEAN

9

Map Key

————————	road
━━━━━━━━	route on road (various colours)
————————	route (various colours)
●●●●●●●●●●●●	alternative route (various colours)
- - - - - - - - - -	other tracks or paths
▥▥▥▥▥▥▥▥▥	tunnel
⌒⌒◯⌒⌒	river/reservoir
▭▭▭▭▭▭	airport
Ⓢ Ⓕ ⓈⒻ	start point/finish point/start-finish point
ⒶⓈ ⒶⒻ	alternative start/alternative finish
◉	town/village
■	building
▲	peak
▣	parking
●	water feature
→	direction arrow
→	route direction arrow
●	other feature
⚲	church

```
0          1          2          3
|━━━━━━━━━━|██████████|██████████| km
```

The above scale applies to all the routes in the book.

Contour Key

▨	800-1000m	▨	1800-2000m
▨	600-800m	▨	1600-1800m
▨	400-600m	▨	1400-1600m
▨	200-400m	▨	1200-1400m
▨	0-200m	▨	1000-1200m

PREFACE TO THE SECOND EDITION

Madeira has undergone many changes since the first publication of *Walking in Madeira* and most are for the good. A tortuous road system once made it difficult to reach the start of many walks, but now a splendid network of road tunnels enables quick and easy access to many formerly remote places. Bus companies have adapted and altered their schedules, with more frequent services, more destinations and rapid access through the new tunnels.

While a handful of bars and restaurants have closed, many more have opened and there are more places offering accommodation around the islands in places that are popular with walkers. No longer should anyone feel confined to Funchal or the 'Hotel Zone', as they can walk from one hotel to another on long-distance routes. Walkers have not been forgotten as the island authorities have waymarked and signposted some splendid walking routes, improved and restored others, provided safety fencing and opened completely new trails.

All these changes meant that *Walking in Madeira* was ready for a complete overhaul. All the routes have been walked again and the route descriptions brought up to date. New routes have been added and all the relevant facilities have been checked. More and more walkers are seeking longer and more sustained routes across Madeira. Some routes are now structured so that they serve not only as day walks, but can also be linked end-to-end to create splendid long-distance walks. Improved full-colour mapping, more information and more photographs should allow walkers to get more enjoyment out of their visit to Madeira.

Paddy Dillon

Impossibly steep terraces and tiny cultivated plots produce abundant crops of fruit and vegetables

INTRODUCTION

Madeira and Porto Santo rise steep, rocky and remote in the Atlantic Ocean off the coast of Europe and Africa. The nearest island groups are the distant Azores and Canary Islands. All these islands enjoy a subtropical climate that many walkers find acceptable throughout the year. A compact and mountainous island, Madeira is criss-crossed by old paths and tracks, and is remarkably scenic and accessible. Water is conveyed round the island in charming flower-fringed channels called *levadas*, which offer anything from gentle strolls to extremely exposed cliff walks. Richly wooded valleys, rocky slopes, cultivated terraces and impressive cliff coasts can be explored, along with one of the best *laurisilva* forests in the world. This book describes a rich and varied selection of 60 walks to suit all abilities, covering the whole of Madeira and Porto Santo, as well as a cruise to the Ilhas Desertas.

LOCATION

Madeira is a small island of 750km^2 (290 square miles). It lies at 32°46'N/17°03'W in the subtropical Atlantic Ocean, about 600km (370 miles) from Morocco in North Africa, and about 950km (590 miles) from Portugal, to which it belongs. Its closest neighbours are Porto Santo, about 40km (25 miles) away, and the Ilhas Desertas, about 20km (13 miles) from Madeira at their closest point. Other islands are far from view, such as the Azores and Canaries, with which Madeira is loosely associated, since they all lie along the same huge fracture in the Earth's crust.

GEOLOGY

Madeira is essentially a volcanic island, although volcanic activity has long ceased. Basalt from deep within the earth spewed onto the ocean floor around 130 million years ago. Gradually, enough material built up for land to appear above the water, so that Madeira raised itself from the ocean about 2.5 million years ago. Some corals established themselves round the fringe of the island as it grew, and these are preserved as fossils in very limited areas.

The overwhelming bulk of the island is made up of ash and basalt lava flows shot through with dolerite dykes. It is thought that volcanic activity ceased around 25,000 years ago and the rock is now heavily weathered. Porto Santo is older and more weathered than Madeira. Although mostly basalt, Porto Santo features a central band of calcareous sandstone that produces a fertile soil in the middle of the island that has

Madeira is made up of thick layers of volcanic ash and lava flows criss-crossed with basalt dykes

eroded to form a magnificent golden beach.

HISTORY

The true story of Madeira's 'discovery' may never be known, but early records agree it was a densely-wooded uninhabited island. The many fanciful tales of Madeira's discovery don't tie in easily with historical documentation. Some early maps show the island and there is a suspicion that the Phoenicians may have been the first to set eyes on Madeira. Others say the Genoans discovered it. Some records state that the Spanish were in the habit of stopping off at

Porto Santo on trips between Spain and the Canary Islands. A strange story relates how an Englishman, Walter Machim, along with his wife and a companion, were marooned on Madeira and thus became the first temporary settlers.

Reliable records date from 1418, when Prince Henry 'The Navigator' of Portugal patronised voyages to seek new territories. João Gonçalves Zarco and Tristão Vaz Teixeira were leading one of these voyages around Africa in 1419, when they were blown off-course onto Porto Santo. While checking out possibilities for settling the island, they also discovered Madeira. In 1425 great fires were started to clear Madeira's native woodlands and open up sunny slopes for settlement and cultivation. In 1452 slaves were drafted in to work the land and dig a network of irrigation channels, or levadas. Christopher Columbus is said to have visited Madeira and Porto Santo in 1478, convinced that by sailing ever-westwards he would find India.

Madeira and Porto Santo, being remote from Portugal, were open to attack by pirates from Europe and Africa. The islands suffered several raids, resulting in the destruction of property, looting and the capture and killing of inhabitants. Fortifications were constructed, including a wall around Funchal in 1542, but most island communities were unprotected. In calmer times good trade links were developed, along with agriculture, and Madeira became known for producing fine wines. By 1662, following a marriage between Charles II of England and Catherine of Braganza, English merchants settled on Madeira and took key positions in the wine trade. English troops were stationed in Madeira in 1807 as Napoleon conquered more and more territory. In more settled times, during the 1850s, cholera wiped out thousands of islanders, while disease destroyed their vines. Banana cultivation developed, with the 'dwarf banana' proving the most suitable type for Madeira's climate.

Tourism has developed since 1890, with the climate making it a favourite winter destination for rich Europeans. Although Portugal was neutral in the War years, it suffered under a dictatorship and many Madeirans emigrated to other parts of Europe, or to Angola, Brazil and Venezuela. Madeira has been an autonomous region since 1976 and, following Portugal's entry into the EU, vast sums of money have been applied to its infrastructure. Tourism continues to boom and walking is an important pursuit for many visitors. A lively way to appreciate Madeira's history and heritage is to visit the Madeira Story Centre on Rua Dom Carlos I in Funchal, www.storycentre.com.

LANDSCAPE

Madeira's landscape is one of exceptional beauty and ruggedness. The first thing visitors notice is the steep slopes. Between the airport and Funchal these slopes are well-settled and dotted with white buildings. However, there are also plenty of trees and shrubs along with a splendid array of colourful flowers. Bananas and palms jostle with bird-of-paradise flowers and amaryllis, while further uphill there are stands of pine and eucalyptus. Exploring beyond Funchal, quiet wooded valleys feature exceptionally steep and rugged

Stone steps and paved paths were constructed through the forbiddingly steep and rocky mountains

slopes, with bare mountains at a higher level. The steepness of the slopes is always apparent, and anyone exploring on foot needs to find routes with acceptible gradients.

On the northern side of Madeira there are damp and green *laurisilva* forests. Water is abundant and in many places it is siphoned off along levada channels, through awesome rock tunnels beneath the mountains, to generate power and to irrigate cultivation terraces on the drier southern slopes of the island. Old roads, tracks and paths twist and turn so much that they present ever-changing views, while the network of new tunnels offers no views at all!

Variety is one of the great charms of the island, and there is plenty of variety beside the levadas, through the wooded valleys, over the mountain tops and along the rugged coastline. Old paths and mule tracks have been hacked from bare rock and constructed by hand to reach all parts of the island.

TREES AND FLOWERS

The moment Madeira rose from the ocean, terrestrial plants strived to gain a roothold. Maybe lichens and mosses eked out an existence in tiny crevices, sometimes thriving, then overwhelmed by later lava flows. A variety of plants, including flowers and trees, will have become established later. When Madeira was first discovered it was referred to as a well-forested

island. Unusually, most of the trees were *laurisilva* species, once common in the tropics millions of years ago but now much less common. Porto Santo was famous for its primeval 'dragon trees'. The first seeds to reach the islands could have arrived after floating on the ocean currents, borne on the wind or deposited in bird droppings. No one can know for sure.

Madeira has one of the largest *laurisilva* forests in the world, featuring the mighty til tree, bay tree and Madeira mahogany. There are delightful lily of the valley trees and intriguing wax myrtles, or candleberry trees. The mountains are covered in gnarled tree heather and tall bilberry. Those who trample heather and bilberry moors in Britain are surprised to find it grows so tall and dense on Madeira that it blocks the sunlight! The *laurisilva* is also termed 'cloud forest' as it draws moisture from mist or fine drizzle, condensing it and dripping it onto the ground, keeping Madeira well-supplied with water. This is especially the case on the densely-forested northern slopes. The 'cloud forest' is rich in ferns, mosses and liverworts, some of them endemic to Madeira, or known only from fossil records elsewhere in the world. Large areas are covered in ubiquitous bracken, especially the plateau of Paúl da Serra.

The bird-of-paradise flower is Madeira's national flower, while the 'Pride of Madeira' and amaryllis are popular. Entire books have been written on the endemic flora of Madeira;

Tree ferns and a host of smaller ferns grow abundantly in the dense and moist laurisilva 'cloud forests'

A delightful display of 'angel's trumpets' grow from a bush and are commonly seen early in the year

Madeira is blessed with lovely flowers including the 'bird-of-paradise', Madeira's national flower

Agapanthus was imported from African deserts and its tough root mass is used to bind steep earthen banks

200 species are indigenous to Madeira, the Azores, Canaries and Cape Verde islands, while 120 of these are endemic in Madeira. Add to this the number of plants that have been introduced, growing in gardens or under cultivation, and the species count becomes bewildering. Notable non-native plants include the soil-binding agapanthus and hydrangeas that flourish beside many levadas.

Porto Santo was almost rendered uninhabitable when rabbits were introduced, stripping the island of vegetation. Much of the island's plant life has been lost and some badly-eroded areas have had to be reforested. Non-native trees on Madeira include the invasive eucalyptus, mimosa and acacia, and efforts are being made to stop them spreading into the *laurisilva*. Vines grow on some lower, sunny slopes and there are plantations of 'dwarf bananas'. All kinds of fruit and vegetables are grown on terraces hacked from the mountainsides. Long-established gardens and parks are planted with exotic trees, shrubs and flowers. In some of the parks trees and shrubs are labelled, to help the visitor identify them in the wild.

To delve deeply into Madeira's wonderfully extensive and complex flora, visit the many botanical gardens around Funchal and elsewhere, or try the following books: *Plants and Flowers of Madeira,* by António da Costa and Luis de O Franquinho; *Endemic Flora of Madeira,* by Roberto Jardim and David Francisco; *Parks and Gardens of Funchal,* by Raimundo Quintal and Margarida Pitta Groz.

BIRDS

Creatures could only reach the 'new' volcanic islands of Madeira and Porto Santo unaided if they could fly, and such creatures included insects, bats and birds. While the species count is low, and some species are becoming alarmingly scarce, some birds are endemic to the islands. The long-toed pigeon lives in the most secluded parts of the *laurisilva* and is notoriously difficult to spot. Other birds include the tiny firecrest, smallest of Madeira's birds, as well as Madeiran varieties of chaffinch, grey wagtail, pipit and rock sparrow. The Madeiran storm petrel spends most of its time far out to sea and is rarely spotted, while other rare petrels choose remote and inaccessible cliffs as nesting sites. Specific bird-watching trips are available but if planning to do your own thing a useful book is: *Where to Watch Birds in the Madeira Archipelago,* by Claudia Delgado.

ANIMALS

Apart from lizards, which often over-run sunny spots and may have arrived clinging to driftwood, most land animals were brought to Madeira by settlers. The sea around the islands teems with large mammals, including several whale species, half a dozen species of dolphin and rare monk seals. There was once a thriving whaling industry operating out of Caniçal, where the Museu de Baleia, or whaling museum, echoes with the epic tale of 'Moby Dick'. Among the invertebrates there are delightful butterflies and honey bees, while small millipedes are seen almost everywhere.

The introduction of animals to these islands created problems, such as the plague of rabbits that stripped Porto Santo bare, or the goats that over-grazed the Ilhas Desertas. Madeira has such steep and dangerous cliffs that free-range farm animals are rarely seen. Cattle, sheep, goats and pigs tend to be confined indoors or kept on short tethers outdoors, while farmers cut and carry huge bundles of vegetation for fodder and bedding.

Madeira's 'crocodiles' – the coachloads of slow walkers sent out by the hotels every morning – are not dangerous, but should be avoided if at all possible! Try and cover as much distance as you can along popular levadas before they emerge. They travel very slowly and it is almost impossible to overtake them on the narrow paths.

PARQUE NATURAL DA MADEIRA

Much of the central and high ground in Madeira is designated as a vast 'Parque Natural' (www.pnm.pt). It includes virtually all the uncultivated

and uninhabited wild areas and especially the lush, dense *laurisilva* forest. The few buildings in the park are generally owned by the government, including the occasional 'Posto Florestal' or Forestry Post. Of prime importance is the conservation of the remaining *laurisilva* forest as a living ecosystem. Special areas include Fanal with its huge and ancient til trees, and the Parque Ecológico do Funchal, where native trees are being replanted. The bare, arid and rocky Ponta de São Lourenço is also protected. Its flowers are being conserved and badly-eroded slopes are being stabilised and revegetated.

The Ilhas Desertas are rich in bird-life and contain a breeding colony of monk seals, so the land and the sea bordering it are protected. A marine reserve has been established east of Funchal, the Reserva Natural Parcial do Garajau. Walkers should cause as little disturbance to the wildlife as possible.

FUNCHAL AND MONTE

Funchal is the biggest settlement in Madeira so familiarise yourself with it straight away.

Pick up a free town plan from the tourist information office and carry it with you always. All facilities are available, but anything that can't be obtained here has to be sought in mainland Europe! The town comes in three parts which are, from west to

Funchal is the largest settlement in Madeira and the buildings are stacked steeply above the sea

east, the Hotel Zone, Town Centre, and Old Town. If you are based in the Hotel Zone and walk into town you will pass the Parque de Santa Catarina and Jardim Municipal. Exotic trees and flowers can be studied free of charge at both. Other popular gardens around Funchal may charge an entry fee.

21

Throughout the Town Centre shops sell wine, embroidery and specific Madeiran souvenirs. The town centre is always busy and bustling, with flower-sellers on the streets, but there are also quiet pedestrian streets and charming squares. The Madeira Wine Company at Avenida Arriaga 28 is worth a visit. There are plenty of churches, ranging from the central Cathedral, or Sé, to the secluded English Church. Museums focus on topics as diverse as history, natural history, contemporary art, sacred art, photography, electricity and sugar! Start with the Madeira Story Centre on Rua Dom Carlos I. The fort on the Avenida do Mar is the seat of the government.

The main coastal road, and the narrow streets running parallel, lead to the Old Town, or Zona Velha, where the fort of São Tiago can be seen. The Old Town is very atmospheric, with its narrow streets, crumbling buildings and relaxed air.

Walking up the steep roads to Monte is very tiring; instead you can go there cheaply by bus, or use the more expensive *teleférico* from the coast. Attractions include a fine church above a shady square, and the Jardim Tropical Monte Palace. The most unusual and expensive way back to Funchal is to be pulled down a steep road in a wicker basket, or 'toboggan'.

Staying in Funchal

If your accommodation base is in Funchal, build up your knowledge of the place before and after each day's walk. Even if you choose a quieter base, you are likely to need to change buses there. All the bus companies on Madeira are based in the town, so it makes sense to spend an hour or so discovering where the bus stations and important bus stops are located. Time can be wasted, and buses missed, when walkers are wandering around aimlessly looking for this information at the last minute. Make it a priority!

Free town plans will be available from your hotel or from any place displaying tourist literature. There is no need to purchase a detailed town plan, although they are available. Most visitors are interested only in the narrow coastal strip between the Hotel Zone, town centre and Old Town. Shops and services are generally located in that strip, but you may wish to explore further inland, bearing in mind that there are some very steep and tiring roads.

Many visitors opt to stay in the Hotel Zone, obtaining a package deal that includes all meals. Others may take self-catering apartments or may be looking for a selection of fine restaurants serving evening meals. There are far too many restaurants to list, but visitors need to decide whether they want a cosmopolitan choice, or local fare. Tourists will frequently swap notes, but for decent local specialities, talk to local people. Generally speaking, if a menu comes in many languages, then prices are likely to be high. The restaurants favoured by Madeirans are down-to-

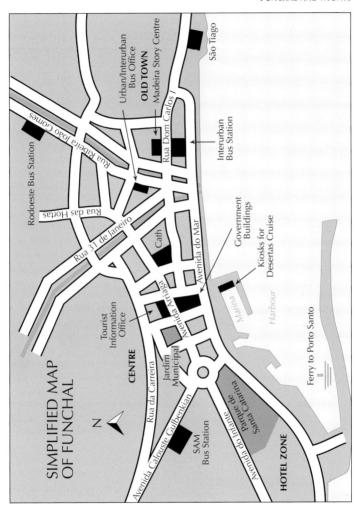

SIMPLIFIED MAP OF FUNCHAL

N

Rodoeste Bus Station

Rua Ribeira João Gomes

Rua das Hortas

Rua 31 de Janeiro

Urban/Interurban Bus Office
OLD TOWN
Madeira Story Centre

Rua Dom Carlos 1

São Tiago

Interurban Bus Station

Cath

Avenida do Mar

Government Buildings

Kiosks for Desertas Cruise

Marina

Harbour

Tourist Information Office

CENTRE

Rua da Carreira

Avenida Arriaga

Jardim Municipal

Avenida Calouste Gulbenkian

SAM Bus Station

Avenida do Infante

Parque de Santa Catarina

Ferry to Porto Santo

HOTEL ZONE

earth and remarkably cheap. Beware of the taxi driver who knows 'just the place you're looking for' as it will be miles from anywhere, and you'll be stuck there until he comes back!

PRACTICALITIES

GETTING TO MADEIRA

Flights

Madeira is very well served by charter and scheduled flights. Most visitors choose a package deal, so their flight, accommodation, meals and maybe even car hire are all included. This is fine for a first-time visit, but such an arrangement would limit anyone wishing to explore more extensively. Flight-only deals are possible, using the national carrier, Air Portugal (www.flytap.com), British Airways (www.britishairways.com), other national carriers or budget operators such as Easyjet (www.easyjet.com). Shop around as prices vary enormously. To fly to Porto Santo it is usually necessary to fly to Madeira first, then take a 15-minute 'hop' to the island.

Ferries

There are no ferries from mainland Europe to Madeira. Cruise ships and naval vessels berth at Funchal, but never give passengers long enough for a decent walk.

GETTING AROUND MADEIRA

Car Hire

Cars can be hired at the airport or delivered to you, but hiring a car is not recommended and can actually ruin a walking holiday. Despite recent improvements, there are still many narrow, steep, tortuous roads with blind bends and the danger of rockfalls. While a car is essential for walks on the plateau of Paúl da Serra, most of the walks in this guidebook are linear, in deference to the nature of the terrain. Arriving by car means returning to the car afterwards, which can be inconvenient and frustrating.

Bus Services

Madeira has a comprehensive and remarkably cheap bus network, providing vital lifelines to the most distant villages. You can buy a 'Bus Guide' from a tourist information office but it is not comprehensive. It is well worth visiting the various bus offices to pick up more information. Study timetables a day or two in advance of your walks and always be aware of your options.

Some services are fast and frequent while others may be slow and irregular. Service numbers are quoted in this guide, but they can and do change, so always seek the most up-to-date timetables. Fares can be paid as you get on the bus, but at bus stations you can buy a ticket before boarding. Bus stops are marked by a sign reading 'Bus' or 'Paragem', but sometimes the stop is indicated by a couple of yellow lines painted on the road. If in doubt about the location of

Madeira is best explored by bus, but you need to find where the bus stops are and obtain an up-to-date timetable

a bus stop, ask a local person for help and advice. Buses were used extensively to research the walking routes in this guide.

Horários do Funchal – Urban

Funchal is particularly well served by Horários do Funchal buses, which are yellow with a white stripe (www.horariosdofunchal.pt). Visit the office at the Centro Commercial Anadia to pick up a free 'urbanos' timetable and route map. In this guide these services are referred to as 'urban bus'.

The company operates information kiosks and kiosks dispensing tickets. Departures are from stops all around Funchal but are especially concentrated on or near the busy coastal Avenida do Mar. Refer to the 'urbanos' map to locate your stop, then watch for the route numbers displayed on the buses.

Horários do Funchal – Interurban

The far-flung suburbs of Funchal are also covered by Horários do Funchal buses – but grey and white with a yellow stripe (www.horariosdofunchal.pt). Services run to Camacha and Santo da Serra, to Monte and Poiso, then down to Faial, Santana and São Jorge, as well as to Curral das Freiras. Visit the office at the Centro Commercial Anadia to pick up a free 'interurbanos' timetable and route map. In this guide these services are referred to as 'interurban bus', and they operate from a small bus station with a nearby kiosk, just off the Rua Dom Carlos I in Funchal.

Sociedade de Automóveis da Madeira

This company's buses are green and cream with a white stripe (www.sam.pt). Services cover towns and villages east of Funchal to Machico, Caniçal and Ponta de São

25

Lourenço. Buses also climb from Machico to Santo da Serra and reach Porto da Cruz and Faial. In this guide these services are referred to as 'SAM bus'.

The company operates two bus stations, one on the Avenida Calouste Gulbenkian on the west side of Funchal and the other near Machico. Go to either station to collect free timetables.

Rodoeste

The Rodoeste bus company serves the whole western half of Madeira (www.rodoeste.pt). Bus colours are changing from grey and white with a red stripe to white with grey and red stripes. The most regular services run to Jardim da Serra and Ribeira Brava, decreasing in frequency as they extend further west and north. In this guide these services are referred to as 'Rodoeste bus'.

There is a bus station on the Rua Ribeira de João Gomes on the east side of Funchal, as well as roadside kiosks, and another kiosk at Ribeira Brava. Visit any of these for free timetables, or go to the Rodoeste office at Rua do Esmeraldo 50 in Funchal.

Taxis

Hire a taxi to move faster than a bus, or to reach a remote or awkward location. Taxi drivers operate meters on short runs, or work to an 'official' table of fares for long-distance runs, but it may be possible to negotiate a fare. Taxis are nearly always yellow Mercedes with a blue stripe, though some are minibuses suitable for small groups. Many taxis will provide drop-off and pick-up services at either end of linear walks but may apply a 'day rate' for the service. Some offer mini-tours with a commentary if required. If you see a taxi in a remote location, simply flag down the driver. Even if the car is full a message could be relayed to another driver.

Helicopter

For many years a helicopter has been parked by the harbour in Funchal and is available for hire. Charges are sky-high and time in the air is limited, but to see the island from the air and check out remote walking locations, this is a distinct possibility; tel 291-232882.

ACCOMMODATION

Accommodation in Madeira is mostly concentrated around the 'Hotel Zone' to the west of Funchal and a large hotel complex at Garajau, but there is plenty more around the island. Walkers looking for small and simple places to stay will find several options at a range of prices. Tourist information offices can supply a 'Hotel Guide' but addresses are arranged according to a grading system rather than location. Anyone using the guide to find accommodation in a specific location will find it frustratingly complex.

There are remarkably cheap pensions in the centre of Funchal, as well as an English B&B at Trejuno, halfway up to Monte at Livramento. Mountainside lodgings include the Pousada dos Vinhàticos and Residencial Encumeada above Serra de Água, or the Hotel Pico da Urze high on Paúl da Serra. Most towns and several villages offer small hotels and pensions, so there are great opportunities for long-distance walks from one place to another.

Campsites are very limited and wild camping is forbidden. Check the main tourist information website to find accommodation.

CURRENCY

The Euro is the currency of Madeira. Large denomination Euro notes are difficult to use for small purchases, so avoid the €500 and €200 notes altogether, and the €100 notes if you can. The rest – €50, €20, €10 and €5 – are the most useful. Coins come in €2 and €1. Small denomination coins come in values of 50c, 20c, 10c, 5c, 2c and 1c. The availability of banks and ATMs in particular areas is given within the walk descriptions. Many accommodation providers will accept major credit and debit cards.

LANGUAGE

Madeira's language is Portuguese and if you know Portuguese you will notice that Madeirans have their own accent and colloquialisms. Some Portuguese place-name origins have been lost, but most are highly descriptive and it is worth checking common ones in the

The Hotel Pico da Urze is the highest hotel in Madeira, at 1350m (4430ft) on the plateau of Paúl da Serra

Join the queues on Saturdays at popular roadside bakeries to sample the very filling Madeiran bread

language notes and topographical glossary in Appendix 2. Learn a few key phrases to negotiate a bus journey, ask for basic directions or order food and drink, but many Madeirans have a good grasp of English. Don't be afraid to practise the language; as so many islanders speak English, you can pick up words very quickly as someone can always explain things to you. No matter how bad you think you sound, be assured that the islanders have heard much worse.

FOOD AND DRINK

Food and drink are abundantly available around Madeira and the locations of bars and restaurants are given for each of the walking routes. Some

bars are very small and supply only a small range of refreshments, but they are always likely to serve bottled beer, wine, soft drinks, coffee and water. Restaurants vary enormously, with some catering very much for an international clientele, while others are very definitely pitched at local people. No matter what is on the menu, it is likely to be good and wholesome, and even if unfamiliar, is unlikely to upset anyone's stomach. If you have special dietary requirements, or allergies to certain things, such as seafood or gluten, then feel free to ask questions about items on the menu.

Two similar-sounding, traditional Madeiran dishes could cause confusion – *espada,* or black scabbard fish, and *espetada,* or spicy skewered beef.

Try them both and they may well become firm favourites. Be warned that traditional Madeiran bread, *bolo do caco,* can contain considerable quantities of meat! Other typical food and drink items are listed in the language notes in Appendix 2.

Ordinary tap water is perfectly safe and drinkable everywhere in Madeira. The water comes from occasional rainfall, or is condensed from the mist by the *laurisilva* 'cloud forest', filtering through great thicknesses of volcanic ash before being drawn off along levadas to water treatment plants, and from there into the domestic supply. It really couldn't be cleaner, but if you prefer to buy bottled water, that too is available. On Porto Santo the tap water comes from a desalination plant. Again, it is perfectly safe to drink, but some people dislike the taste and prefer to buy bottled water.

WEATHER

Madeira is generally hot and humid, but not excessively so, and is an all-year-round destination. That said, the summer months can be too hot and winter brings a slight risk of snow in the mountains. Some places look arid, but on the whole Madeira is remarkably green and well-watered. Porto Santo is hotter, drier and more brown than green. A typical day on Madeira starts sunny and clear, then during the afternoon clouds begin to form which may completely blanket the mountains. In the evening the cloud may break up, but not before the mist has dampened the 'cloud forest' on the high mountains.

The greater the altitude, the more likely there is to be cool air, mist and light rain, but it is seldom so severe that it forces walkers to retreat, and often it is sunny and clear all day long. However, Madeira is a subtropical island and, depending on the direction of the wind and the amount of moisture it carries, there can occasionally be prolonged or torrential rain, causing rivers and levadas to flood, which can result in rockfalls and landslides. Water also soaks deep in the bedrock, enabling many rivers to flow throughout the year. Porto Santo is lower and has less rain, so sea-water has to be desalinated, while the Ilhas Desertas have no permanent running water at all.

TOURIST INFORMATION

The main Tourist Information Office in Madeira is located centrally at Avenida Arriaga 16 in Funchal. It is usually open from 0900 to 2000 Monday to Friday and 0900 to 1800 at weekends. English-speaking staff can assist with queries about accommodation, transport, tours and visitor attractions, tel 291-211902, www.madeiraislands.travel. Small tourist information offices are found throughout Madeira and a list with contact details can be found in Appendix 3.

HEALTH ISSUES

There are no nasty diseases in Madeira, or, at least, nothing you couldn't contract in Britain. There are no venomous creatures apart from occasional bees, wasps and mosquitoes. However, Madeira's weather is generally hot and humid, which can cause excessive sweating, leading to distressing conditions such as prickly heat, dehydration and sunstroke. The sun can be very strong indeed on clear days, so it is sensible to wear long-sleeved, light-coloured clothing, and cover exposed skin adequately with sunscreen.

The health service on Madeira is good, as any ex-pat will happily confirm. There are two hospitals in Funchal and dozens of health centres and pharmacies scattered around Madeira, with a health centre also on Porto Santo. Treatment for EU citizens is free, but obtain and carry a European Health Insurance Card and consider taking out adequate insurance cover.

EMERGENCIES

Don't over-exert yourself on very steep and rocky slopes when it is hot and humid; this will leave you tired and weary when faced with a steep and rocky descent, when accidents are more likely to happen. Be alert to the danger of landslips and rockfalls, especially in wet and windy weather. Check the weather forecast and wear appropriate clothing. Walking in full

30

sun requires the use of a sun hat and sunscreen, and plenty of water needs to be carried. It is a good rule to walk in the sun, but rest in the shade. Carry a first-aid kit to deal with any cuts or grazes along the way. Madeira has no specific mountain rescue service. If you need assistance the Ambulance, Fire Service or Police could be involved in your rescue. All three services are contacted via the same emergency telephone number – 112.

PORTO SANTO

Three walks are offered on the island of Porto Santo for those who want to visit somewhere close, but quite different, to Madeira. The island is small and seems bleak and barren, but has all sorts of hidden places well worth seeking out. The three walks could be covered in one energetic weekend, or sampled bit by bit throughout a week. A long, golden, sandy beach is one of the highlights of Porto Santo, and each of the three walks can be extended along it for a very pleasant finish.

Flights

Very short flights operate between Madeira and Porto Santo. These can be booked online through Air Portugal (www.flytap.com), through a tour operator, or simply by turning up at the airport without booking, though this could involve a long wait until a seat is available. They take only 15mins.

Ferry

The Porto Santo Line ferry, the Lobo Marinho, runs daily between Madeira and Porto Santo, taking about 2½hrs per crossing. Day trips do not allow enough time ashore for a decent walk, though it might be possible to rush up and down Pico Castelo. Either book through a tour operator, or book directly with the ferry company, www.portosantoline.pt.

Moinho Bus

Moinho operates a bus service on Porto Santo. Obtain a timetable from the kiosk in Vila Baleira and study it carefully as services are quite limited.

Taxis

Taxis can be hired in Vila Baleira, conveying walkers quickly and cheaply anywhere on Porto Santo.

Accommodation

A few hotels are available on Porto Santo, notably in Vila Baleira and at Cabeço da Ponta. There is also a campsite. While it is possible to organise travel and accommodation separately, good deals are available if you book a ferry crossing with the Porto Santo Line and let them organise accommodation in one of the hotels at the same time. Assistance can also be sought from the Tourist Information Office, tel 291-982361.

MAPS OF MADEIRA

Maps of a quality similar to Ordnance Survey Landranger and Explorer maps of Britain are not available in Madeira. The Portuguese 'Serviço Cartogràfico do Exército' produces the 1:25,000 'Carta Militar', or military maps of

Several walking routes have been designated as 'PR' trails and are equipped with signposts and waymarks

Madeira. These are grossly out-of-date, but remain a good reference for walkers. Nine sheets cover Madeira, but they aren't sold on the island and so must be obtained before you go. The 'Instituto Geogràfico e Cadastral' produces the 1:50,000 'Ilha da Madeira' on two sheets, but this is also grossly out-of-date. The 1:50,000 Kompass map of Madeira and the 1:40,000 Madeira Tour & Trail map have good detail, are fairly up-to-date and use a grid system. Free tourist maps tend to be bland and lacking in detail.

Order your maps well in advance from British suppliers such as: Stanfords (12-14 Long Acre, London WC2E 9BR, tel 0207 836 1321, www.stanfords.co.uk), The Map Shop (15 High Street, Upton-upon-Severn WR8 0HJ, tel 01684 593146, www.themapshop.co.uk) or Cordee (3a De Montfort Street, Leicester LE1 7HD, tel 0116 254 3579, www.cordee.co.uk).

MAKING MULTI-DAY TRIPS

Walkers who hire cars on Madeira are quickly frustrated when they realise that most of the walks on the island are linear. The steep and rugged mountainsides of Madeira do not easily support circular walks. There are some circular walks in this guidebook, but the ascents and descents are sometimes formidable so most of the walks are linear, and most of them start and finish on bus routes. The end of one walk is frequently the start of

another walk, giving you the opportunity to keep walking, day after day, week after week, as long as you can spot the opportunities.

The walking routes in this guidebook are presented as a series of one-day walks, but they are also loosely grouped into areas for convenience. Within these areas, if you look carefully at the overview maps, you will see that some routes cross other routes, or have stretches that run in common. Once you have spotted this, it is a simple matter to chop and change between routes, to extend a route or choose a different destination, in the sure and certain knowledge that you have all the information to complete the walk, and know what facilities and services are available on the way.

The main issue for a long-distance walker on Madeira must be knowing in advance whether food, drink and accommodation are available along a route. This information is in the route descriptions. There is nothing to stop adventurous walkers altering and adapting routes to walk from hotel to hotel, for example from Encumeada to Paúl da Serra and Porto Moniz, or from Ponta do Pargo to Prazéres, Ponta do Sol and Ribeira Brava. There is no need to feel confined to the Hotel Zone in Funchal. Break free and walk from place to place. Madeira's accommodation guide isn't arranged logically for such an approach, but it still contains all the contact information you need. Wild camping isn't permitted on Madeira, but it still happens.

Bananas are grown in the southern parts of Madeira; the 'dwarf banana' is best suited to the climate

USING THIS GUIDE

This guide begins with easy, popular, shaded levada walks that are handy for Funchal. These 'starter' routes have good bus services and useful facilities along the way, so are suitable for cautious walkers.

More levada walks follow in eastern Madeira, as well as rugged coastal walks, taking walkers into steeper, rockier and more exposed locations. Old roads to Porto da Cruz and Santana offer insights into how people travelled long ago. Mountainous levadas are followed around Funchal and some of these cross particularly exposed cliffs. Always read the route descriptions carefully and don't tackle anything beyond your ability.

This guide uses strip maps, concentrating on features close to the walking routes. The routes are sometimes shown in groups, and are colour-coded to distinguish between them. *Colour is used only to distinguish between different routes and not to signify difficulty or any other feature.* Walkers can quickly see how to link one route with another, something that walkers are increasingly doing as they trek long-distance from hotel to hotel across Madeira.

Madeira is a place of steep and rocky slopes, and in deference to the nature of the terrain, very few of the walks are circular. Using a car is a great handicap on linear walks, and many walks run downhill rather than uphill, although there are exceptions. Some routes are roller-coasters with several ascents and descents. Cautious walkers should start with easy levada walks before tackling strenuous mountain walks.

The timings in this guidebook are only a rough estimate. Some walkers go faster than others and no-one is ever going to match them all the time. Giving precise timings on routes where all kinds of things can affect progress is difficult, but walkers need some sort of guidance if they are hoping to catch a bus late in the day. Take note of the timings and assess your progress. If you keep beating the stated times, then you probably always will, and you might safely plan to walk longer and further each day. If you keep falling well short, then you probably always will, and you should work out how much extra time you need in order to compensate. Pencil notes into the margins and refer to them!

The timings are purely *walking* times and do not take any account of time spent resting, stopping for lunch, or taking more than a few snaps with the camera along the way. Any time spent motionless, maybe contemplating an exposed cliff or levada walk, must be taken into account, so that by the end of the day you might find another two or three hours need to be added.

Walks in the central mountains take in rugged ridges and the highest peaks, sometimes on steep and rugged slopes and sometimes deep in the *laurisilva* forests. Again, levada routes can be mountainous and there are some particularly exposed cliffs. Some of the levadas feature long, dark, narrow tunnels where a torch (and even a spare torch) is essential. Buses giving access to and from the walks are always mentioned, but there are no buses over the plateau of Paúl da Serra, so a car or taxi must be used for access.

Rugged levada walks can be followed down from Paúl da Serra towards Ribeira Brava and Porto Moniz in the extreme north-west of Madeira.

The lengthy Levada Calheta/Ponta do Pargo can be followed for days through one of the quietest parts of Madeira, and indeed, this could be linked with more levadas to provide an even longer route. In fact, most of the walks in this guide can be linked with other walks, so that anyone who wants to walk long-distance from place to place has all the information they need.

Three walks explore almost the whole of Porto Santo, and there is a final chapter covering a short cruise to the Ilhas Desertas, where walking opportunities are very limited, but where it is possible to spot some of the rarest of Madeiran wildlife.

Always read the route descriptions carefully, carrying appropriate maps and equipment, not forgetting a torch if there are tunnels, and the most up-to-date bus timetables to get to and from the starting and finishing points. Step-by-step route descriptions are provided and many of the features shown in **bold** can be found on the sketch maps to aid navigation. Any shops, bars and restaurants along the way are mentioned; otherwise you need to be self-sufficient in remote locations and carry food and drink for the day. Bear in mind that on Saturdays bread is traditionally baked at roadside stalls.

There are plenty of splendid opportunities to explore Madeira and Porto Santo on foot, either by searching for your own routes, using this guide or taking part in a guided walking holiday.

Looking back towards Porto da Cruz and Penha d'Águia while climbing towards Larano

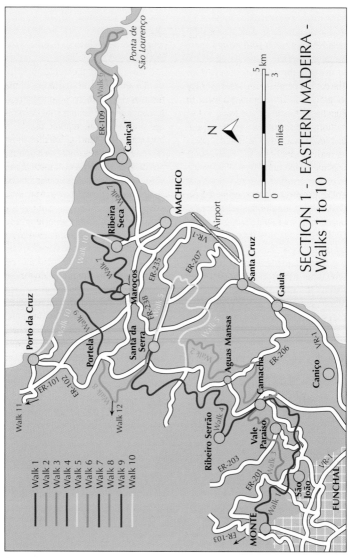

SECTION 1 - EASTERN MADEIRA - Walks 1 to 10

SECTION 1
Eastern Madeira

The eastern part of Madeira is very easy to get around for anyone based in Funchal or Machico. The walks in this section include some of the most popular levada walks on the island, as well as two stunning coastal walks and a convoluted route that offers the chance to explore a fine 'laurisilva' forest. It is unlikely that you will have any of these walks to yourself, and in the case of the hugely popular Levada dos Tornos, you could end up stuck at the end of a long 'crocodile' of walkers.

If visiting Madeira for the first time and staying in Funchal, then most of these walks are served by regular buses. Use urban and interurban buses from Funchal to reach different parts of the Levada dos Tornos and Levada da Serra. The main bus company for eastern Madeira is SAM, and they serve all the other walking routes. Always remember to check bus timetables carefully, preferably the day before you walk, to ensure that your outward and return buses suit your walking schedule.

Funchal and Machico were the first two urban settlements on Madeira, so naturally they have plenty of facilities and there are regular bus links between them. Funchal has the largest range of accommodation on Madeira, much of it lying west of town in the Hotel Zone. Those who want more peace and quiet can stay in Machico.

Cautious walkers, unsure of their ability, should sample some of the easier levada walks before attempting the more rugged coastal walks. The latter require a sure foot and a head for heights, and anyone lacking these attributes will have difficulty when they begin to explore the more mountainous parts of Madeira. First time visitors might prefer level levada walks until they feel more comfortable with the heat and humidity, and understand how the buses work. Keen walkers, however, will easily spot opportunities to link walks together in this region to create longer routes.

Bilberry grows as a tall and slender bush on the high mountains, often among heather trees

WALK 1

Levada dos Tornos: Monte to Camacha

Start	Monte, above Funchal – 219167
Finish	Camacha – 273170
Distance	16km (10 miles)
Total Ascent	330m (1080ft)
Total Descent	130m (425ft)
Time	5hrs
Map	Carta Militar 9
Terrain	Apart from short ascents and descents at the start and finish, mostly level walking on wooded or cultivated slopes, with one avoidable tunnel.
Refreshments	Snack bars and/or cafés at Monte and Babosas, around Lombo da Quinta and Nogueira. Plenty of choice at Camacha.
Transport	Urban bus 20, 21 & 48 serve Monte. *Teleférico* from Funchal to Monte. Urban bus 22 serves Babosas. *Teleférico* from Jardim Botânico to Babosas. Urban bus 29 serves Curral Romeiros. Urban bus 47 serves Hortensia Gardens and Jasmin Tea House. Interurban bus 110 serves Nogueira. Interurban bus 29, 77, 85 & 110 serve Camacha. Taxis at Monte and Camacha.

The popular Levada dos Tornos carries water from north to south through Madeira. The northern parts are largely confined to tunnels, but the southern part runs in the open and the general altitude is 600m (1970ft). The levada path is about 27km (16¾ miles). Strong walkers could cover it in a day, but most take two days, detouring into the basket-making centre of Camacha.

Snack bar, café, souvenir stalls and toilets.

Start at the bus stop at **Monte**' where a cobbled square at 550m (1805ft) is shaded by tall plane trees. ◀ Head for a candle-lit shrine and a drinking fountain dating from the 16th century. Walk up steep and cobbly steps to an imposing church. Enjoy views over Funchal then walk down steps to the Belomonte Restaurante Snack Bar. Wicker 'toboggans' are stacked ready to whisk people down to Funchal. Follow a level, cobbled road signposted Largo das Babosas. Pass the Jardim Tropical Monte Palace (www.montepalace.com) and follow the road past a *teleférico* station. ◀

Café do Monte, Restaurante Casa de Chá and toilets.

Walk gently downhill to a little chapel at **Babosas**. Café and tickets for *teleférico* to Jardim Botânico da Madeira. This shady spot has tall plane trees and views over a steep, wooded valley. Follow a cobbled track, the Caminho Rev Padre Eugénio Borgonovo, signposted downhill for the Levada dos Tornos and Curral dos Romeiros. Stop at a path junction. Either turn **left** up a path for the Levada dos Tornos, or turn **right** down a track instead. Both routes join at Curral dos Romeiros.

The rugged path on the **left**, signposted for the Levada dos Tornos, is broad and clear, climbing beside a rocky cutting. Eucalyptus and mimosa are followed by pines, then the **Levada dos Tornos** emerges from a tunnel. Follow the water downstream

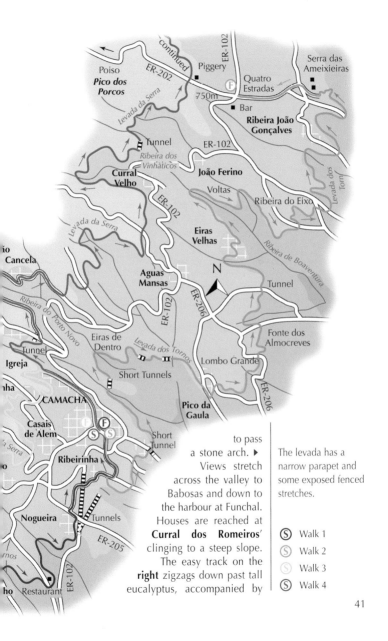

to pass a stone arch. ▶
Views stretch across the valley to Babosas and down to the harbour at Funchal. Houses are reached at **Curral dos Romeiros'** clinging to a steep slope. The easy track on the **right** zigzags down past tall eucalyptus, accompanied by

The levada has a narrow parapet and some exposed fenced stretches.

- Ⓢ Walk 1
- Ⓢ Walk 2
- Ⓢ Walk 3
- Ⓢ Walk 4

Walkers follow the Levada dos Tornos from
Choupana towards the popular Jasmin Tea House

street lights crossing a bridge over a bouldery river. The track climbs a slope of laurel and mimosa to reach another junction. Zigzag up to the left past tall eucalyptus to reach **Curral dos Romeiros**. Take an obvious track through the village, concrete or cobbled, avoiding turnings to right and left until almost on a road near a bus stop. ▶ Watch for a sign on the left and climb up steps for the **Levada dos Tornos**.

Urban bus 29

The levada is covered and flows beneath a house. Walk down steps and turn left to walk along a cobbled track. Watch for a sign and steps leading up to the levada. After leaving the village, the next valley has dense laurel cover. Mimosa and eucalyptus appear later, while agapanthus and brambles flank the path.

After looping round small valleys, the levada runs under a road and enters the **Choupana Hills** resort. Stay on the path as the facilities are private. A fence runs beside the levada and a few houses are passed. Cross a steep road near **Quinta do Pomar**, then pass a couple of houses and a water intake. ▶

Infrequent
Urban bus 94

Cross another steep road later, pass eucalyptus and a small farm, then make tight turns to cross a couple of streams. After a wooded stretch, the path runs beneath a road, ▶ then a battered road is reached near the delightful **Hortensia Gardens** tea house. Follow the levada further with views of Funchal and the Ilhas Desertas. Walk through woods and cross the ER-201 road on a bend at **Lombo da Quinta**. Eucalyptus and pines flank the path and there is a break in the trees near the **Jasmin** tea house. Walk into a quiet wooded valley, passing a pink house with apples alongside. The levada reaches a bend on the busy **ER-102 road**, so cross carefully. ▶

Urban bus 47

Urban bus 36A

Pass a water intake and keep left of the 'Tecnialia' building. Cross a road and turn left to continue along the levada (Bar 1 Maio is uphill). Apple trees give way to dense eucalyptus and mimosa.

Reach a **tunnel** entrance and either walk through it or over it. To go through, use a torch, noting that the path is narrow and the roof is low. The latter half drips and is wet before the tunnel exit. To go over, climb up earth

Urban bus 37 and
Bar Levada dos
Tornos.

steps and cross a wooded slope. Follow a concrete road to a tarmac road at **Pinheirinho** ◀ Turn left up the road, then right down the Estrada do Pinheirinho. Turn left along a narrow concrete access road to reach a house set back from the road. Walk down concrete steps and turn left down a steep path on a wooded slope to reach the levada near the tunnel exit.

Continue through woods to a road called the Rua do Pomar (Restaurante Casa de Chá) and turn right. The levada drifts away to the left and is less wooded. Chestnut and oak are seen while traversing the valley, and there is a knot of canes at the valley head. Cross the Vereda da Nogueira, then as the levada passes houses at **Nogueira**, the channel is covered in slabs. Don't follow it beyond the village, as there is a **tunnel** too low for comfort. Follow a dirt road and tarmac road uphill instead, passing the Pastelaria Candeeiro snack bar.

Interurban bus 110

Walk straight up through a housing estate, avoiding turnings to right and left. ◀ There are bus stops, if an early finish is needed; otherwise walk to a road junction facing the large 'Biofábrica Maderia' building. Turn left up the **ER-205 road**, then right along the Travessa João Claudio Nobrega. Walk straight downhill from a crossroads along the Caminho Fonte Concelos. The road winds down through **Ribeirinha**, passing a number of houses, pines and eucalyptus trees. Follow the road uphill, and note a sign on the right marking the continuation of the **Levada dos Tornos**. Take this turn if continuing directly with Walk 2, otherwise stay on the road.

The road climbs over a wooded rise. Turn left to along the Caminho Fonte Concelos, which later swings left and climbs steeply among tall trees. Cross a busy road and climb straight past a modern church to reach a fine square in the centre of **Camacha**.

CAMACHA

A monument on the square declares that the first game of football played on Portuguese territory took place here in 1875. Just off the square is a fine basket factory well worth a visit. There is accommodation, as well as shops, bars, restaurants and a bank with ATM. Interurban bus 29, 85 & 110 link Camacha with Funchal while bus 77 links with Funchal and Santo da Serra.

WALK 2

Levada dos Tornos:
Camacha to Quatro Estradas

Start	Camacha – 273170
Finish	Quatro Estradas on the ER-102 – 288204
Distance	18km (11 miles)
Total Ascent	150m (490ft)
Total Descent	100m (330ft)
Time	5hrs 30mins
Maps	Carta Militar 6 & 9
Terrain	Apart from short descents and ascents at the start and finish, mostly level walking on wooded or cultivated slopes. Some short rugged stretches.
Refreshments	Plenty of choice at Camacha. Basic bar at Quatro Estradas.
Transport	Interurban bus 29, 85 & 110 link Camacha with Funchal while bus 77 links Quatro Estradas with Funchal and Santo da Serra. Taxis at Camacha.

The second and less popular half of the Levada dos Tornos runs from Camacha into a series of well-wooded valleys. It ultimately reaches a dead-end, although it could be extended along the Levada Nova with reference to Walk 5. To finish, it is necessary to follow roads up to Quatro Estradas, with a view to catching the bus that links Santo da Serra with Funchal.

See map on pages 40–41.

45

A small waterfall and pool are seen on the Ribeira do Porto Novo while following the Levada dos Tornos

Head downhill from the modern church in **Camacha** to cross a busy road and continue straight down a quiet road, the Caminho Fonte Concelos. Turn right along this road, then right again to cross a wooded rise before dropping down towards **Ribeirinha**. Watch for a sign on the left, where a path leads down a slope of pines to the **Levada dos Tornos**. Turn left to follow the levada path.

Cross a steep road, then cross another steep road at some houses. Continue through woods and along a concrete path to reach more houses and a short tunnel, where the water from the levada runs through a pipeline. The path is good, but the tunnel roof is low. Emerge to follow the pipeline past a couple of houses on the side of a wide valley below **Camacha**. There are views in places, but other parts are well-wooded. Cross a footbridge and follow the pipeline through another **tunnel**, with good headroom.

Don't trip over concrete blocks supporting the pipeline as it runs towards the head of the valley, and the path may be wet and slippery as it narrows. Pass a water intake building then cross a step-footbridge over the **Ribeira do Porto Novo**, whose overspill may form a slender waterfall. Pass a weeping wall and turn round a densely wooded spur below **Eiras de Dentro** to enter a side valley. Watch for rocks overhanging the path, turn round the valley, then walk past chestnut and pine trees. Go under a little bridge to reach another short **tunnel**. There is a good path and good headroom, then a brambly corner. The next **tunnel** is curved, so a torch is useful, though the path is good and there is good headroom. ▶

The tunnel can be avoided by taking a path gently downhill, but climb steps up to the left later.

Later, there are some short exposed stretches, as well as views back across the valley to Camacha. Pass a mixture of trees and shrubs before crossing a steep and narrow road at **Pico da Gaula**. Follow a concrete path with street lights alongside and cross another steep and narrow road. ▶

Pass by a water intake and small reservoir; the path is broad as it turns round **Lombo Grande**. Cross the **ER-206 road**.

Agapanthus and tall pines grow alongside the levada.

47

Continue walking into denser woods then cross a narrow road where there are a few buildings at **Fonte dos Almocreves**. The levada passes pines to reach the head of a little valley where there are chestnuts and willows. The valley is mostly cultivated and, on leaving it, a steep concrete track is crossed. Turn into the next little valley, which is also cultivated, with a view down to the airport. Go through a short **tunnel** under a road, where the path is uneven and headroom is limited. Follow the levada onwards, passing a house and stands of pine and eucalyptus. ◄ Enter another little valley where the vegetation is tangled and willow grows at the head.

There are a few chestnuts here, and some of the pines later have charred trunks.

After turning round a tiny valley with a few houses and terraces at Eiras Velhas, pass a derelict house. ◄ The path then narrows and drops below the levada for a short while and the view down the valley reveals the Ilhas Desertas. Take care on a narrow concrete parapet along the rocky edge. Head into a steep-walled, well-wooded gorge, and cross a step-footbridge over the Ribeira dos Vinháticos. There is another rocky edge to negotiate. Turn into a side valley and admire the terraces in the main valley. Willows grow at the head of the side valley, then pines and eucalyptus. The path becomes concrete and has street lights, leading past houses to cross a concrete road at **Ribeira do Eixo**.

Masses of agapanthus grow beside the levada.

Follow the levada past nurseries, taking in loops before passing a circular reservoir and crossing a road. After a short walk, cross another road, then turn round a blunt nose on a hillside into a little valley. ◄

On leaving the valley turn a corner, with a view down to the airport and the Ilhas Desertas beyond. Walk past pines and chestnuts before gaining another view, with more mimosa and tall eucalyptus, and agapanthus alongside. There is a rocky stretch before another turn into the next little valley, where willows grow around the valley head. On leaving the valley the mixed woodlands include laurels. Cross a steep tarmac road and pass a house below **Ribeira João Gonçalves**.

Tall pines, mimosa and eucalyptus grow on the hillside, and tall mimosa in the valley.

Head into the next little valley, where there are views of small farm buildings. The head of the valley is a jungle, but there is later a view down the main valley, drained by the Ribeira de Santa Cruz. To leave the **Levada dos Tornos**, watch for a pylon line above. When standing immediately beneath it, turn left to cross the levada and climb cobbled steps. A path rises beside a field and reaches a couple of houses at **Serra das Ameixieiras**. Turn left up a steep cobbled road, then rise more gently to a crossroads. Climb steeply up the Caminho de Pedreira, passing tall pines and cedars. Turn right up the Rua Mary Jane Wilson, climbing from woods to reach a junction with the ER-102 road at **Quatro Estradas** at 750m (2460ft). There is a very basic bar off to the left in the direction of Camacha.

WALK 3

Levada da Serra:
Campo do Pomar to Camacha

Start	ER-201 road above São João de Latrão – 242157
Finish	Camacha – 273170
Distance	10km (6¼ miles)
Total Ascent	120m (395ft)
Total Descent	100m (330ft)
Time	3hrs 15mins
Maps	Carta Militar 6 & 9
Terrain	The levada path is clear, level and easy to follow; generally well wooded with some cultivated areas.
Refreshments	Bar at Achadinha. Plenty of choice at Camacha.
Transport	Urban bus 47 to São João. Interurban bus 111 serves Achadinha. Interurban bus 29, 85 & 110 link Camacha with Funchal while bus 77 links with Funchal and Santo da Serra. Taxis at Camacha.

The Levada da Serra do Faial can be walked in a day but most walkers break halfway and head for

See map on pages 40–41.

Camacha. The full length of the well-wooded levada path measures 23km (14¼ miles) and rises from 750m (2460ft) above Campo do Pomar to 800m (2690ft) above Camacha. The levada itself was drained many years ago and in recent years a water pipeline has been buried beneath the path.

No bus runs to the start, so use Urban bus 47 to reach a point at 630m (2065ft) on the ER-201 road above **São João de Latrão**. When the bus turns downhill, continue along the bendy high road to pass the football stadium at **Campo do Pomar**. Turn right at a crossroads up the cobbled, well-wooded Caminho do Pico do Infante. Turn right after a bendy stretch, but as the way is not signposted, watch for little manholes and the concrete edge of the disused **Levada da Serra** at 750m (2460ft).

Walkers follow the wooded Levada da Serra, seen here with a fringe of agapanthus which binds the earth banks

There is no water in the narrow channel and the slopes are covered in eucalyptus, chestnut, laurel and pine. Later the levada passes through mostly eucalyptus,

which grew up on the slopes of **Pico Alpires** after a fire, though a few charred chestnuts survive.

The ground cover is bracken and brambles, with agapanthus beside the path. There are glimpses of Funchal before a ruined stone building is passed. Walk round a valley above **Lombo da Quinta**, noting a few habitations below the levada and a view of the Ilhas Desertas. ▸ Leaving the valley, cross a cobbled track and a short tunnel at the same time.

Walk through dense woodlands and cross a bridge over the bouldery **Ribeiro da Abegoaria**. Swing round a bend where there are tall pines, oaks and laurels, covered in ivy. Pass a blocked gateway on the left, then cross a track leading up to the grand old house of **Quinta de Vale Paraiso**. Views from this point take in the Ilhas Desertas. The track beside the levada runs though lovely mature woodlands. Cross the **ER-203 road** near a house called Casa do Reviver ▸

The levada path is flanked by trees, with a few houses above and below, and tangled terraces. Swing round across two streams, later crossing a steep road, the Caminho Ribeira Grande. A house called Quinta Proteas is just uphill. Continue along the wooded path, noting pines growing in the valley, though there are other well-established trees, including oaks with scorched trunks. ▸ Pass close to a massive concrete buttress that holds a sports ground in place. The path is pleasantly wooded and crosses a narrow road called the Caminho da Madeira above the **Casais de Alem**.

There are plenty of eucalyptus trees, though oaks also grow alongside the levada, as well as banks of gorse. Camacha is seen, but the levada describes great loops and the village doesn't get any closer. A slope covered in pines gives way to denser woods. Later, drop down steps onto a road and turn left to reach **Achadinha**. ▸

Walk straight through a crossroads signposted 'Levada da Serra – Faial'. A concrete road passes a few houses, with the levada to the left. A rugged track and clear path lead into lovely mixed woods. A track leads past houses and reaches a crossroads with the Caminho

Later, you can see what the slopes were like before the fire, passing well-established chestnut, oak, mimosa and laurel woodland.

Infrequent interurban bus 112 to Funchal.

The higher parts of the valley feature rampant bracken and gorse.

Snack Bar Moisés and interurban bus 111.

51

If the Levada da Serra is broken at Camacha, have a look inside the basket-making factory in the village

Municipal da Portela (bar uphill). Either continue to Santo da Serra via Walk 4, or turn right and follow the road down to **Camacha**.

WALK 4
Levada da Serra:
Camacha to Santo da Serra

Start	Camacha – 273170
Finish	Santo da Serra – 298218
Distance	20km (12½ miles)
Total Ascent	120m (395ft)
Total Descent	140m (460ft)
Time	6hrs 15mins
Maps	Carta Militar 6 & 9
Terrain	The levada path is clear, level and easy to follow; generally well-wooded with some cultivated areas.

Refreshments	Plenty of choice at Camacha. Two bars at Ribeira Serrão. Plenty of choice at Santo da Serra.
Transport	Interurban bus 29, 85 & 110 link Camacha with Funchal while bus 77 links Santo da Serra with Camacha and Funchal. SAM Bus 20 links Santo da Serra with Machico and Funchal. Taxis at Camacha and Santo da Serra.

See map on pages 40–41.

The second part of the Levada da Serra do Faial runs from Camacha to Santo da Serra. Apart from the initial climb from Camacha, the levada rises gradually from 800m to 820m (2625ft to 2690ft). A road is used at Ribeira Serrão, but for the most part the levada runs round quiet, often well-wooded valleys. At the end, either drop to Santo da Serra or continue along the Levada da Portela.

Leave **Camacha** by walking up the road signposted for Santo da Serra, known locally as Santa da Serra. Turn left at the Super Mercado Vila da Camacha and follow the quiet Caminho Municipal da Portela uphill. Turn right at a crossroads to follow the **Levada da Serra**. The track is wooded, with street lights alongside, crossing a stream and traversing the other side of a valley, where there are more houses. Follow the track onwards when the levada suddenly ducks into a **tunnel** on the left. Walk up to a road, which is followed only a few paces downhill before turning left at a junction. Walk down the road a short way to see the **tunnel** again on the left. The Levada da Serra is buried beneath the road for 3km (2 miles). Eucalyptus and oak grow beside the road, though later there is more terracing and cultivation, with plenty of houses stacked on the sunny slopes. The road eventually swings round to the right and crosses a bridge over the Ribeira do Porto Novo at **Ribeiro Serrão** (two bars). Keep to the road and pass through a cutting surmounted by a small bridge at **Cancela**, then swing into a couple of side

53

valleys. When the road begins to run downhill, turn left along another road. It quickly leads onto a track and the levada is seen again on the left.

The track crosses a slope of pine and eucalyptus, though a line of oaks march beside it. Enter a pleasant little valley and cross a concrete road. ◄ There is another wooded stretch, as well as a bare landslip area. The levada makes a pronounced left bend in the trees and crosses a road. Keep following the clear path alongside. Passing above **Curral Velho**, mounds of crushed stone can be seen down in the valley. The levada runs to the head of the wooded valley, with oaks beside the track, as well as broom and tree heather. Cross a stout bridge over the **Ribeiro dos Vinháticos** and walk on top of a massive stone buttress. There are denser woodlands around a derelict building, then vigorous growths of hydrangeas beside the levada, while the next valley is richly wooded. ◄

Walk through a short **tunnel** and continue along the levada path. Cross a bridge in the next valley and note how the water is drawn off along a lower levada. Keep

The oaks are a trademark for the route, while the slopes carry plenty of broom.

Views down the valley frame the Ilhas Desertas.

Another well-wooded stretch of the Levada da Serra, with a regular line of oak trees planted alongside

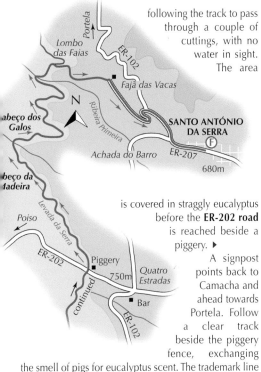

following the track to pass through a couple of cuttings, with no water in sight. The area

map continued from pages 40–41

Ⓕ Walk 4

is covered in straggly eucalyptus before the **ER-202 road** is reached beside a piggery. ▶

A signpost points back to Camacha and ahead towards Portela. Follow a clear track beside the piggery fence, exchanging the smell of pigs for eucalyptus scent. The trademark line of oaks and hydrangeas still march beside the levada. ▶ Eucalyptus trees have been felled near the **Ribeira da Serra de Agua**, beyond which grow denser stands of laurel and tree heather, some of them hoary with lichens. The levada makes a series of loops through rampant vegetation then reaches a broad and clear track at **Lombo das Faias**. The levada is abandoned here but can be followed to Portela by referring to Walk 8.

To finish at Santo da Serra, turn right and follow the track down through wonderfully mixed woods. There are a couple of houses to the left on leaving the woods, then a minor road swings left and right to drop down to the main **ER-102 road**. Turn right and follow the road

To leave the walk here, go down to Quatro Estradas for buses to Santo da Serra or Funchal.

There are fine views across the eastern parts of Madeira, with pleasant loops and laurel trees further along.

carefully round a right-hand bend. There are bus stops here; otherwise turn left along the **ER-207 road** as signposted for **Santo da Serra**.

SANTO ANTÓNIO DA SERRA

Commonly abbreviated (as in this guide) to Santo da Serra, this long and straggly village has a whitewashed church at its centre and offers accommodation, shops, bars, restaurants and an ATM, as well as a popular park and nearby golf course. Interurban bus 77 runs to Camacha and Funchal, while SAM Bus 20 runs to Machico and Funchal.

WALK 5

Levada Nova:
Quatro Estradas to Santo da Serra

Start	Quatro Estradas on the ER-102 – 288204
Finish	Santo da Serra – 298218
Distance	13km (8 miles)
Total Ascent	260m (855ft)
Total Descent	190m (625ft)
Time	4hrs
Map	Carta Militar 6
Terrain	Steep roads and a difficult path down into a valley, then the levada is easy, level and well-wooded. The road-walk up to Santo da Serra starts steep and gradually levels out.
Refreshments	Basic bar near Quatro Estradas. Plenty of choice at Santo da Serra.
Transport	Interurban bus 77 links Funchal with Quatro Estradas and Santo da Serra. SAM Bus 20 links Santo da Serra with Machico and Funchal. Taxis at Santo da Serra.

The Levada Nova offers a pleasant walk across wooded and cultivated slopes high above Santa

Cruz and the airport. Buses don't cross the levada, but it can be reached from Quatro Estradas and Santo da Serra. The levada path runs at a general level of 500m (1640ft), but access to it involves walking downhill first, later finishing with a road-walk up to Santo da Serra.

Quatro Estradas is a crossroads at 750m (2460ft) on the ER-102 road between Camacha and Santo da Serra. Follow a road downhill, the Rua Mary Jane Wilson, passing mimosa, eucalyptus and pine. Turn left down the steep Caminho de Pedreira, passing tall pine and cedar. Go straight through a crossroads to walk more gently down a cobbled road. Turn left round a steep bend to reach houses in fields at **Serra das Ameixieiras**. Turn right down a narrow cobbled path beside a field and follow cobbled steps down a wooded slope to the **Levada dos Tornos**.

Turn left along the levada to follow its bendy course across a densely wooded slope. Watch carefully to spot a narrow path descending to the right. This is steep, worn and awkward, leading to a concrete footbridge over the **Ribeira de Santa Cruz** at 490m (1610ft). Stone steps lead quickly up to a levada. Turn right, or maybe consider a short detour left to see how water is drawn from the river. The **Levada Nova** runs downstream through a wonderfully wild and wooded valley. It can be wet in places with a slippery path. There is a rocky stretch and a view of a little waterfall, then a cultivated slope is crossed. After picking a route along another rocky edge, pass a water intake and cross a steep concrete road at **Moinhos da Serra**. ▶

An earth path is flanked by agapanthus and mimosa as the levada curves round a small valley. Cross a step-footbridge in tall mixed woods and cross another steep concrete road, passing a water intake and a house above **Achada da Morena**. Swing round into the next valley, with a good view before eucalyptus blocks it.

Agapanthus flanks the path and the trees are mostly tall eucalyptus.

Agapanthus and brambles flank the path on leaving the valley, with mimosa below. Turn round the slope and enter another valley, crossing another step-footbridge. Mimosa and eucalyptus flourish on leaving the valley. Continue towards the head of the

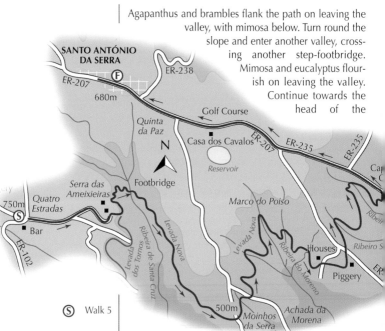

main valley, crossing a short exposed rocky slope. The **Ribeira do Moreno** is spanned by a step-footbridge.

Cross a short, exposed, rocky stretch as you leave the valley, passing tangled eucalyptus in a little side-valley. Turn round a slope bearing burnt tree trunks, with mimosa and eucalyptus. Enter another little side-valley full of eucalyptus and cross another step-footbridge. Pass a couple of **houses**, then head back into woods. Mimosa, then agapanthus and brambles flank the path. Cross a concrete road above a piggery, then cross the **ER-207 road**.

The levada passes a building and enters the valley of the **Ribeiro Seco**. Eucalyptus grows at the head of the valley, where a final step-footbridge is crossed. Mimosa grows as the levada leaves the valley. Walk round the valley of the **Ribeiro do Lugarinho** where mixed woodlands give way to pine, which in turn gives way to more mimosa and eucalyptus. The levada makes a couple of tight turns, reaching a road above the white **Capela dos Cardais** where there is a view of Ponta de São Lourenço. To omit the final road-walk arrange to be met by car at this point.

Turn left to follow the road steeply up a wooded slope. Turn left along the ER-235 then turn right along the ER-207, passing a large golf course and the **Casa dos Cavalos** (a horse-riding centre with a classic car show-room and a bar-restaurant). Keep following the road, enjoying views east to the rugged Ponta de São Lourenço and west to Pico do Areeiro. Pass a road junction at **Quinta da Paz** and continue along a more wooded stretch of road to finish in **Santo da Serra** at 680m (2230ft). ▶

For facilities see page 56.

The final stretch of the Levada Nova leads to the Capela dos Cardais and the road up to Santo António da Serra

59

WALK 6
Baia d'Abra and Ponta de São Lourenço

Start/Finish	ER-214 road at Baia d'Abra – 410237
Distance	7km (4¼ miles)
Total Ascent	450m (1475ft)
Total Descent	450m (1475ft)
Time	2hrs 30mins
Map	Carta Militar 7
Terrain	Good paths and steps cross steep slopes and cliff edges. Several stretches have safety fencing.
Refreshments	Possible snack van at the Baia d'Abra. Bars and restaurants back along the road to Caniçal.
Transport	SAM bus 113 serves Baia d'Abra from Funchal, Porto da Cruz, Machico and Caniçal.

The Ponta de São Lourenço is the shattered, battered easternmost point of Madeira, a place of sheer cliffs, rocky coves and jagged edges. The area is protected on account of its wild flowers, while bird-watchers hope to spot the rare Berthelot's pipit. The further east the walk proceeds, the more remarkable the scenery, but there is no way across the rocky gap of Boqueirão.

Start from the road-end car park at **Baia d'Abra**. There is a view of a lighthouse on Ilhéu do Farol, as well as a pierced headland beneath the furthest point reached on this walk. The Ilhas Desertas lie far out to sea. A signpost names the trail as the PR8 to Sardinha. Visitors are requested to stay on the marked paths, as the area has been extensively re-vegetated. ◀

Rocky areas teem with lizards on sunny days.

Walk down a clear path and cross a **footbridge** then climb up broad wooden steps. Pass through a tumbled wall where there is a 'Parque Natural' sign. The path is quite obvious and runs down to a gap where there are remarkable cliff views and stacks of rock at **Pedra Furada**, all protected by fencing. ▶ Follow the path up a rocky slope and head down to another gap in the cliffs, where the towering rock of Ilhéu do Guincho is framed by the rocky arms of a dramatic cove, with colourful, contorted, banded cliffs. The distant island of Porto Santo can be seen. The path roughly contours round a slope and reaches a remarkably narrow and exposed rocky ridge at **Estreito**. The path is fenced on both sides and views are exceptional. ▶ Drop down from the ridge to reach a path junction on a gentler slope.

Keep left and follow the path across an easy slope, reaching yet another gap featuring great views. Signs beg visitors to stay on the path, so turn right and pass above the solitary palm-shaded house of **Casa do Sardinha**.

▶ Another junction is reached just beyond the house, where a sign warns that the path running uphill can be dangerous. It is certainly steep, and the gravelly pumice underfoot is slippery so tread on bare rock wherever possible. The top of the hill boasts twin summits at 150m (490ft). There is a splendid view across the yawning gulf of Boqueirão, which cannot be crossed. The Ilhéu do Farol and its lighthouse can be seen, as well as the Ilhas Desertas, Porto Santo and much of eastern Madeira.

Note how varied the rock is, with crumbling pumice, knobbly breccia and tough lava.

Look left while following the ridge for complex cliff views.

An early 20th-century residence reached by boat from a nearby quay, this is now used as a centre for the Reserva Natural da Ponta de São Lourenço.

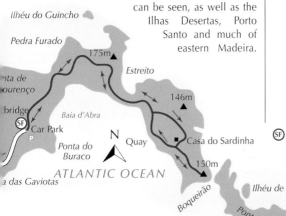

Ilhéu do Guincho
Pedra Furado
175m▲
Estreito
nta de
ourenço
146m▲
bridge
Baia d'Abra
SF Car Park
N
Quay
Casa do Sardinha
SF   Walk 6
Ponta do Buraco
150m▲
ATLANTIC OCEAN
a das Gaviotas
Boqueirão
Ilhéu de Agostinho
Ponta de São Lourenço

A path crosses steep slopes, followed out onto the rugged Ponta de São Lourenço and back again

Descend and keep left at the path junction, heading down a bouldery slope to reach a footbridge and a spur path leading to a **quay**. Cross the footbridge and climb to a higher junction, then turn left. All that remains is to retrace steps back to the road-end, enjoying all those wonderful views in reverse.

WALK 7

Levada do Caniçal: Maroços to Caniçal

Start	Maroços – 318232
Finish	Caniçal tunnel – 350226 or Caniçal – 375232
Distance	13km or 20km (8 or 12½ miles)
Total Ascent	50m (165ft)
Total Descent	210m (690ft)
Time	4hrs or 6hrs 30mins
Maps	Carta Militar 6 & 7
Terrain	The level levada crosses steep wooded or cultivated slopes. The path is good, but narrow and more exposed above Caniçal.
Refreshments	Bars at Maroços. Bar on the route above Ribeira Seca. Bar near the Caniçal tunnel. Plenty of choice at Caniçal.
Transport	SAM Bus 156 serves Maroços from Funchal and Machico. SAM Bus 113 serves the Caniçal tunnel and Caniçal from Funchal and Machico.

The Levada do Caniçal offers a pleasant route through the Machico valley at around 220m (720ft). Fruit and vegetables grow on the sunny, south-facing slopes, but the levada also runs into shady, well-wooded side-valleys. Either finish at the Caniçal tunnel, or walk through the tunnel and enjoy a rather more exposed stretch of the levada to finish in the coastal village of Caniçal.

Walk up the road from the Snack Bar Estevão at **Maroços** and turn right up the steep Caminho do Lombo do Talho. Step to the right at the second pedestrian crossing to find a concrete ramp leading onto the **Levada do Caniçal**. From here the levada runs downstream through the Machico valley and is almost level.

Listen to people talking and children playing, dogs barking and cockerels crowing. Few valleys are as populated and lively as this!

One by one, the Ilhas Desertas sail into view out at sea.

◀ The broad concrete path beside the levada gives way to a narrower path heading into a side-valley, passing small houses and cultivation terraces. Cross the Ribeira das Cales at the head of the valley, then look down on Maroços while turning a pronounced bend. Note the flight of steps called the Vereda do Lombo da Roçada, part of the PR5 trail described in Walk 9.

The path is concrete as it passes houses then it becomes earth as it passes through a narrow side-valley where a mossy cliff drips water. Leave the little valley for a fine view down the main valley to Pico do Facho, which rises between Machico and Caniçal. ◀ The path becomes concrete and crosses the Vereda do Cabecinho then swings into another side-valley drained by the **Ribeira Grande**. All kinds of fruit and vegetables grow on the terraces. Turn round the head of the valley and follow an earth path, rocky in places, with mimosa growing alongside pine and eucalyptus.

Turn round another little valley and meander past small houses. Another rocky stretch leads past a cave and through a short **tunnel**. Emerge with a view of Machico and continue walking.

Ⓢ Walk 7

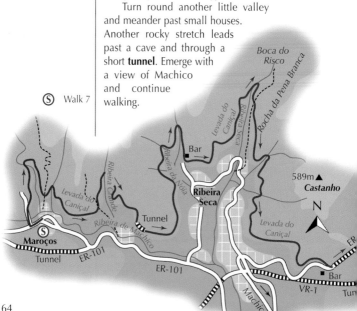

Although the levada has been cut from rock, there is no real sense of exposure, despite overhanging rock. Turn left round a corner at a water intake building to see a big valley drained by the Ribeira Seca. Several little side-valleys are negotiated while walking round this valley. The first little valley is under cultivation, while the next is dense with mimosa trees. The valley of the **Ribeira da Nóia** is long and cultivated, with only small huts and terraces and no habitations in view. Overlook the bustle of the main valley while crossing the concrete Caminho da Nóia beside the **Bar O Jacaré**.

Turn round into another little valley, passing Vivenda João de Gois, then turn a rocky corner and cross the Vereda dos Loureiros on the way into the next valley. The head of the valley, where the **Ribeira Seca** is crossed, is cultivated, but also features plenty of mimosa. Only a few huts are seen on the terraces around the head of the valley. Walk past a rocky cut, then notice a path called the Vereda da Boca do Risco slicing downhill to the right, marked with street lights. ▶

Bar Boca do Risco and buses are at the bottom of this path, which is used on Walk 10.

Stay on the levada path to continue, with rock overhanging the channel later, though again there is no real sense of exposure. A pronounced left bend takes the path into a side-valley

The Levada do Caniçal on a steep slope before the Caniçal tunnel, where the walk can be cut short

where more mimosa grows. Turn round the head of the valley and traverse another rocky cut. Meander in and out of folds on the steep slopes of **Castanho**. There are views down to Machico but also wooded areas with mimosa, pine and eucalyptus. Cross a wooded slope and pass a few houses, to reach the **ER-109 road** at the mouth of a tunnel. ▶

To follow the levada to Caniçal, walk through the **tunnel** using a path on the left side where the water runs through a pipe. The tunnel has lighting and runs 800m (875yds) through the Pico de Nossa Senhora, though most traffic now uses the deeper **VR-1** road tunnel. Emerge to follow the levada away from the road, but beware of rockfalls from a quarry at **Feiteiras**. The path is less trodden and clings to a cliff that some might find unnerving, but it gets better later. There are odd mimosa trees, prickly pears and malfurada bushes. Turn round a rocky corner for views of Caniçal and the Ponta de São Lourenço.

The path can be overgrown but is cut from time to time. It is easy to follow by keeping the levada in view. Cross a hillside, then cross a red-earth track and enter dense woods of mimosa, pine, oak and eucalyptus. Turn round a little valley where a small bridge over the **Ribeira do Serrado** needs to be crossed with a straddling manoeuvre. Later, the levada suddenly turns right and rushes downhill. Follow a broad track alongside and quickly leave the woods at **Silveira** to pass a covered reservoir. A road called the Rua das Feiteirinhas leads down to a crossroads. Either catch a bus here, or walk further downhill along the Estrada da Banda d'Além, turning right to finish in the centre of **Caniçal**.

Bus stop nearby with the Restaurante O Tunel down the road.

CANIÇAL

This former fishing village is now flanked by industrial sites, but has a sandy beach. There is a bank with ATM, post office, shops, bars and restaurants. SAM bus 113 serves Machico, Porto da Cruz and Funchal. Taxis are also available. The Museu de Baleia, or whaling museum, is well worth visiting.

WALK 8

Levada da Portela:
Santo da Serra to Portela

Start	ER-102 / ER-207 junction at Santo da Serra – 291221
Finish	ER-102 / ER-212 junction at Portela – 293244
Distance	8km (5 miles)
Total Ascent	150m (490ft)
Total Descent	160m (525ft)
Time	2hrs 30mins
Map	Carta Militar 6
Terrain	Paths and tracks are generally easy and clear. The higher parts are well-wooded. Some steep paths on the descent are slippery when wet.
Refreshments	Two bar/restaurants at Portela.
Transport	Interurban bus 77 serves Santo da Serra from Funchal. SAM bus 20 serves Santo da Serra from Machico. SAM bus 53 serves Portela from Funchal, Machico and Faial. Taxis at Santo da Serra.

The Levada da Portela takes a convoluted, but fairly level route across a well-wooded slope around 830m (2725ft). The descent comes in a series of abrupt drops, with the water racing down to Portela faster than walkers can follow it, ending at a fine roadside viewpoint.

This route could be started at **Santo da Serra**, but the road-walk can be limited by starting at the junction of the ER-102 and ER-207 roads outside the village. Follow the road signposted for Portela, turning carefully round a left-hand bend. A minor road leaves on the left, runs up round a sharp bend and later passes a couple of houses. Continue up a broad track into mixed woodland. The track bends as it climbs at **Lombo das Faias**.

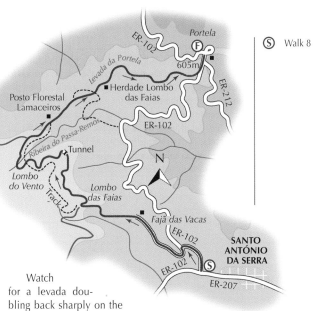

Watch for a levada doubling back sharply on the right. This is the **Levada da Serra**, around 820m (2690ft). Follow it a short way round a corner to reach a flat area beside a water tower. Pointers for Portela and Ribeiro Frio are painted on the tower. ▸ The path is easy at first, but the parapet beside the levada becomes very narrow across a rocky outcrop, so use a path running below for a while. The rest of the path broad and clear, flanked by more tall cedars. There is a pronounced left bend passing a small tunnel then the levada describes little curves as it crosses the wooded slopes of **Lombo do Vento**.

Cross a broad track then cross a bouldery streambed at **Ribeira do Passa-Remos**. Reach a junction of paths around 830m (2725ft) where signposts point in all directions (including ahead to Ribeiro Frio, see Walk 12). Turn right down a clear sunken path, with the **Levada da Portela** out of sight but running parallel. ▸ The path switches from side to side, landing on a dirt road at a toilet block, garden and picnic site at the **Posto Florestal Lamaceiros**.

This is a popular place for walkers to take a break. Curiously contorted cedars march beside the levada and dense laurisilva forest blocks the sunlight.

When seen, the channel is narrow and steep, so the water races down it.

69

Follow the dirt road gently downhill, with the levada channel on the left, but note an older channel running down the middle of the road. When the levada crosses to the right, either follow it through woods and drop steeply later, or stay on the dirt road for a more gradual descent. The levada meets the dirt road again at a junction.

Turn left along a track signposted as the PR10 trail for Portela. The track runs beside a tall fence surrounding the **Herdade Lombo das Faias**. Don't follow the levada where it runs through a very narrow cut, but cross over

the channel later at a corner. ▸ Woods obscure views as the levada runs across a slope around 700m (2300ft). Suddenly, the water rushes downhill again from a ruined building, and the path has steps flanked by hydrangeas and agapanthus. Pass a stand of mimosa and tall cedars, taking care not to trip over tree roots.

Land on the **ER-102 road** at a notice-board and turn left down the road. A short path on the left leads to a pillar-like shrine and viewpoint, which is likely to be quieter than the popular viewpoint further down the road at **Portela**, at 605m (1985ft).

There are good views of Penha d'Águia, Porto da Cruz and the coast, as well as up to Pico do Areeiro and Pico Ruivo.

PORTELA

A fine view takes in Penha d'Águia, Porto da Cruz and the north coast, as well as the high peaks of Madeira. The Restaurante Miradouro da Portela and Restaurante Portela à Vista offer food and drink. SAM bus 53 serves Portela from Funchal and Machico. There may be taxis. Portela is the starting point for Walk 9 along the Vereda das Funduras to Maroços and Walk 12 along the Levada do Furado to Ribeiro Frio.

WALK 9

*Vereda das Funduras:
Portela to Maroços*

Start	ER-102 / ER-212 junction at Portela – 293244
Finish	Maroços – 318232
Distance	10km (6¼ miles)
Total Ascent	150m (490ft)
Total Descent	580m (1900ft)
Time	4hrs
Map	Carta Militar 6
Terrain	A broad and easy forest road, followed by a narrow, convoluted forest path. A steep descent on paths and tracks ends on cultivated terraces.
Refreshments	Two bar/restaurants at Portela. Bars at Maroços.

Transport	SAM bus 53 serves Portela from Funchal, Machico and Faial. SAM Bus 156 serves Maroços from Funchal and Machico.

The Miradouro da Portela Restaurante and Restaurante Portela à Vista offer food and drink at the start and there is a fine roadside viewpoint.

The waymarked PR5 trail, or Vereda das Funduras, explores an area of lush *laurisilva* forest high above the Machico valley. Access is from Portela, using a forest road running parallel to the Levada da Portela. Later, the forest road is left in favour of a narrow path, becoming like a jungle trek. In the end, a steep descent leads down from the forest to finish on cultivated terraces at Marços.

Start the junction of the ER-102/ER-212 roads at **Portela**, at 605m (1985ft). ◄ Follow the road signposted as the PR5 for Maroços, passing a noticeboard beside the Caminho das Funduras. Follow the road round a bend and turn left. Stay level to pass another notice,

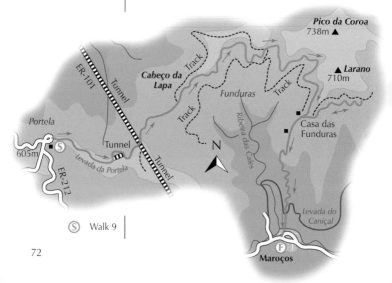

avoiding a route dropping steep and grassy on the left. A track runs gently downhill across a steep slope of mixed forest, with the narrow concrete channel of the **Levada da Portela** alongside. The levada runs through a **tunnel**, but stay on the track to find it again on the other side of a ridge. Keep straight ahead at a track junction, still with the levada alongside. ▶

Watch for a path heading off to the right, signposted 'Serra das Funduras Percurso Pedonal'. This leads into dense *laurisilva*, but don't worry about how remote it suddenly seems, since there is only one path. Roughly contour across a steep slope, or at least follow an undulating course, and steps eventually lead up to a **forest track**. Turn right to walk down through a cutting then turn left up a path signposted 'Percurso Pedonal', passing a picnic site.

The path crosses another slope of dense *laurisilva*, undulating more as it passes lush ferns and tree ferns, with mosses and liverworts in wet areas. There are more pines later then the path suddenly lands on a forest track at the **Casa das Funduras**. ▶ The forest track is signposted 'Percurso Pedonal' and a detour is possible at this point, returning to the *casa* later. Follow the track, avoiding a broad path down to the right, but take a narrower

The forested crest gives occasional views from coast to coast.

Enjoy fine views across the forested head of the Machico valley to the high peaks of Madeira.

The Casa das Funduras marks the start of an easy spur route and a long and steep descent to Maroços

Views reveal Machico at the mouth of the valley and the Ilhas Desertas far beyond.

path down to the right as marked. This roughly contours across a slope of *laurisilva* and ferns until log steps lead up to the track at a picnic site below **Larano**. ◄ Use either the path or the track to return to the **Casa das Funduras**.

Walk straight downhill from the building as signposted for Maroços, using a narrow path with log steps. The path becomes steep and may be slippery. When a track is reached, cross it and step up a little to continue along the path. Pass a **building** on the forested ridge and drop steeply again. Watch carefully and step to the right near an abandoned car. Turn right to go down a track, then left down a clearer track. Avoid two left turns, catching a glimpse of Maroços before dropping steeply down a rugged, rutted track.

Street lighting appears beside the track, along with a few buildings, but it remains a steep descent. Go down a concrete path from a house, the Vereda do Lombo da Roçada, which features hundreds of steps. There are 325 steps before the path crosses the **Levada do Caniçal** (described in Walk 7), with another 225 steps down past a narrower levada to reach a road beside the **Ribeira de Machico**. There is a notice about the PR5 trail, but to finish the walk cross a bridge over the river and walk up to the Snack Bar Estevão in **Maroços**. A bus stop stands a little further up the road.

WALK 10

North Coast:
Porto da Cruz to Ribeira Seca

Start	Porto da Cruz – 291271
Finish	Bar Boca do Risco, Ribeira Seca – 342227
Distance	10km (6¼ miles)
Total Ascent	400m (1310ft)
Total Descent	250m (820ft)
Time	4hrs

Map	Carta Militar 6
Terrain	Paths and roads climb uphill. A well-wooded path crosses a steep slope, becoming rocky and exposed, then wooded again. An easier valley path leads downhill at the end.
Refreshments	Bars and restaurants at Porto da Cruz. Small bar at Larano. Bar at Ribeira Seca.
Transport	SAM bus 53 serves Porto da Cruz from Funchal and Machico. Interurban bus 56, 103 & 138 serve a tunnel above Porto da Cruz from Funchal, but study timetable details carefully as not all of them do. SAM bus 113 links Ribeira Seca with Machico. Taxis at Porto da Cruz.

A fine cliff path heads east from Porto da Cruz on the north coast of Madeira, but it takes time to reach the best parts. Winding paths and roads climb uphill and the first stages of the path are well-wooded. The cliffs are revealed quite suddenly and a few places wouldn't suit vertigo sufferers. Beware of rock-falls, especially after rain. Head inland from Boca do Risco to end at Ribeira Seca.

PORTO DA CRUZ

An interesting little coastal settlement with a landmark church and a sugar factory built in 1927. Facilities include a bank with ATM, post office, bars and restaurants.

Start at the church in the centre of **Porto da Cruz** and walk down to the sea wall. To the left is the sheer cliff face of Penha d'Águia (see Walk 11), while to the right a broad dirt road runs along the foot of cliffs, subject to rockfall. Walk with care to a water treatment works and cross the mouth of the Ribeira da Maiata beside a bouldery beach. Follow a track uphill and cross a road, picking up a narrow cobbled path to climb higher.

75

Look back to see Madeira's highest mountains in the distance.

Continue along a level terrace, or use a slightly higher path with street lights alongside. Both paths lead to a concrete path on a gap where there is a good view back to Porto da Cruz and Penha d'Águia. Climb up concrete steps, passing a few houses to reach a road at **Larano**. Turn left uphill to pass a small shop/bar.

Keep climbing straight ahead up the road, avoiding a turning on the left. Later, the road turns left and right and overlooks the wooded valley of **Ribeira do Seixo**. ◄ Tarmac gives way to a concrete road that suddenly reaches a gap overlooking the sea. A *teleférico* drops 350m (1150ft) at **Cova das Pedras**, allowing access for farmers to remote cultivation terraces.

Ilhéu

PORTO DA CRUZ

ER-102

Water Treatment

ATLANTIC OCEAN

Espigão Am.

Bar

Larano

Teleférico

Cova das Pedras

Ribeira do Seixo

Pico da Coroa
738m ▲

C.

Ⓢ Walk 10

There is another fine view back to Penha d'Águia.

◄ Continue
along a track which ends suddenly, giving way to a path across a slope of pine, laurel and heather. When the path later narrows, climb up a short rocky ramp to continue along the correct line, as the lower path disappears on a steep slope.

The path wriggles in and out of small gullies on a steep, wooded slope, and generally runs around 350m (1150ft) above the sea. Step down a rock outcrop and look back along the coast to Porto da Cruz. There is little ground cover, though pine, mimosa and eucalyptus grow on the slope. Dense heather flanks the path as it turns round a significant point at **Espigão Amarelo**.

Enjoy views back to Porto da Cruz and ahead to the Ponta de São Lourenço and the distant island of Porto Santo.

◄ The path suddenly enters a huge bare hollow that some might find unnerving. Steep slopes of grass and

A cable has been bolted to the cliffs for added security on a particularly narrow and exposed cliff path

crumbling rock drop to the sea. Only a few small trees or clumps of heather are dotted across the slopes, and the path is narrow and crumbling in places. Beware of rockfalls and take particular care crossing a rock-wall with a short length of cable attached, below **Pico da Coroa**. Follow the path past a little pinnacle of rock to reach dense heather, laurel, mimosa, and masses of brambles and bracken, where the sense of exposure lessens.

There are a couple of open areas, but also patches of *laurisilva* woodland so dense that it is quite dark inside. The path is broad and stony as it turns round a rocky headland. Go through another dense patch of vegetation, turn another headland and follow the path through gorse before rising gently to the **Boca do Risco** at 350m (1150ft).

Enjoy the last of the cliff-coast views before following a

path downhill from the gap. Although the valley seems well-wooded, the stony path often crosses grassy slopes and keeps away from denser stands of trees. Heather and laurel increase in size on the way down, and there is a small-holding where there may be a few animals. The path, known as the Vereda da Boca do Risco, passes tall, burnt, snapped-in-half pines. Continue descending easily, though it is rockier in a rugged side-valley. Trees give way to more cultivated slopes and there are little sheds below.

Cross over the **Levada do Caniçal** around 220m (720ft) (see Walk 7). The path is rough and stony as it descends, with some parts under concrete, and there are street lights all the way down to **Ribeira Seca**. At the bottom, go down a flight of steps to reach the road at the Bar Boca do Risco. If a SAM bus 113 isn't due for a while, **Machico** can be reached easily on foot by walking down the road.

MACHICO

A bustling coastal town with an intriguing history, Machico is supposedly named after an Englishman called Walter Machim. During the early settlement of Madeira this was the main base for Cristão Vaz Teixeira. The cobbled streets are delightful and old buildings stand beside new ones, with everything cosy and compact. The easiest way between the bus station, town centre and cobbled beach is to follow a paved path beside a river, which is full of croaking frogs in Spring. A full range of services is available, including banks with ATMs, post office, hotels, shops, bars, restaurants and taxis. The Tourist Information Office is in an old fort near the beach, tel 291-962289.

SECTION 2
Funchal to Santana

In this part of Madeira, the rugged uplands rise above steep, forested slopes. The valleys are deep and steep-sided. Levadas have been cut across precipitous slopes, sometimes tunnelling through rock to avoid cliff faces. Obviously, walkers need to tread carefully and ensure that they choose walks that are within their ability. The peak of Penha d'Águia might only be a 'little hill' by Madeiran standards, but it is surrounded on almost all sides by cliff faces and its paths are very steep.

Despite the nature of the terrain, Madeira's early settlers hacked and slashed their way through forests, constructing stone-paved highways from coast to coast. Two of these old roads, or 'Caminhos Velha' can be traced from Poiso to the rugged north coast – one leading to Porto da Cruz and the other leading to Santana. The northern slopes of Madeira are well-watered and covered in lush green vegetation.

On the southern side of the high crest, the ground is more arid and the urban sprawl of Funchal needs all the water it can get. Some of the oldest levadas on the island were constructed to carry water into town. Four levadas are followed downstream, including two from Poço da Neve to the high suburbs of Funchal and two more at a lower level that feature exceedingly steep and exposed sections that are quite unsuitable for anyone who suffers from vertigo or clumsy feet.

Funchal is an obvious base for these walks, and there are interurban buses running back and forth between Funchal, Santana and Porto da Cruz. Those who wish to experience the quieter parts of Madeira should base themselves in Santana. Those looking to create long-distance walks will find good links with routes in eastern Madeira, at Monte, Santo da Serra and Porto da Cruz, as well as links with other mountain paths from Curral das Freiras, Pico do Areeiro and Santana.

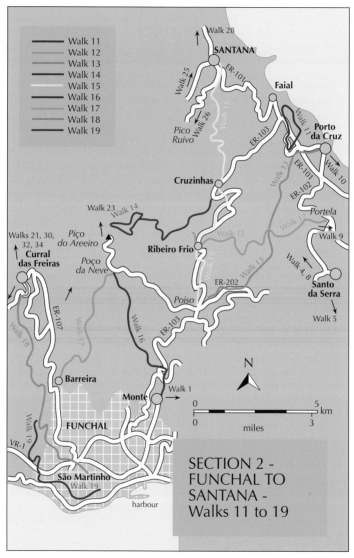

Walk 11
Walk 12
Walk 13
Walk 14
Walk 15
Walk 16
Walk 17
Walk 18
Walk 19

SANTANA
Faial
Porto da Cruz
Walk 28
ER-101
Walk 25
Walk 26
ER-103
Pico Ruivo
Cruzinhas
Walk 11
ER-101
ER-102
Walk 10
Portela
Walk 9
Walk 23
Walk 14
Walk 12
Ribeiro Frio
Piço do Areeiro
Walks 21, 30, 32, 34
Curral das Freiras
Poço da Neve
ER-107
Walk 18
Walk 17
Walk 16
ER-103
Poiso
ER-202
Walk 13
Walk 4, 8
Santo da Serra
Walk 5
Barreira
Monte
Walk 1
FUNCHAL
VR-1
São Martinho
Walk 19
harbour

N

0   5 km
0   3 miles

SECTION 2 -
FUNCHAL TO
SANTANA -
Walks 11 to 19

WALK 11
Vereda da Penha d'Águia

Start/Finish	Between Moinhos and Faial – 273284
Distance	6km (3¾ miles)
Total Ascent	550m (1805ft)
Total Descent	550m (1805ft)
Time	3hrs
Map	Carta Militar 6
Terrain	Steep and narrow steps and paths may be rocky, crumbling or overgrown in places. Densely forested on top. The final stage is along a road.
Refreshments	Two bars before the main ascent. Bar at Cruz after the main descent. Two more bars between Cruz and Moinhos.
Transport	SAM bus 53 & 156 run from Funchal and Machico to Cruz and Moinhos. Interurban bus 56, 103 & 138 serve Moinhos from Funchal.

Penha d'Águia looks inaccessible from all sides. The seaward cliffs are vertical and cliffs appear to be wrapped all round the landward sides. In fact, a narrow path reaches the summit from the north-west, and a steep zigzag path descends roughly south-west to Cruz. This walk is not really suitable in wet weather as the paths can become treacherously slippery.

Start on the ER-101 road below **Moinhos**, at a bus stop just before the bridge spanning the Riberia de São Roque. A flight of 380 uneven steps rises directly from the bus stop, made of concrete or stone, zigzagging steeply uphill with street lights alongside. ▶ The path levels out and drops between two small buildings to land on a road. Follow the road gently downhill from the Bar Ar & Sol to the **Restaurante Galé**.

There is a sheer cliff above, and a few pines and malfurada bushes on the slope.

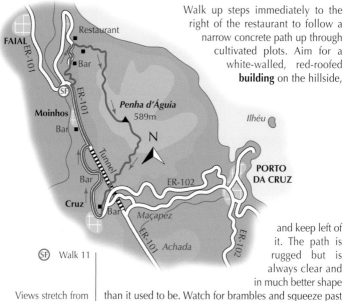

Walk up steps immediately to the right of the restaurant to follow a narrow concrete path up through cultivated plots. Aim for a white-walled, red-roofed **building** on the hillside,

and keep left of it. The path is rugged but is always clear and in much better shape

(SF) Walk 11

Views stretch from the sea to Faial and the high mountains.

than it used to be. Watch for brambles and squeeze past clumps of heather and malfurada. Steps have been installed but there is also bare rock in places. ◄

Climb above old terraces to enter pine forest, where the path is narrow and crumbling on a steep slope with annoying brambles. Climb more easily, but still steeply up a slope of pines. A gap is reached on the crest of the hill, where a left turn is made. The crest is well defined, undulating gently past pine, mimosa and eucalyptus. Views to the right reveal a sheer cliff. The path is narrow but easy, with some wooden steps. There is a tiny clearing on top of **Penha d'Águia**, with most of the space taken by a tall trig point at 589m (1932ft). There are small pines, laurels, heather, gorse, brambles and bilberry around the clearing. ◄

There is no view of the sea but the mountains rising inland look impressive.

A narrow path continues along the crest, descending with a view through the trees to the Ponta de São Lourenço and the distant island of Porto Santo. Squeeze past gorse and heather and note how pines are crowded

82

out by eucalyptus. The path is narrow and crumbling, leading to a clearing on a gap. An old **winch cable** stretches downhill, marking the line of descent along a steep, narrow, crumbling, zigzag path. Take great care all the way down. Don't be tempted to short-cut or leave the path.

Things get better while passing a few mimosa trees. The path is less steep and there are fine coastal views. Although the road can be seen below, care is still needed on the path. When the gradient eases on a crest, watch out on the left to drop down to a narrow levada on a cultivated terrace. Turn right to follow it across the hillside to reach the ER-102 road at **Cruz**. ▸

Snack Bar Adega da Cruz and small shop

Looking up towards Pico do Areeiro from the road-walk back to Moinhos on the descent from Cruz

A signpost points back for the 'Vereda da Penha d'Águia' if the route is ever considered in reverse.

Either turn left to walk down the road to Porto da Cruz, linking with Walk 10 for a longer trek, or turn right to walk back to where the walk started. Taking the latter, there are a couple more small bars down the road, one well below Cruz and the other beyond the tunnel mouth before reaching **Moinhos**.

WALK 12

Levada do Furado:
Portela to Ribeiro Frio

Start	ER-102 / ER-212 junction at Portela – 293244
Finish	Ribeiro Frio – 236232
Distance	11km (6¾ miles)
Total Ascent	190m (625ft)
Total Descent	10m (30ft)
Time	4hrs
Map	Carta Militar 6
Terrain	Paths, tracks and steps are used on the ascent. There are a few short tunnels and some parts are exposed, rocky and slippery. Most is well-wooded. The path towards the end is clear, level and easy.
Refreshments	Two bar/restaurants at Portela and two more at Ribeiro Frio.
Transport	SAM bus 53 serves Portela from Funchal and Machico. Interurban bus 56, 103 & 138 serve Ribeiro Frio from Funchal and Santana.

The Levada do Furado was cut in the 1820s across a very steep slope of *laurisilva* forest, linking with the Levada da Portela and Levada da Serra. There are sheer cliffs along the way, though the dense forest masks the exposure, and there are a few short tunnels. Maps often show the levada wrongly, which roughly follows the 850m (2790ft) contour to Ribeiro Frio.

Start at 605m (1985ft) at **Portela**. ▶ Follow the ER-102 road uphill towards Santo da Serra. A path on the right leads to a pillar-like shrine and viewpoint, but continue up the road to reach a notice and signpost for the PR10 trail. Climb crude steps and watch for tree roots. The **Levada da Portela** races through a narrow channel and is followed upstream past tall cedars. Pass a stand of mimosa and climb more steps flanked by hydrangeas and agapanthus. The path is on the left of the levada as it climbs a wooded slope, but switches to the right after passing a ruined building. A gentler path leads onwards from around 700m (2300ft), reaching an open corner.

▶ The levada cannot be followed through a narrow cut so follow a broad path ruinning parallel. Walk beside a tall fence surrounding the **Herdade Lombo das Faias** to reach a track junction with several signposts. Turn right as signposted for Ribeiro Frio, then either follow the levada steeply uphill through woods, or follow a broad dirt road more gradually uphill. The levada and dirt road meet later and run at a gentle gradient to a toilet block, garden and a picnic site at the **Posto Florestal Lamaceiros**.

Keep right of the track and follow the levada steeply uphill from the toilet block. The path climbs beside the levada at first, then a sunken path to the left is used while the water, running parallel, is out of sight. Reach a junction of paths around 830m (2725ft) where signposts point in all directions. Turn right for Ribeiro Frio, passing a water tower just round a corner, where the **Levada do Furado** is followed upstream.

The levada channel slices through mossy rock and runs through dense *laurisilva*. ▶

Marvel at the engineering of the watercourse, which includes a few **small tunnels** – most for walking through

For facilities see page 71.

There is a good view of Penha d'Águia and Porto da Cruz, as well as to Pico do Areeiro and Pico Ruivo.

Trees often obscure the fact that the levada clings to a very steep and rocky slope.

85

but a couple for walking past. In the middle of this series is a fine view down the valley to Porto da Cruz. The levada parapet is narrow and exposed, often with fencing alongside, and there may be rock overhanging the channel. The last of the tunnels is more like a narrow rocky chasm cut through the spur of **Cabeço Furado**, though part of it is roofed. ◀

The path is broad and well-wooded then becomes rough and uneven, turning left round a pronounced rocky corner into the valley of **Pedra Rachada**, where there are well-established laurels and tree heather. The valley head is moist and dripping; then the path

Note Walk 13 crosses over the tunnel roof on Walk 12.

Ⓢ Walk 12

Ⓢ Walk 13

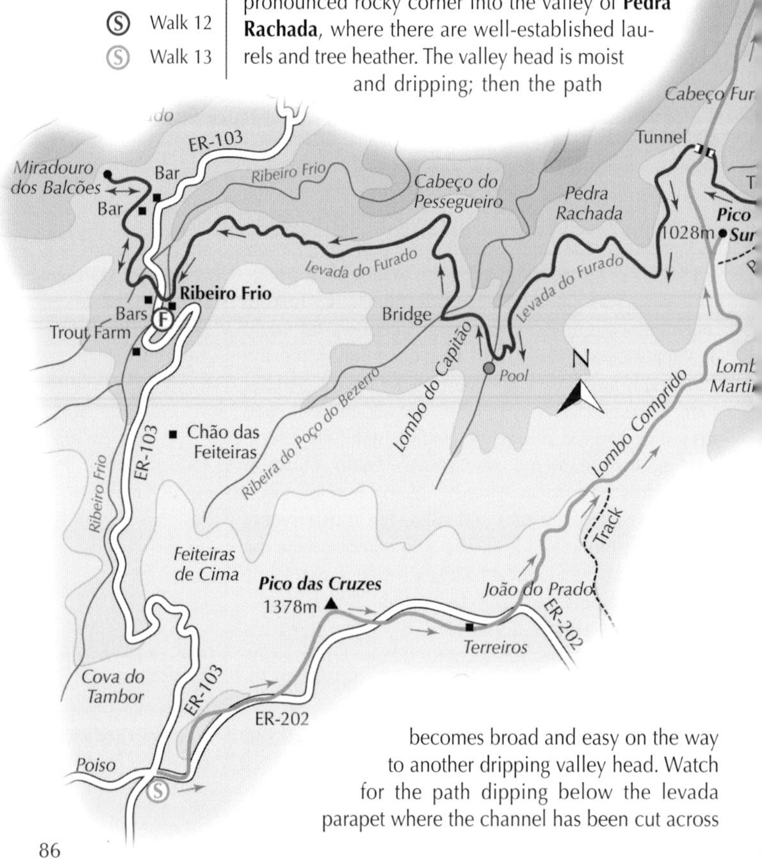

becomes broad and easy on the way to another dripping valley head. Watch for the path dipping below the levada parapet where the channel has been cut across these wet areas. After turning left round another pronounced corner, the levada runs through narrow rock cuttings where walkers must step on slabs placed across the channel.

Follow the path into a couple of damp, mossy, fern-clad valleys, where the path dips

Walk 13 map continued to Porto da Cruz on page 91

There is a deep green pool in the second valley.

below the parapet to cross streambeds. ▸ The path is narrow as it curves round the **Lombo do Capitão**, but it becomes easy and well wooded. Cross a wide **bridge** over the **Ribeira do Poço do Bezerro**. The path is broad and well-wooded as it leaves the valley and there is a pronounced swing into the next valley. The path narrows and has a fence alongside. After passing a weeping wall, swing round a rocky corner at **Cabeço do Pessegueiro**. ▸

The surroundings remain forested, but there are a couple of fine views of the highest peaks on Madeira.

The path is rough and rocky, passing through a rocky notch and often equipped with fencing. After another rugged stretch, things get easier and hydrangeas grow alongside. An old mill is seen across the river before a bridge is crossed. A notice-board explains about the PR10 trail, then a flight of steps leads up to the road at **Ribeiro Frio**, around 870m (2855ft).

Extension to Balcões

It is well worth seeking the continuation of the levada, which offers a pleasant and easy extension to the popular Miradouro dos Balcões. The path is well signposted, turns round a well-wooded valley, passes a small bar and

A view of Torres and Pico Ruivo, seen from the Levada do Furado as it approaches Ribeiro Frio

goes through a rocky cutting. A paved path on the right later leads to a rocky tor, which is a perch for a splendid viewpoint. Look down the Metade valley to Penha d'Águia and up the valley to Pico do Areeiro, Pico do Gato, Torres, Pico Ruivo and Achada do Teixeira. There is also a view of the generating station at Fajã da Nogueira (start of Walk 14). The walk to Balcões and back to Ribeiro Frio is almost level and measures 3km (2 miles).

RIBEIRO FRIO

The Restaurante Ribeiro Frio is immediately to hand, while a bar and a souvenir shop lie across the road. The Posto Aquicola trout farm is just up the road, across the river. An interesting garden can be explored across the road from the trout farm, where plants have name tags to assist identification.

WALK 13

Caminho Velha:
Poiso to Porto da Cruz

Start	ER-103 / ER-202 junction at Poiso – 234206
Finish	Porto da Cruz – 292272
Distance	13km (8 miles)
Total Ascent	100m (330ft)
Total Descent	1500m (4920ft)
Time	4hrs
Map	Carta Militar 6
Terrain	Intermittent paths give way to a good track on increasingly forested slopes. Steep and narrow paths later may be rocky, crumbling or overgrown. Road-walking towards the end.
Refreshments	Bar/restaurant at Poiso. Bar at Cruz. Bars and restaurants at Porto da Cruz.
Transport	Interurban bus 56, 103 & 138 serve Poiso from Funchal or Santana, as well as a tunnel at Maçapez. SAM bus 53 & 156 serve Cruz and Porto da Cruz from Funchal and Machico.

See map on pages 86–87.

The old road, or *Caminho Velha*, can still be followed from a high crest at Poiso down to the sea at Porto da Cruz. This route includes fine views of the mountains from easy paths then descends through dark and dense *laurisilva* forest where views are limited. The final stages involve tracks and roads dropping down past cultivation terraces and tiny farms to reach the coast.

Start high on the ER-103 road near the Casa de Abrigo restaurant at **Poiso**. Turn right at a flowery junction at an altitude of 1412m (4633ft). Follow the **ER-202 road**, signposted for Santo da Serra. The road climbs gently and turns left, overlooking the south coast. When it bends right and has white bollards alongside, watch for a grassy path on the left. This rises between pines, heather and gorse, to cross a gentle rise and head back down to the road.

Walk down the road until a small quarry is seen on the left then follow a track downhill to reach a broad, grassy area used as a picnic site. Make a very easy ascent of **Pico das Cruzes**, at 1378m (4521ft), for views stretching from Madeira's highest peaks all the way down to the coast. Further along, the crest becomes forested, so cross the road and pick up a narrow path running roughly parallel, reaching a picnic area and animal pens at **Terreiros**. Come back onto the road at a building and walk down the road as far as a bend.

Watch for a path heading off to the left between trees, continuing across the heather-dotted slopes of **João do Prado**. The path wiggles around, but is always clear underfoot, running along **Lombo Comprido**, where views stretch from the high mountains to the rugged peninsula of Ponta de São Lourenço. The path later turns

The view from Pico das Cruzes takes in Madeira's highest mountains – Pico do Areeiro, Torres and Pico Ruivo

sharp right and drops down to a broad track. Turn left to follow it down across increasingly well-wooded slopes.

Keep left at junctions with other tracks until a wooded gap is reached. ▶ The main track rises easily from a stone water trough to the summit of **Pico do Suna** at 1028m (3373ft). There is a watch-tower here with a view straight down to Penha d'Águia and Porto da Cruz.

Retrace your steps to the water trough and turn sharply right to follow a clear path further downhill. This is broad at first, running through dense *laurisilva* forest, then it drops steeply and ruggedly and may be slippery when wet. When it levels out at **Cabeço Furado**, there are less obvious paths leading down to the right and left. Don't take them, but just note that they lead to the **Levada do Furado**, which runs through a tunnel directly beneath the path (see Walk 12).

The path continues easily, but becomes quite narrow as it traverses the steep and well vegetated slopes around 750m (2460ft). ▶ Watch for brambles as the path undulates and runs through a rocky notch. Faial can be seen down through the valley. The path then runs alongside a fence bounding an area marked as private property. Zigzag down from the forested peak of **Pedreiro** while views take in Porto da Cruz for a while.

Tall eucalyptus forest limits the views further downhill even when the path follows the crest of Cabeço do Rochão. There are a few pines on the slopes, but there was a blaze in the past and eucalyptus grew afterwards. The path is plain and obvious as it zigzags further downhill, and is paved with cobbles before it reaches a narrow tarmac road. Simply follow the road straight ahead and downhill,

Just before this point, a path heads down to the right, which can be used to reach a junction of three levadas.

A fire opened up views across the valley to the high mountains, but these will be lost as the vegetation recovers.

map continued from pages 86–87

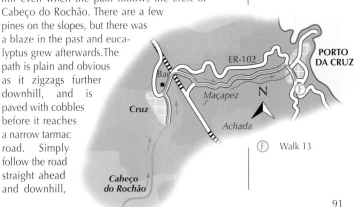

91

*The bouldery beach at Porto da Cruz is backed
by the sheer cliffs of Penha d'Águia*

passing a couple of little shops on the way to the main ER-102 road, around 240m (790ft), at **Cruz**. ▶

The walk could be ended at this point or continued by turning right to head down to Porto da Cruz. Avoid the main road by walking down the Caminho do Massapêz. Buses can be picked up close to a tunnel mouth or later, down at **Porto da Cruz**. ▶

Snack Bar Adega da Cruz

For facilities see Walk 10.

WALK 14

*Fajã da Nogueira
and Levada da Serra*

Start/Finish	Fajã da Nogueira – 217241, or bridge below Cruzinhas – 242252
Distance	9km or 18km (5½ or 11 miles)
Total Ascent	390m or 640m (1280ft or 2100ft)
Total Descent	390m or 640m (1280ft or 2100ft)
Time	4hrs or 7hrs
Map	Carta Militar 6
Terrain	Broad and clear tracks at the start and finish, on steep and wooded slopes. A narrow and exposed levada walk includes ten small tunnels.
Refreshments	None closer than a small bar at Cruzinhas.
Transport	Interurban bus 56, 103 & 138 serve the bridge over the Ribeira da Metade below Cruzinhas from Funchal and Santana.

Fajã da Nogueira can be reached by following a broad dirt road into the Metade valley. It is a long way to walk there and back, but it can be approached carefully by car. Starting from the generating station, a clear track leads up through *laurisilva* to the Levada da Serra, which offers an exciting and exposed walk round the head of the valley, including a series of tunnels.

Whether approaching on foot or by car, start from a bridge over the **Ribeira da Metade** below Cruzinhas, on the ER-103 road. The Central Fajã da Nogueira is signposted from bridge and the tarmac quickly gives way to a broad dirt road. Follow it onwards and gently uphill through the well-wooded valley, passing a few cultivated plots along the way. ◄ The road bends and climbs round the **Cova do Rocha Machado**.

There are glimpses of the peak of Torres high above the head of the valley.

Cabeço do Gavino

Tunnels

Levada da Serra

Tils

Tunnels

Footbridge

Fajã da Nogueira

Tunnels

Pico da Nogueira

Cova do Rocha Machado

Ribeira da Metade

Miradouro dos Balcões

N

Chão das Faias

(SF) Walk 14

A lengthy side-valley has to be turned at **Chão das Faias**, where a building and a tunnel mouth are passed. Cross a bridge over a bouldery river and follow the dirt road to the generating station at **Fajã da Noguiera**. If driving to this point, park off the road.

The peaks of Torres and Pico do Gato (traversed on Walk 23) can be seen briefly from the generating station. Follow the last part of the road towards some houses, but turn right up a stony track before reaching them. The track climbs in easy loops on a well-wooded slope. ◄ Turn right at a junction of tracks and climb past more big old tils. The track leads to the **Levada da Serra**, around 970m (3180ft), which is covered with slabs in both directions. The route turns left, but it is worth turning right first to enjoy a fine view down the Metade valley then return to the same point to continue. After walking left along the slab-covered stretch, there is an open stretch where the water is followed downstream. The path is wide at first, then passes through two little **tunnels** before more care and attention is needed.

A sign points out that two enormous til trees on the left are the oldest discovered on the island. Admire them, but note how much damage they have suffered over the centuries.

Turn round an exposed ravine and go through another little **tunnel**. The next **tunnel** is curious and bendy, with a 'window' partway through. The parapet path is both fenced and unfenced as it slices across a cliff face. Go through a short and low **tunnel**, which has a 'window' part-way through. The levada channel is covered and the path is uneven as it crosses an open slope. Go through another bendy **tunnel**, which has a low entrance and exit, with a couple of 'windows' along its length. The levada is quite bendy afterwards. Walk along the parapet path then walk below it for a while.

There is no need to enter the next **tunnel**, as a

The first part of the Levada da Serra is covered, while later parts can be exposed as it crosses sheer cliffs

rugged path runs round the rock face instead. Tree heather grows on the slopes and a fenced path runs below the levada parapet. Enter the next bendy **tunnel**, which has a double arch at its exit. Step up onto the parapet path, then step down to enter yet another bendy **tunnel**, which is quite low and has another 'window'. The path leads round a rocky gully that is both unfenced and exposed, but there are short lengths of fencing later. Walk on and off the parapet as required, passing big til trees. Look for Pico do Gato above the head of the valley.

Cross a bouldery ravine and pass a tin hut, then turn an exposed corner. The path is mostly fenced and runs

beside the parapet to cross a stone-arched bridge over the Ribeira da Fajã da Nogueira at the head of the valley.

Walk along or beside the parapet as required, with or without fencing alongside. Curve round an undercut cliff that drips with water, where the levada is unfenced but covered with slabs. Go through a little **tunnel** after which he path is mostly fenced. There is another slab-covered stretch and good views down through the valley. Go through a small cutting and curve round another dripping cliff, noting how water enters from a tunnel. Go through a short, tall **tunnel** and continue walking on and off the parapet, where the path is fenced and unfenced, until another **tunnel** is reached.

Instead of entering this last tunnel go down some stone steps on the left, followed by some crude wooden steps, zigzagging down a slope of tall tils. Turn left at a track junction and walk down to the Ribeira da Fajã da Nogueira. Either ford the river or use a rickety footbridge. The track drifts away from the river and climbs with less woodland alongside, reaching the junction of tracks passed earlier in the day. Turn right to walk downhill, passing the two enormous **til trees**, to return to the generating station at **Fajã da Nogueira**.

If a car was used, then simply drive back down through the valley towards Cruzinhas. If walking, maybe someone will offer you a lift. If there is any length of time to wait for a bus back at the bridge over the **Ribeira da Metade**, it may be worth walking up to **Cruzinhas** for a break at the little Bar das Cruzinhas.

WALK 15
Caminho Velha: Poiso to Santana

Start	ER-103 / ER-202 junction at Poiso – 234206
Finish	Santana – 243309
Distance	20km (12½ miles)
Total Ascent	630m (2065ft)
Total Descent	1630m (5350ft)
Time	7hrs
Maps	Carta Militar 3 & 6
Terrain	Forested and cultivated ridges and valleys. Steep cobbled paths and tracks can be slippery when wet. Some road walking at intervals.
Refreshments	Bar/restaurants at Poiso and Ribeiro Frio. Bars at Achada do Cedro Gordo and Cruzinhas. Plenty of choice at Santana.
Transport	Interurban bus 56, 103 & 138 serve Poiso, Ribeiro Frio, Achada do Cedro Gordo, Cruzinhas, Lombo Galego and Santana from Funchal.

The modern mountain road between Funchal and Santana is remarkably convoluted. The old road, or *Caminho Velha*, was more direct, but featured steeper gradients and had tight zigzags. Much of the old road can still be followed between Poiso and Santana, but start early and expect to finish late as a series of steep-sided valleys need to be crossed along the way.

Start high on the ER-103 road near the Casa de Abrigo restaurant at **Poiso**. Walk straight through a flowery junction at an altitude of 1412m (4633ft). Follow the road downhill in the direction of Ribeiro Frio, but turn left down a cobbled track. This is the *Caminho Velha*, flanked by tall pines and out of sight of the main road.

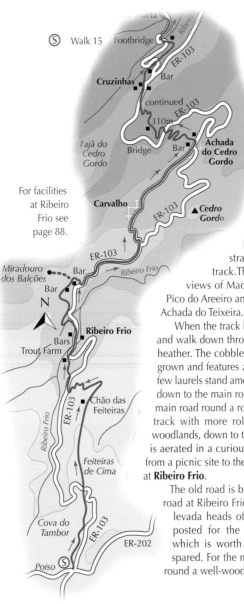

For facilities
at Ribeiro
Frio see
page 88.

Walk downhill, straight
through a junction with
another track, crossing
over the **ER-103 road**
soon afterwards.

A broad dirt
road runs through
a recreation area
that was once a
landfill site, then the
cobbled road runs
past tree heather onto
level ground. Pass
buildings and sheep-
pens at **Chão das
Feiteiras** and continue
straight along a grassy
track. The track affords splendid
views of Madeira's highest peaks from
Pico do Areeiro and Torres to Pico Ruivo and
Achada do Teixeira.

When the track bends right, turn sharp left
and walk down through a gate into dense tree
heather. The cobbled road is steep and grass-
grown and features zigzags and rolled steps. A
few laurels stand among the heather on the way
down to the main road. Turn right to follow the
main road round a rocky bend, then go down a
track with more rolled steps through mixed
woodlands, down to the main road again. Water
is aerated in a curious stepped levada, flowing
from a picnic site to the Posto Aquicola trout farm
at **Ribeiro Frio**.

The old road is buried beneath the modern
road at Ribeiro Frio, but just round a bend a
levada heads off to the left. This is signposted for the Miradouro dos Balcões,
which is worth a detour if time can be
spared. For the moment, follow the levada
round a well-wooded valley and pass a small

bar to reach a rocky cutting. Don't go through the cutting, but turn right along a concrete path and go down steps to return to the **ER-103 road** beside the Restaurante Snack Bar Faisca.

Turn left and the road rises gently away from Ribeiro Frio. Mimosa grows above the road and there is a fine view back to Pico do Areeiro. Pass a picnic site on a bend and follow the road down past a bus shelter. A road on the left is signposted as the Caminho Municipal da Achada do Cedro Gordo. Walk down this road, through **Carvalho**, enjoying a fine view of the high peaks above the Metade valley. All kinds of fruit and vegetables grow in small plots. Reach a church, Bar Zeca, bus stop and the main road at **Achada do Cedro Gordo**, at 610m (2000ft).

Walk straight ahead then turn left along another stretch of the old cobbled road. This passes a house and becomes quite steep and well-vegetated as it zigzags down a well-wooded slope. Some parts are wet and slippery, subject to rockfall and landslip. Cross over the **ER-103 road** to continue downhill. Turn right down a concrete road and right again at a house to go down a cobbled track. Pass a fine house, formerly a mill, and cross a substantial arched bridge over the **Ribeira da Metade**, around 310m (1015ft).

Zigzag up a narrow road on the other side of the valley, looking down to the rugged hill of Penha d'Águia. Just before road runs downhill, turn sharp left up 14 concrete steps to a cobbled path, which is the old road again. Cross a tarmac road and climb 14 more concrete steps to climb a concrete path laid on top of the old cobbled road. Turn right up the main road, but quickly leave it on the left to follow a

short stretch of old road into the tiny village of **Cruzinhas**, around 420m (1380ft).

The old road is immediately below the one sign-posted for Fajã da Murta, and is more direct, though the modern road has the Bar das Cruzinhas alongside. The steep concrete road has steps down the middle and its own street lights. Grass-grown cobbles lead further downhill then the road is concrete as it crosses the tarmac road. Go down steps and continue down a path, swinging left to land on the tarmac road near the bottom of the valley. Follow the road down round a bend, then either cross the road bridge over the **Ribeira Seca**, or cross an old footbridge hidden among old houses around 260m (855ft). ◄

Pico do Areeiro is seen one last time at the head of the valley.

Follow the road up through **Fajã da Murta**, round a bend and across a bridge. Go round another bend, but don't cross the next road bridge. Instead, climb up concrete steps with street lights alongside and cross an old bridge in a steep-sided valley. Continue up a cobbled track with a view of Penha d'Águia. Nearby slopes are well cultivated and dotted with houses. Climb round a tarmac road bend then go straight up a broad flight of concrete steps at the next bend. Walk up a cobbled track then climb steps back onto the tarmac road.

Just before a **footbridge** spans the road, turn sharp left up a cobbled path with street lights alongside. The path turns right and later continues

A road bridge and an older footbridge cross the Ribeira Seca

straight onto a narrow concrete road. This road rises and falls gently, then rises and falls to the tarmac road again. Climb round a bend to cross a bridge over the Ribeira do Lombo Galego. Follow the road uphill, but before it begins to fall gently, turn left up a steep concrete road signposted for Cova da Roda and Santana.

Keep zigzagging up the clearest concrete track, above all the houses at **Lombo Galego**, finally passing a concrete water tank before patches of the old cobbled road show through the concrete. Only a few storage sheds stand on the last cultivated terraces before a fine view of Penha d'Águia and Porto da Cruz. Views are lost as the track swings left round a corner into a valley dominated by eucalyptus trees. When the track suddenly swings left up through a rocky cutting, don't follow it, but keep straight ahead along a grassy track. This is the old road but its cobbles are not immediately seen. The track leads down to an old grass-grown bridge over the **Ribeira da Albelheira**, where there may be waterfalls and rock pools.

Zigzag up from the bridge among mixed woodlands, where *maracujá* fruit hang low enough to pick. The grassy track becomes a broad dirt road leading to a crossroads and picnic site at **Cova da Roda**. Views from this point, around 690m (2265ft), stretch from Poiso down to Penha d'Águia. A signpost points back to Cruzinhas, while a cobbled track uphill is signposted for Pico das Pedras (see Walk 26). A tarmac road runs downhill, leaving only a track running straight ahead for Santana.

Follow the cobbled track past a cultivated area and continue through forest on gentle gradients to reach a junction with a tarmac road. Turn left to follow the road a little uphill, then downhill. ▶ Follow the road steeply down through forest, turning left before climbing past a **stoneworks**. Continue along the road to pass a **football ground** then keep right at a junction beside the Auto Chapinha building. Walk downhill and keep left to pass a fruit depot. The Bar Azevedo is on the left later, while further down the road, a cemetery stands on the right. Reach a junction with the **ER-101 road**, where there are

The **Parque Empresarial** is off to the left but isn't visited.

bar/restaurants. Either turn left or head straight downhill to reach the main part of **Santana**.

SANTANA

Santana sprawls, but the centre is well defined. The Hotel Colmo is handy, while other hotels lie further from the centre. Services include banks with ATMs, post office, shops, bars and restaurants. Several tiny thatched houses are dotted around the village, mostly painted red and white, and one of them serves as the Tourist Information Centre, tel. 291-572992. Interurban bus 56, 103 & 138 serve nearby São Jorge and distant Funchal. There are two departure points for buses, so study the timetables at *both* stops to be sure of being in the right place for a particular service. Taxis are also available.

WALK 16

Levada do Barreiro:
Poço da Neve to Monte

Start	Poço da Neve, near Pico do Areeiro – 200222
Finish	Monte, above Funchal – 219167
Distance	9km (5½ miles)
Total Ascent	50m (165ft)
Total Descent	1140m (3740ft)
Time	3hrs
Maps	Carta Militar 6 & 9
Terrain	Paths are vague at first, becoming rugged and slippery. Wooded slopes can be overgrown. Old roads and tracks are used towards the end.
Refreshments	Bars and cafés around Monte.
Transport	Taxi to Poço da Neve. Urban bus 20, 21 & 48 link Monte with Funchal. Taxis at Monte.

The Levada do Barreiro offers a fine route down from the slopes of Pico do Areeiro to Monte, above

Funchal. The levada is mostly confined to the Parque Ecológico do Funchal. This area is slowly having its original forest cover re-established and is popular with Madeiran school parties. The levada crosses bare and forested areas, with roads and tracks finally leading to Monte.

Use a taxi to reach **Poço da Neve**, at 1640m (5380ft), where there is a small roadside parking space. A signpost and a gate reveal a paved path leading down to a stone **ice-house** covering a deep and dark pit.

POÇO DA NEVE

There is a view all the way down to the harbour at Funchal. The ice-house was filled with compacted snow whenever it fell on the mountainside, which would be conserved throughout the hot summer months. Before the advent of refrigeration, runners would carry precious ice at speed down to Funchal, where it commanded a high price and was used for some medical treatments.

A grassy path runs downhill from the ice-house, bearing red and yellow marker posts. Cross a track and continue down a slope of grass and bracken, with some boulders dotted about. Keep right at a junction, following

The ice-house at Poço da Neve, with a view down towards the harbour at distant Funchal

red and yellow markers. Cross a stony track and notice the very narrow **Levada do Barreiro**. Walk past tall tree heather and pick a way down towards a stand of pines, aiming to the left of them. Follow the levada, now waterless, turning left round a corner to pass a solitary, gnarled specimen of tree heather. The channel descends past a few tall pines then drops over a rocky lip, while the path goes down log steps to cross a little **footbridge** over a small stream.

The water in the levada sometimes flows through a black plastic pipe which is occasionally seen on the surface. A path traces it through tree heather, crossing a steep and stony slope. Drop down towards the river, but watch for the levada channel where a sign points back uphill to Poço da Neve. A better path runs beside the channel through tree heather. Pass a junction where another path climbs uphill, but keep to the levada. The path swings round to cross a stream then picks its way across another slope of tree heather. ◄

The path steepens and the levada is fenced where the slope is exposed or slippery. Take care at these points and continue through dense woodland. ◄ The path is sometimes level, sometimes steep, and can be rugged. There are some open slopes and views across the valley or down towards Funchal. The Estrada Florestal, a loop of forest road, can be reached on the left and offers easy walking towards Poiso.

Walk steeply down a ridge, taking care where log steps are a bit rickety. Cross a track and walk down a narrow levada path, landing on the track further down. ◄ Signposts point back uphill for Poço da Neve. Turn left to leave the levada and follow the track round the valley to pass white buildings at **Casa do Barreiro**, at 960m (3150ft). The track leads through green gates to leave the Parque Ecológico do Funchal and a tarmac road leads onwards. Cross a slope of tall eucalyptus and pine then pass a **quarry** on the left, and a house on the right. The road leads to green gates at a junction with the **ER-103 road** on a hairpin bend. Follow the main road up to a higher bend then turn right down a very steep cobbled

Fine views stretch across the valley of the **Ribeira de Santa Luzia,** taking in a nearby waterfall.

The woods here are of pine, mimosa, holm oak and tree heather.

Alternatively, follow a path along a crest to a hilltop viewpoint first, then drop down to the levada.

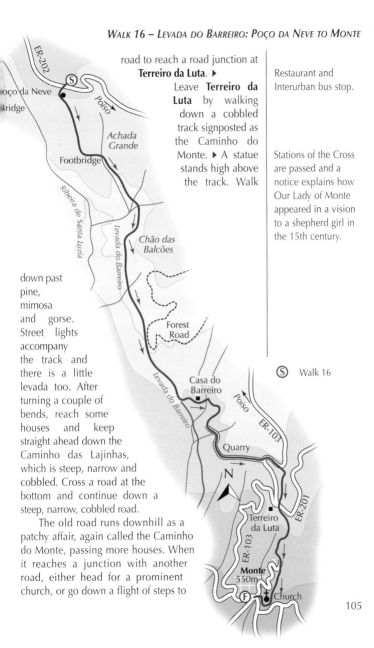

road to reach a road junction at **Terreiro da Luta**. ▶

Leave **Terreiro da Luta** by walking down a cobbled track signposted as the Caminho do Monte. ▶ A statue stands high above the track. Walk

Restaurant and Interurban bus stop.

Stations of the Cross are passed and a notice explains how Our Lady of Monte appeared in a vision to a shepherd girl in the 15th century.

down past pine, mimosa and gorse. Street lights accompany the track and there is a little levada too. After turning a couple of bends, reach some houses and keep straight ahead down the Caminho das Lajinhas, which is steep, narrow and cobbled. Cross a road at the bottom and continue down a steep, narrow, cobbled road.

The old road runs downhill as a patchy affair, again called the Caminho do Monte, passing more houses. When it reaches a junction with another road, either head for a prominent church, or go down a flight of steps to

105

reach a fine cobbled square at **Monte**, shaded by tall plane trees, at 550m (1805ft). Snack Bar Alto Monte, Café do Parque, souvenir stalls, toilets, taxis and Urban bus to Funchal.

CAMINHO DE FERRO DO MONTE

Madeira never developed a railway network, but an idea for a short funicular railway was promoted in 1893. The line was fully operational between Funchal, Monte and Terreiro da Luta by 1912. It closed in 1943, though recently there have been plans to restore at least the top part of it. There is a small museum about the railway at Terreiro da Luta, while down at Monte the old station is being restored to its former glory as a refreshment house.

WALK 17
Levada da Negra:
Poço da Neve to Barreira

Start	Poço da Neve, near Pico do Areeiro – 200222
Finish	Barreira, above Funchal – 176175
Distance	8km (5 miles)
Total Ascent	50m (165ft)
Total Descent	1040m (3410ft)
Time	2hrs 30mins
Maps	Carta Militar 5, 6 & 8
Terrain	The path is narrow and stony in places, occasionally exposed, crossing steep and rocky mountain slopes. Woodland near the end gives way to a track and a steep road.
Refreshments	None on the route, but plenty around Funchal.
Transport	Taxi to Poço da Neve. Urban bus 10A links Barreira with Funchal.

The narrow channel of the Levada da Negra carries water at speed from the flanks of Picos do Areeiro and Cedro to thirsty Funchal. This walk starts at the Poço da Neve ice-house, and the levada is picked up on the other side of a rugged valley. In reverse, and despite its steepness, this route offers the easiest ascent from the suburbs of Funchal to the highest peaks on Madeira.

Use a taxi to reach **Poço da Neve**, at 1640m (5380ft), where there is a small roadside parking space. A signpost and a gate reveal a paved path leading down to a stone **ice-house** covering a deep and dark pit, with a glimpse of the harbour down at Funchal. ▸

A grassy path runs downhill from the **ice-house**, bearing red and yellow marker posts. Cross a track and continue down a slope of grass and bracken with boulders dotted about. Keep right at path junctions, regardless of marker posts, to land on a broad and stony track. Turn right to follow the track down to a concrete bridge spanning the **Ribeira de Santa Luzia**. Normally, the riverbed is dry and boulder-strewn, but note the walls built at intervals along its course to control flash floods.

Follow the track uphill and notice how the slopes have been planted with tree saplings and shrubs in an effort to regenerate the forest cover. The track reaches a junction on a broad gap at 1540m (5050ft). ▸ The narrow **Levada da Negra** is encountered, so just follow the water downstream. Route-finding couldn't be easier, but the path can be rough and rocky.

The narrow channel is flanked by short grass and boulders, dropping in a straight line, allowing the water to pick up speed. Stone steps have been laid on a steeper stretch. The levada suddenly pours into the bouldery bed of the **Ribeira de Santo António de Madalena**, around 1280m (4200ft). Rather than flowing *downstream* with the river, the water actually flows *across* the river to continue along the levada.

The channel is less steeply inclined as it slices across the valley side. The valley itself, however, falls

For more information about the ice-house see page 103.

There is a view of Pico do Areeiro, which will not be visible from this walk again, the next big mountain in view being Pico do Cedro.

Look to the right to see several round, dry-stone structures which were formerly ice-houses.

When there is a good flow of water there are fine waterfalls.

(S) Walk 17

The slope is steep and rocky, but the path is often wide and supported by a stout dry-stone buttress, and some parts are level and grassy.

dramatically and features rocky gorges and deep pools. ◄ Turn round a corner to look down to Funchal and the sea. Look for traces of an older levada cut into the rock just above the current one. The path hugs the **Levada da Negra**, except when a bouldery gully is reached, when it runs a little lower. Lush clumps of heather grow on the rocky slopes and a descent features steps. While some parts of the path are narrow and rocky, other parts are easier and a fairly level stretch passes a few pines on a steep slope. These are all that survived a fire, along with a few chestnuts beside the river. The water picks up speed for another downhill run, levelling out after turning a corner. ◄ Enjoy a last view back up the valley, then go through a gate into dense eucalyptus forest.

A narrow path runs beside the levada, reaching a concrete hut at an intersection with another narrow levada. Keep level, in effect curving to the right to continue following the **Levada da Negra** downstream. The path leads in and out of a little valley, then turns sharply to enter another little valley, making a tight turn to leave it. A broader path curves more gently, passing eucalyptus and tall chestnut. Head downhill and swing left to join a broad, cobbled road. Follow this along a crest with a narrow levada on either side. Pass a farm where the tree cover diminishes and street lights appear.

The narrow Levada da Negra traverses steep and rugged slopes, but always has a good path alongside

Walk downhill to pass a water intake building and continue down a steep concrete road with steps in the middle. When tarmac is reached at **Barreira**, there are bus stops. ◀

Fork right and walk down a very steep concrete road, reaching a round water tank and around 650m (2130ft). ◀

Infrequent urban bus 91

Regular urban bus 10A to Funchal

WALK 18

*Levada do Curral:
Curral das Freiras to Funchal*

Start	Curral das Freiras – 161216
Finish	São Martinho, Funchal – 188137
Distance	15km (9½ miles)
Total Ascent	15m (50ft)
Total Descent	400m (1310ft)
Time	5hrs
Maps	Carta Militar 5 & 8
Terrain	The levada path is uneven in places as it crosses steep, wooded slopes and sheer, exposed cliffs. Beware of rock-falls at first, then steep and slippery rock at Fajã. The final stretch into Funchal is without difficulties.
Refreshments	Plenty at Curral das Freiras. Restaurants at Santo Quitéria. A couple of bars are passed on the way to São Martinho.
Transport	Interurban bus 81 serves Curral das Freiras from Funchal. Urban bus routes proliferate between Santo Quitéria and São Martinho.

This is one of the more frightening levadas on Madeira, slicing southwards from Curral das Freiras through an impressively steep-sided gorge. The levada clings to sheer cliffs and there is a notoriously awkward stretch at Fajã where it has been hacked from a cliff that continually weeps with water, so it is treacherously slippery. The continuation into Funchal is much easier.

CURRAL DAS FREIRAS

Translated as the 'Nuns' Valley', the name recalls how the nuns from the convent at Santa Clara fled from pirates in 1566 and re-settled far inland, deep in the valley. A badly thought-out geological theory states that the valley is a volcanic crater, but this is nonsense. It is simply a deeply eroded valley cut into thick volcanic rock. The village has a few shops, bars and restaurants, as well as an annual autumn chestnut festival. Interurban bus 81 runs to and from Funchal, passing through a tunnel almost 2.5km (1½ miles) long.

Start at the church in **Curral das Freiras** and follow the bendy road downhill. (The bus runs this way but the start of the walk could easily be missed.) A garage bearing a number 92 stands to the right of the road, while the **Levada do Curral** is on the left of the road and passes above a building with a corrugated roof. The levada path is concrete as it runs above vegetable plots, then it turns into a little side-valley and is covered by earth and stones. ▶

Landslips and rockfalls are common from the cliffs near **Eira do Serrado**!

After passing through mixed woods, views overlook the main valley from a short stretch of fencing. Turn round another side-valley and proceed without the security of a fence across a steep slope of chestnut. There are some big boulders and still a danger of rockfall! Chestnut gives way to a stand of pines and a view of the sheer cliff that spawns the boulders. Don't loiter, but follow the levada onwards and step round the outside of a little **tunnel**. The channel is covered for a while. ▶ Chestnut and eucalyptus grow on old cultivation terraces, along with malfurada and prickly pears. Turn round a bare hollow of steep rock, where the levada rushes beside an uneven path with brambles alongside. After passing a few chestnuts and more thorny scrub, turn a steep-sided rocky gully by negotiating a short, bent **tunnel**.

There are splendid valley and peak views before turning a corner into woods again.

111

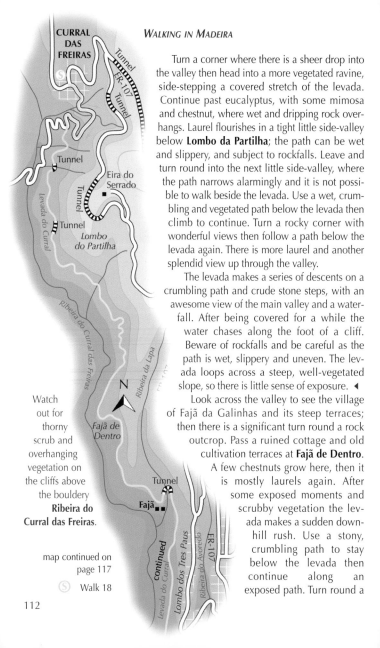

CURRAL DAS FREIRAS

Tunnel

ER-107

Tunnel

Tunnel

Eira do Serrado

Levada do Curral

Tunnel

Lombo do Partilha

Ribeira do Curral das Freiras

Ribeira da Lapa

N

Fajã de Dentro

Ribeira do Avoredo

Tunnel

Fajã

ER-107

continued

Levada do Curral

Lombo dos Tres Paus

Turn a corner where there is a sheer drop into the valley then head into a more vegetated ravine, side-stepping a covered stretch of the levada. Continue past eucalyptus, with some mimosa and chestnut, where wet and dripping rock overhangs. Laurel flourishes in a tight little side-valley below **Lombo da Partilha**; the path can be wet and slippery, and subject to rockfalls. Leave and turn round into the next little side-valley, where the path narrows alarmingly and it is not possible to walk beside the levada. Use a wet, crumbling and vegetated path below the levada then climb to continue. Turn a rocky corner with wonderful views then follow a path below the levada again. There is more laurel and another splendid view up through the valley.

The levada makes a series of descents on a crumbling path and crude stone steps, with an awesome view of the main valley and a waterfall. After being covered for a while the water chases along the foot of a cliff. Beware of rockfalls and be careful as the path is wet, slippery and uneven. The levada loops across a steep, well-vegetated slope, so there is little sense of exposure. ◀

Look across the valley to see the village of Fajã da Galinhas and its steep terraces; then there is a significant turn round a rock outcrop. Pass a ruined cottage and old cultivation terraces at **Fajã de Dentro**. A few chestnuts grow here, then it is mostly laurels again. After some exposed moments and scrubby vegetation the levada makes a sudden downhill rush. Use a stony, crumbling path to stay below the levada then continue along an exposed path. Turn round a

Watch out for thorny scrub and overhanging vegetation on the cliffs above the bouldery **Ribeira do Curral das Freiras**.

map continued on page 117

Ⓢ Walk 18

corner and walk down exposed steps to reach a stand of eucalyptus. ▶

Turn another corner, where the levada is covered with rockfall detritus, then the water rushes downhill. If the concrete path is wet and slippery, take care, though the steeper stretches have steps built into them. Rampant growths of cane and brambles fill old cultivation terraces at **Fajã**. ▶

Reach a gateway and pause to study an awesome side-valley, which is the most dangerous part of the walk, so take great care. Walk down the path and pass a wedged boulder. Enter a high and wide **tunnel**, with the water rushing noisily through it. The tunnel is bent and the exit can't be seen, but there are a series of 'windows' allowing light to enter. A waterfall pours down outside the first 'window' and there are ten 'windows' to pass. Leave the tunnel and walk carefully down 35 steep and exposed steps with a fence alongside. The levada is hidden and an overhang continually streams with water. Use water-proofs or an umbrella, or get soaked, then continue along a fenced parapet to reach dry ground. The path beyond has a fence and passes a small rock arch. Pass another gateway to reach safer ground. Take a break, get a few things dried and look back into the deeply-cut valley.

The deserted houses at **Fajã** are seen from this stance. Later, a vine trellis straddles the levada and a good path leads through woods and along a cliff, with views from Fajã da Galinhas down to the sea. The levada goes through a tiny rock arch, but the path stays outside.

There is a view back up the valley to Fajã da Galinhas.

One of the old houses is seen and there is a view down the Socorridos valley to the sea.

A flight of 35 very steep and exposed steps drop down from a tunnel onto a wet and dripping parapet path

Looking back towards the old houses at Fajã, once the Levada do Curral runs along an easier path

Turn round a corner where it doesn't feel so exposed with trees growing alongside. Go through a rock cutting where slabs lie over the channel for a short stretch, then look down along the **Ribeira dos Socorridos**, which is quite industrial.

Pass a few houses near **Pico dos Cardos** and the levada is covered in slabs as it swings left into another valley. ▸ Cross a concrete and iron footbridge over the bouldery **Ribeira do Arvoredo**, where eucalyptus grows. The paved levada path is now the Vereda de Santa Quitéria, and is cut into a cliff as it passes more houses.

After crossing a steep concrete road the path is the Travessa do Tanque. Water is seen in the levada until the next steep concrete road, where it is covered again. Pass vine trellises and bananas, then join and follow a bit of road round into the next valley. The channel is covered in slabs, but the water is seen again on leaving a little valley. Join a road and head straight through a roundabout, passing below the large 'Maxmat' building at **Santa Quitéria**. ▸ The levada is buried beneath the road, but watch on the right to see it surface beside the Entrada do Tanque on the way to a main road at **Tanque**. ▸

Follow the Caminho do Pico do Funcho, then turn left along the Vereda da Levada do Poço Barral. The levada here runs beneath more slabs. Cross a road and continue slightly downhill, still signposted for the *vereda*. Beware of holes in the path, passing bananas and crossing a concrete path, the Rampa do Poço Barral. There may be a tiny bar available. Continue along the path, passing more bananas and the Recheio Cash and Carry.

Emerge on the busy Caminho do Esmereldo, use a pedestrian crossing and turn right. ▸ Turn left along the Travessa do Moinho, where the levada is covered at first, but turn right down steps later to find it in a concrete aqueduct. Cross the **VR-1 motorway** using a blue aqueduct footbridge and continue between a tall wall and more bananas. Descend a flight of steps to the left to reach a road called the Rua do Ninho. Turn right to follow it downhill and it becomes quite narrow at the end. ▸

Bananas dominate the scene, but all sorts of fruit and vegetables grow. The paved stretch of the levada is called the Vereda da Viana, and some slabs are wobbly and broken.

Madeira Shopping, banks, ATMs, post office, restaurants, bus and taxi

Bruno Bar, Bar Mariano

Restaurante O Moinho

Snack Bar O Ninho

Turn right along the Rua do Doctor Barreto to reach the busy Caminho de São Martinho and catch any bus into **Funchal**.

WALK 19

Levada dos Piornais:
Lombada to Funchal

Start	Lombada – 163141
Finish	Estádio dos Barreiros, Funchal – 195131
Distance	7km or 12km (4½ or 7½ miles)
Total Ascent	35m (115ft)
Total Descent	25m (80ft)
Time	2hrs 15mins or 4hrs
Maps	Carta Militar 8 & 9
Terrain	The first stage crosses exposed cliffs and passes through tiny tunnels. The second stage is easier, crossing cultivated and urban slopes.
Refreshments	Small shops and bars at Lombada, Quebradas and Amparo.
Transport	Urban bus 1 & 3 serve Lombada. Urban bus 2 & 3 serve Quebradas. Urban bus 2 serves Caminho do Areeiro. Urban bus 4 & 48 serve Caminho do Amparo. Urban bus 45 serves the Estádio dos Barreiros.

This is one of the oldest levadas on Madeira, dating from the 15th century. It has been overhauled many times and carries water from the Socorridos valley to the sunny slopes around São Martinho. Sugar was once grown extensively, but bananas now cover the slopes. This walk can be rocky, difficult and exposed, or short, simple and easy, depending on a choice made at the start.

Start at **Lombada**, on the Caminho da Lombada, near the shop/bar Cantinho do Sousa. There is a view into the industrial Socorridos valley, spanned by the VR-1 motorway bridge. Climb steeply up the Rua do Pico da Lombada and cross a bridge over the motorway. The **Levada dos Piornais** is immediately beyond and can be followed left (difficult) or right (easy). Look at an information board detailing some of the plants seen along the way. The endemic Madeiran plant 'piorno' gave the levada its name.

Turn left to head upstream if you are agile, sure-footed and have a head for heights, because the exposure gets worse with distance. The levada is covered and protected by railings at first, but soon afterwards a narrow parapet path passes bananas

Ⓕ Walk 18
Ⓢ Walk 19

map of Route 18 continued from page 112

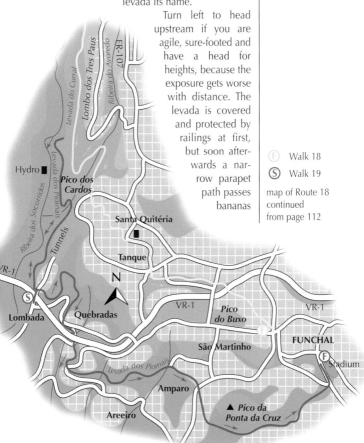

117

and mimosa, a few eucalyptus and pine. Note a flight of steps leading downhill, allowing a difficult and spectacular stretch to be avoided. The levada is partly cut into an overhanging cliff and partly supported on stone arches.

There are railings, but some walkers find the exposure unnerving.

Crouch low, or even crawl through a complex gash of a **tunnel**. ◄ Slabs lie across the levada where the parapet is too narrow to walk. Continue through another small tunnel, then cross a stone aqueduct arch. Walk on slabs through short rock cuttings, then cross another arch. A low, fractured tunnel comes next, then walk on slabs across another arch.

The levada crosses a stepped concrete path with street lights, then the parapet path leads into a side-valley,

The upper half of the Levada dos Piornais is very exposed and crosses a number of cliff faces

passing eucalyptus. There are railings, but it is exposed in places. Railings also stand either side of a narrow, arched stone bridge over the bouldery **Ribeira do Arvoredo**. ▸ Swing round into the main Socorridos valley again, taking care where the smooth concrete parapet turns into an uneven stone parapet. There is a tunnel with good headroom and three 'windows', then the levada crosses a sheer cliff. A pipeline is passed and a cliff has to be negotiated opposite a **hydro-electric station**. After passing a house and cultivation terraces, a sign warns 'perigo/danger' though the path isn't difficult. However, after turning a corner, there is a locked gate surrounded by spikes and further access is denied. Turn round and retrace steps to the information board above **Lombada** where the walk started.

There are no railings on leaving the valley, no matter how narrow or exposed the path becomes.

Leaving the motorway bridge, the **Levada dos Piornais** is covered in concrete and runs between walls, houses and extensive banana terraces. Views can be described as *bananoramic!* Cross over a road at the head of a valley (Urban bus 16A). Walk round another little valley drained by a small stream. ▸ The levada crosses a road bend at **Quebradas** then a short stretch leads to a road bridge spanning the **VR-1 motorway**.

Mountain views include the summit of Pico do Cedro.

There are views from the bridge, but don't cross to the other side. Instead, follow the levada beside the motorway then climb beside a slip road to reach the Caminho das Quebradas. ▸ Turn right to pass a shop/bar, the Super das Quebradas. (Urban bus 2, 3, 16A & 50)

Bar Restaurante Santa Rita to the left

Turn right again as signposted for Funchal and follow the road under the motorway. Turn right down the Caminho das Quebradas de Baixo, then almost immediately left down steps to regain the levada.

The channel is covered and there is a tall wall alongside. A house sits on the levada, so go down steps and continue along a cobbled road. When the road rises a little, go down a couple of steps to the right to continue along the slab-covered channel. Climb up a few steps and cross a road bend on the Caminho do Areeiro. ▸ Walk between a wall and a slope of prickly pears, then the slabs finish and water is seen again.

Urban bus 2

Vegetables and bananas grow down towards the sea at **Areeiro,** where big hotels and apartments are seen.

A wall stands left of the levada. ◄ A steep concrete road crosses the levada on a bend, whereafter the water is covered. A flight of steps forms an arch on another bend, when the levada becomes open. Pass a cave and go under a small stone arch while turning a slab-covered corner. The church tower at **São Martinho** is seen on a hill, while terraces fill the valley below.

The levada parapet is polished stone for a while, then concrete again. Cross a busy bend on the Caminho do Amparo. ◄

Bus, small shop/bar

The levada leaves **Amparo** and continues between houses, partly covered by slabs and partly open. Cross a minor road and walk along a slab-covered section, then follow the open levada using a stone parapet. Looking back, there is a view of the summit tor on Pico Grande. The parapet features slabs that ring musically when anyone walks on them! ◄ While following another slab-covered stretch, there are views of the Ilhas Desertas, as well as the built-up southernmost point of Madeira at Ponta da Cruz.

Look down on large buildings near the sea, while the **Pico da Ponta da Cruz** rising above is thick with prickly pears and crowned with masts.

The levada drops a little while passing under a concrete road, then goes through a flowery cutting. The parapet path leads round a slope offering views over Funchal and its harbour. The levada is covered in slabs for a short way until it crosses a road. Continue along a short slab-covered stretch and an open stretch then walk alongside a busy road. Steps lead up onto this road close to a stadium, the **Estádio dos Barreiros**. Keep left of stadium to finish (bar and Urban bus 45, though the centre of **Funchal** is not too far away.)

ESTÁDIO DOS BARREIROS

Observe the view from the stadium if considering further levada walks near Funchal. Looking left of the stadium, the highest suburb of Funchal is Barreira, terminus of Walk 17 on the Levada da Negra. Look for the twin spires of the church at Monte, terminus of Walk 16 on the Levada do Barreiro and start of Walk 1 on the Levada dos Tornos. Spot the floodlights of the Campo do Pomar, starting point for Walk 3 on the Levada da Serra.

SECTION 3
The High Mountains

Looking back along the stone-paved path during the descent from Pico Ruivo to Achada do Teixeira (Walk 25)

Many walkers want to climb the highest mountains in Madeira, and the two highest peaks are remarkably easy to visit. Pico Ruivo can be climbed in an hour or so by following a stone-paved path from a high car park to the summit. Pico do Areeiro can be climbed in mere seconds using a flight of steps from a car park.

Walkers venturing far into the mountains must be aware that they are phenomenally steep, rather unstable, prone to rock-falls, with a limited number of paths available. However, given good weather, good stamina, a head for heights and a sure foot, walks through the mountains are astoundingly scenic and incredibly interesting. Paths are often carved from the rock, with thousands of stone steps piled one on top of another. While some areas are bare and rocky, other parts are covered in dense 'laurisilva' that almost blocks out the sunlight.

Walkers can head for the heights and attempt to follow rugged ridges, but this isn't always possible as the paths tend to meander round the shoulders of the peaks. On the northern slopes of Pico Ruivo a couple of fine old paths are best used for long descents. Both of them cross the Levada do Caldeirão Verde, which penetrates into deep, remote, forested gullies, where it is fed by waterfalls. A handful of routes traverse the Boca das Torrinhas - a gap in the middle of Madeira's mountains.

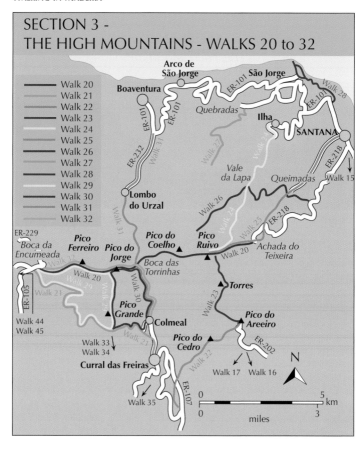

SECTION 3 - THE HIGH MOUNTAINS - WALKS 20 to 32

Approaching the high mountains requires careful planning. Driving a car to Pico do Areeiro or Achada do Teixeira means returning to it, which is frustrating. Careful use of taxis and juggling with Interurban and Rodoeste bus timetables will allow the use some remarkable mountain paths. Keen walkers can link routes together to create tough long-distance routes, especially around the Boca da Encumeada and Curral das Freiras. Links with low-level routes are available around Santana.

WALK 20

*Boca da Encumeada to
Achada do Teixeira*

Start	Boca da Encumeada – 112255
Finish	Achada do Teixeira – 205265
Distance	15km (9½ miles)
Total Ascent	1480m (4855ft)
Total Descent	900m (2950ft)
Time	7hrs
Maps	Carta Militar 5 & 6
Terrain	Mountainous, with paved paths and steps, as well as some steep and stony stretches. Paths are generally clear throughout, but take care at junctions in mist. Dense vegetation cover hampers views on many stretches.
Refreshments	Snack Bar Restaurante Encumeada at the start of the walk. Small bar below Pico Ruivo.
Transport	Rodoeste Bus 6 & 139 serve Boca da Encumeada from Funchal, Ribeira Brava and São Vicente. Taxi from Achada do Teixeira to Santana.

It is possible to walk from the Boca da Encumeada, along the main mountain crest of Madeira, to Achada do Teixeira. If tempted to do this, then be sure to make an arrangement to be collected either by a taxi or by someone else at the end of the day. The route will take a little longer from west to east, than from east to west, since there is considerably more climbing involved.

Start at the Snack Bar Restaurante Encumeada and follow the road through a rock cutting on the **Boca da Encumeada** at 1007m (3304ft). Turn right to follow a stony track uphill, signposted as the PR1.3 trail. The track curves right towards some masts, so keep left to follow a narrow

The dense vegetation is remarkably mixed and includes everything from *laurisilva* species to low-lying brambles.

path further up rough and ready steps. ◄ Climb steep flights of stone steps, often fenced and buttressed, to reach the crest of the mountain range around 1250m (4100ft) near **Pico do Meio**. Continue along the ridge and enjoy good views from a bare shoulder, looking directly down to Ribeira Brava. Cross the gentle, heathery dome of **Pico da Encumeada** to reach a nar-row and well-vegetated gap, where São Vicente and Ribeira Brava can be seen.

Go through a gate and climb stone steps, some of them buttressed and fenced, head-ing left then swinging right to pass a cave with a stone seat. Climb more steps, turning left and right while

At an open corner there are views of the surrounding mountains, particularly Pico Grande.

climbing through tall tree heather. ◄ Pass tall tree heather and ancient til trees and go through a gateway, then pass along the base of a cliff on the southern flank of **Pico Ferreiro**. The path exploits a thin, crumbling layer in the rock and reaches another gateway. Zigzag up a wooded slope to reach a gap on the ridge, around 1420m (4660ft), overlooked by rocky pinnacles.

Climb again, reaching fenced stone steps at a higher level, then enjoy the view, but take care not to be drawn along a path on the right, which is a very rugged route to Pico Grande. The main path climbs more steps on the northern flanks of **Pico do Jorge**, among dense tree heather and bilberry, reaching a shoulder where views take in Pico do Cedro, Pico Grande, Paúl da Serra and

Enjoy a stretch along the crest with good views, looking down from a stout stone buttress to São Vicente.

the north-west coast. ◄ Head downhill to reach a heathery shoulder with fine views. Continue up and along the crest, then cross a gritty gap around 1650m (5415ft) near **Pico Casado**.

Pass a blade-like outcrop of rock and zigzag down-hill, noticing that some of the stones make musical chinking sounds underfoot. Pass a cave and head down steps on a slope of dense heather. The path levels out and squeezes through a rocky cleft full of ferns and exotic plants.

map continued on page 126

Pico do Coelho ▲1733m

Pico das Eirinhas ▲ 1649m

N

▲*Pico da Laje*

iro ▲0m *Pico Casado* ▲1725m 1450m

Boca das Torrinhas

Ⓢ Walk 20

▲1691m
Pico do Jorge

Cove

The way ahead is more rugged but becomes gentler as the path crosses the ridge. Walk down a fenced flight of stone steps to land on the **Boca das Torrinhas** at 1450m (4760ft). ▶

Big, faded signposts give destinations along all the paths that leave this point, which are covered in turn on Walks 30, 31 & 32.

Looking back to the gap of Boca das Torrinhas through a dense covering of heather trees

map continued
from page 125

Unless tempted to switch routes at this point, follow the path up along the ridge and up a ramp-like buttress, enjoying views in most directions before passing through a well-wooded area. Steep flights of stone steps with fencing alongside lead downhill on the sunless northern flank of **Pico da Laje**, where the surroundings are like a jungle. Another long flight of stone steps climbs back uphill, reaching a gap overlooking the Curral valley. Keep left at path junctions to avoid being drawn off-course down into the valley.

Climb easily across the heathery slopes of **Pico das Eirinhas** with views back to Pico Grande and ahead to Pico Ruivo. The path rises and falls, switching from one side of the crest to the other, then runs through dense heather trees and bilberry on the south-facing slopes of **Pico do Coelho**, with a view from one corner. A paved path appears and runs mostly downhill, often with good views of the Curral valley, crossing slopes of broom and heather while avoiding the **Pico da Lapa da Cadela**, then running level. The path climbs through thick heather and swings right along a stony crest of red pumice. Simply follow the paving to reach a junction with another path.

Look along the rugged ridge to Pico do Areeiro, as well as deep down into the valley towards Curral das Freiras. Pico Grande has a prominent summit tor, while the rugged crest of Madeira leads the eye towards the plateau of Paúl da Serra, while densely wooded slopes fall to the north coast.

Turn right to follow a worn path to the top of **Pico Ruivo**. There is a tall trig point at 1862m (6109ft) beside a monument. The summit is entirely covered in wooden decking, surrounded by a wooden fence, with a couple of wooden paths leading off to subsidiary view-points. ◄ Retrace the steps down from the summit, and turn right to follow a well-worn path and crude steps down a heather-clad slope to reach a **refuge** (refreshments available, but it is almost impossible to get permission to stay overnight).

Walk down a flight of stone steps to leave the refuge, reaching another junction of paths. ▶ Keep straight ahead across bare pumice then walk down stone steps to go through a gap in a wall. Pass ancient, gnarled tree heather, big boulders and rocky outcrops, reaching a stone shelter on a gap, where there is a superb view back to the peaks of Torres. Walk down to a signposted path junction and keep straight ahead. ▶ Climb along the paved path to pass another stone shelter and a water source. The path regains the ridge to pass yet another stone shelter. Views take in mountains, valleys and the sea, so enjoy them all before the path finally leads down to the road-end car park at **Achada do Teixeira**, around 1580m (5185ft). (If you reach this point and haven't made any transport arrangements, there are sometimes taxis parked here, waiting for their clients to return from Pico Ruivo. They might be willing to run you down to Santana.)

Right is for Pico do Areeiro, used on Walk 23.

The path down to the left is used on Walk 24.

WALK 21

*Boca da Encumeada to
Curral das Freiras*

Start	Boca da Encumeada – 112255
Finish	Curral das Freiras – 161216
Distance	13km (8 miles)
Total Ascent	680m (2230ft)
Total Descent	1040m (3410ft)
Time	5hrs
Map	Carta Militar 5
Terrain	Mountainous, with a well-wooded path at first, then a paved path, with the danger of rock-falls at a higher level. The descent is along a steep and stony path.
Refreshments	Snack Bar Restaurante Encumeada at the start. Small bar at Fajã Escura. Plenty of choice at Curral das Freiras.
Transport	Rodoeste bus 6 & 139 serve Boca da Encumeada from Funchal, Ribeira Brava and São Vicente. Interurban bus 81 links Curral das Freiras with Funchal.

This walk avoids the peaks, yet includes good views of them from various vantage points. Leaving the Boca da Encumeada, a well-wooded valley has to be crossed before the route climbs around the steep slopes of Pico Grande. Beware of rock-falls on the way to the Boca do Cerro. A steep and winding path leads down into a deep and rugged valley to finish at Curral das Freiras.

Start on the **Boca da Encumeada** at 1007m (3304ft), where the Snack Bar Restaurante Encumeada is available. Follow the road downhill in the direction of Serra de Água, turning left round a bend to reach a junction with a track, where a notice indicates the start of the PR12 trail. ◀ Laurel, heather, broom and brambles grow on the slope, while the track narrows and at one bend features a fine view of Pico Grande. The path passes beneath a pipeline feeding the generating station at Serra de Água.

Buses stop here if given due notice, but it is on an awkward road bend.

Walk down a slope dominated by eucalyptus and cross rocky stream-beds at **Poço**, the last one shaded by laurels. Cross a slope of bracken and brambles with open views. More woodland shade follows, then the path passes cultivation terraces and reaches a footbridge over a bouldery stream-bed. Climb gently through pines, also passing eucalyptus, candleberry and bilberry. The shaded, stone-paved path leads to the head of the valley at **Curral Jangão**, where there are cultivated slopes and plenty of chestnuts. A stone-arched bridge spans a rocky gorge on the **Ribeiro do Poço**.

The path passes a small stone building and undulates, sometimes in dense woods and sometimes with views across the valley. Swing left through tall eucalyptus and pass beneath a frowning rock face, climbing along a stone-paved path to emerge at a corner where broom scrub grows. ◀ Climbing further, the path is flanked by bracken, broom and brambles, passing only a few trees. The route picks out a line of weakness between two cliff faces, working its way round a steep-sided hollow, then

There are good views of the valley and mountains.

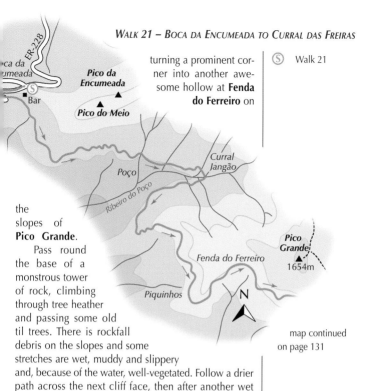

Ⓢ Walk 21

turning a prominent corner into another awesome hollow at **Fenda do Ferreiro** on

the slopes of **Pico Grande**.

Pass round the base of a monstrous tower of rock, climbing through tree heather and passing some old til trees. There is rockfall debris on the slopes and some stretches are wet, muddy and slippery and, because of the water, well-vegetated. Follow a drier path across the next cliff face, then after another wet patch the path levels out on a slope of gorse. There is a fine view ahead to Pico do Serradinho (see Walk 33). For today, turn left up a few stone steps and cross the gorse-covered crest of **Boca do Cerro**. ▶

A narrow path descends gently from the gap with good views into the Curral valley. ▶ A few chestnuts offer shade on the slope, then the path goes through broom scrub and crosses a bouldery stream-bed. Brush past broom, turn round a corner and zigzag down a steep spur at **Eirado**. A well-engineered path, carved from rock or stoutly buttressed, is often stony underfoot. Chestnut and other trees clothe the slope as the zigzag path leads downhill. Go through a gateway on an open slope then pass tall chestnut, eucalyptus and pine. The path joins a forest track on a bend, and this track can be

map continued on page 131

To climb Pico Grande, see Walk 29 or Walk 30.

A pinnacle of rock lies to the right, while views across the valley include Pico Ruivo and Pico do Areeiro.

129

The path squeezes past broom at the start of the long and winding descent into the Curral valley

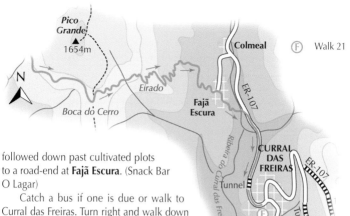

(F) Walk 21

followed down past cultivated plots to a road-end at **Fajã Escura**. (Snack Bar O Lagar)

Catch a bus if one is due or walk to Curral das Freiras. Turn right and walk down the Caminho da Fajã Escura, following a concrete road, a steeper stone track and steps down a wooded slope, with street lights alongside. Cross a bridge over the bouldery **Ribeira do Curral das Freiras**, where a path and steps lead up to the **ER-107 road**. There is a bus stop here, otherwise turn right to keep walking. Cross a bridge over the **Ribeira do Cidrão** then follow the road up through a tunnel to **Curral das Freiras**. ▶

map continued from page 129

For facilities see page 111.

WALK 22

Pico do Cedro and Pico do Areeiro

Start	Ribeira da Lapa on the ER-107 road – 172198
Finish	Pico do Areeiro – 196233
Distance	6.5km (4 miles)
Total Ascent	1070m (3510ft)
Total Descent	200m (655ft)
Time	4hrs
Maps	Carta Militar 5 & 6
Terrain	A steep and rocky ascent with thorny scrub gives way to a grassy ridge with vague paths and a broad track.
Refreshments	Bar/restaurant on Pico do Areeiro.

Interurban bus 81 crosses the Ribeira da Lapa between
Funchal and Curral das Freiras. Taxi from Pico do
Areeiro to Funchal.

From certain vantage points, Pico do Cedro and
Pico do Areeiro look smooth, seeming to offer easy
walking. This isn't quite true, since the ridge falling
from Cedro south-west to the Curral valley ends in
cliffs and the only 'walkable' slope is very steep and
covered in awkward thorny scrub. Apart from this,
the route is delightful, but many walkers may find
the early stage too difficult.

Start this walk from the entrance to a long tunnel at
Ribeira da Lapa, at 950m (3115ft). Take the old road, or
'antiga ER-107' signposted for Eira do Serrado. On the
left-hand side of the road, count past one metal
lamp-post and three wooden ones. Turn right
to climb a little way up a grassy gully,
but turn right again up a vague, old
path, which is marked on some
maps. Chestnut gives way to
tall pines, but this slope was
devastated by a fire and the
old path is easily lost as height
is gained, being covered in
thorny scrub. ◄ The slope is
very steep, with brambles
and gorse proving as awk-
ward as fallen trees and
pine saplings. The idea,
when faced with rocky outcrops at a higher level, is to
drift to the left and spot an over-
head power line leading to a concrete **pylon** on the ridge high above.

Persevere, but if it
proves too difficult,
then abandon
the walk.

Ⓢ   Walk 22

If you reach this point, which could take well over an hour, then lick your wounds in the knowledge that the worst is over!

Follow the narrow, rocky, steep-sided ridge northwards, looking down on the busy hotel and viewpoint at **Eira do Serrado**. A vague path passes occasional charred pines, gorse and broom. Later, either cross over or skirt a rounded hill covered in bracken at 1410m (4625ft). ▶ Turn right to cross a gentle gap and climb the next hill on the broad crest, at 1466m (4810ft),

Enjoy fine views over the Curral valley, with Pico Grande and its summit tor rising steep and rugged on the far side.

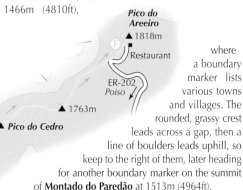

Pico do Areeiro
▲ 1818m

Restaurant

ER-202
Poiso

▲ 1763m

▲ **Pico do Cedro**

where a boundary marker lists various towns and villages. The rounded, grassy crest leads across a gap, then a line of boulders leads uphill, so keep to the right of them, later heading for another boundary marker on the summit of **Montado do Paredão** at 1513m (4964ft).

Cross another little gap and climb a slope covered in boulders, giving way to bare rock on a summit bearing a concrete marker at 1588m (5210ft). Walk

Lumpy pillow lava is passed on a gentle gap before the route climbs onto Pico do Cedro

133

Look ahead to Pico do Areeiro, take in the peaks round the Curral valley to Pico Grande, and note Paúl da Serra and Terreiros beyond.

across easy bedrock towards the next little gap to climb the next rounded hill, which is bare and bouldery. Either keep to the right, or climb to the summit at 1612m (5289ft). Walk down across grass and boulders to reach the corner of a dry-stone wall and fence then follow these uphill. After passing a ladder stile, follow the fence up to the left, reaching a bouldery crest and another boundary marker. Pass newly-planted trees and boulder-hop to **Pico do Cedro**, where a trig point stands at 1759m (5771ft), with good views of the mountains. ◄

Walk down a slope of pulverised pumice to join and follow a clear track across a gap. At the top of the track, turn left along a vague path to reach the next summit, which has a boundary marker at 1763m (5784ft). Follow the fence down along a crest of grass and boulders. Cross a ladder stile at a fence junction to follow a way-marked path up a ridge to a bend on the **ER-202 road**, where slopes fall steep and rugged to the head of the Curral valley. Walk straight uphill from the road bend to reach a car park at the Pousada Areeiro. ◄ Climb steps to the summit viewpoint on **Pico do Areeiro** at 1818m (5965ft), which can be a surprisingly popular place. Either negotiate a lift, arrange to be collected by someone or call for a taxi to leave the mountain. ◄

Shop, bar and restaurant

Keen walkers can continue on to Walk 23.

WALK 23
Pico do Areeiro to Pico Ruivo

Start/Finish	Pico do Areeiro – 196233
Distance	12km (7½ miles) there and back
Total Ascent	1300m (4265ft)
Total Descent	1220m (4000ft)
Time	6hrs
Maps	Carta Militar 5 & 6
Terrain	Mountainous, with a narrow path, flights of steps and a tunnel. Steep, rocky and exposed slopes are often protected by fencing.

Refreshments	Bar/restaurant on Pico do Areeiro. Bar below Pico Ruivo.
Transport	Taxi from Funchal to Pico do Areeiro.

The most popular mountain walk on Madeira is from Pico do Areeiro to Pico Ruivo. It is not suitable in bad weather, being prone to rock-falls, and would upset vertigo sufferers. Apart from that, the engineering of the path is superb. It is carved from rock, offers close-up views of mountains while linking the highest peaks. The walk is there-and-back but could be ended at Achada do Teixeira.

Start at the car park beside the Pousada Areeiro, studying a notice about the Vereda do Areeiro, or PR1 trail. ▶ Climb steps to the summit viewpoint on **Pico do Areeiro** at 1818m (5965ft), which can be a surprisingly popular place. ▶ The path is paved and runs gently down to a gap, then crosses a small hump. Steps lead down to another gap then the path slices across a rocky slope, exploiting a weak and crumbling layer in the basalt bedrock. Detour right to reach a fine viewpoint overlooking the Metade valley, taking the opportunity to spot later stretches of the path.

Continue along the main path, which turns a sharp corner and crosses over a ridge. Fenced steps lead down a steep, sharp, rocky edge to a gap at **São Gonçalo**. Climb a little and cut across a cliff face on **Pico do Cidrão**, then descend with a vengeance using zigzag flights of stone steps. Duck beneath a huge, leaning boulder, pass rocky pinnacles and go down through a hole punched through an upstanding wall-like basalt dyke. An easier terrace path leads to a **tunnel** beneath the sheer-sided **Pico do Gato**. There is good headroom and if you have a torch, use it. Emerge to go down another steep flight of steps, reaching a gap around

Shop, bar and restaurant

Arrive as early as possible for the clearest views.

Refuge

Pico Ruivo ▲
1862m

Tunnel

Closed

Torres
1847m ▲

Tunnel

Closed

1550m
Pico do Gato ▷ Tunnel

**Pico do
Cidrão**
1798m ▲

N

**Pico do
Areeiro**
(SF) ▲ 1818m

Restaurant

(SF) Walk 23

ER-202
Poiso ↓

It is possible to walk
through the tunnel
for a view of the
Curral valley, but
don't follow the path
onwards as another
tunnel has collapsed.

Turning right here
offers the easiest exit
via Achada do
Teixeira, see Walk 25.

1550m (5085ft) where there are splendid views of
the Curral valley and Pico Grande. A fenced-off
path formerly offered an approach to Pico Ruivo,
but one of its tunnels collapsed, so the route is
closed. If it should re-open feel free to use it.

Follow the path downhill across a steep,
vegetated slope overlooking the Metade valley, passing a sign marked 'Fonte'. Later the
path starts to climb, even though the way
ahead seems blocked by sheer cliffs.
Monstrous flights of stone steps have been
carved up these cliffs, but as it isn't possible
to see all the way to the top, just climb
slowly and steadily, enjoying dramatic scenery, until a level
path is reached high on the
shoulder of **Torres**, around
1800m (5905ft). The
path begins to descend
and goes through a
notch on the shoulder.
Stony zigzags and steps
lead downhill and the path
curves down around rocky
ravines, one of which might con-
tain enough water for a shower! Pass beneath a leaning
boulder and follow the path until it reaches the mouth of
a tunnel. ◄

The main path has been carved deeply into a cliff
face, running more or less horizontal with a fence for
protection. It is horribly exposed, but apart from that is
actually quite easy. Follow it gingerly onwards, enjoying
dramatic views but watching for low headroom. Climb
up a winding path and steps through tree heather to
reach a signposted junction of paths. ◄ Turn left to climb
up a flight of stone steps to reach a **refuge** (refreshments
available, but it is almost impossible to get permission to
stay overnight).

Leave the **refuge** to follow crude steps and a well-
worn path up a heather-clad slope. At a junction of

136

paths, turn left to follow a worn path, crunchy with red pumice, to the top of **Pico Ruivo**. There is a tall trig point at 1862m (6109ft) beside a monument. The summit is covered in wooden decking, surrounded by a fence, with a couple of wooden paths leading off to subsidiary viewpoints.   Look along the rugged ridge to Pico do Areeiro, as well as deep into the valley towards Curral das Freiras. Pico Grande has a prominent summit tor, while the rugged crest of Madeira leads the eye towards the plateau of Paúl da Serra. Densely wooded slopes fall to the north coast. Retrace the steps down from the summit and turn right to return to the **refuge**.

To finish this walk, there are four options. The easiest exit is via Achada do Teixeira, only 2.5km (1½ miles) from the refuge along an easy path, but if heading that way, a taxi is needed from a road-end car park high above Santana. The statistics for this walk assume that you will retrace your steps back to Pico do Areeiro, again bearing in mind that a taxi is needed unless you parked a car there. Only the fittest walkers could hope to continue to the Boca da Encumeada, or down to Ilha or Santana. ▶

Look back along the exposed cliff path before climbing to a refuge and the summit of Pico Ruivo

See Walks 20, 24 and 25.

137

WALK 24

Pico Ruivo, Vale da Lapa and Ilha

Start	Pico Ruivo – 184258
Finish	Ilha – 213315
Distance	10km (6 miles)
Total Ascent	30m (100ft)
Total Descent	1530m (5020ft)
Time	3hrs 30mins
Maps	Carta Militar 3, 5 & 6
Terrain	The path down from Pico Ruivo is paved, but the spur to Ilha is vague and rugged at first, becoming clearer as it descends a forested ridge. An old levada, steep paths, steps, tracks and roads finally reach Ilha.
Refreshments	Bar below Pico Ruivo. Small shops and bars at Ilha.
Transport	Taxi from Santana to Achada do Teixeira. Interurban bus 103 occasionally serves Ilha from Funchal, Santana and São Jorge.

Signposts between Ilha and Pico Ruivo point uphill, but this route seems better suited for descending, especially on a hot and humid day. The path is way-marked as the PR1.1 trail, heading down a steep ridge covered in tree heather, becoming easier further downhill. It levels out after crossing the Levada do Caldeirão Verde, but there are further steep drops to Ilha.

The statistics for this walk assume that the summit of Pico Ruivo has been reached by other means, such as Walks 20 or 23, leaving this route purely for the descent. However, the route can be restructured by starting from Achada do Teixeira, either walking 2km (1¼ miles) to the start of the path to Ilha, or 3km (2 miles) to climb to the summit of Pico Ruivo first.

Enjoy wide-ranging views of the mountains of Madeira from the summit of **Pico Ruivo**, at 1862m (6109ft). Walk down through the heather along a worn path, crunchy with red pumice, to reach a junction. Turn right to follow a well-worn path and crude steps down a heather-clad slope to reach a **refuge** (refreshments available, but it is almost impossible to get permission to stay overnight).

Walk down a flight of stone steps to leave the refuge, reaching another junction of paths. ▶ Keep straight ahead to follow the paved path across bare pumice then walk down stone steps to go through a gap in a wall. Pass ancient, gnarled tree heather, big boulders and rocky outcrops, reaching a stone shelter on a gap. Walk down to a signposted path junction and turn left as signposted for Ilha via the PR1.1 trail. ▶ The path is vague, but is marked with red and yellow paint flashes.

Cross a water pipe where the path is a grassy ribbon with crude steps and the slope is liberally scattered with stones. The path crosses a steep and rugged slope, generally descending with good views. Other mountain ridges drop very steeply, but this route heads for the **Lombo dos Bodes**, which is gentler. There are some rocky outcrops,

A paved path passes a shelter on a gap before a less well-used path heads down towards Ilha

Turn right for Pico do Areeiro, see Walk 23.

The path straight ahead is used on Walk 25.

but the path slips off to the left down steps, passing a rock-face, then switches to the right down into tree heather on a lower part of the ridge. Here the path is good, with earth and log steps. Reach a junction in denser tree heather, where a signpost points back to Pico Ruivo and left for Semagral, but keep right to continue downhill.

There are good views across Caldeirão Verde and Caldeirão do Inferno. The path swings right and drops down log steps through a deep rut where the

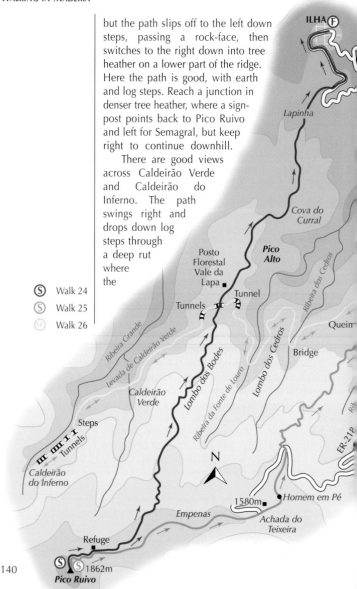

Ⓢ Walk 24

Ⓢ Walk 25

Ⓢ Walk 26

ILHA Ⓕ

Lapinha

Cova do Curral

Pico Alto

Posto Florestal Vale da Lapa

Tunnel

Tunnels

Ribeira dos Cedros

Quein

Bridge

Ribeira Grande

Levada de Caldeirão Verde

Caldeirão Verde

Lombo dos Bodes

Ribeira da Fonte de Louro

Lombo dos Cedros

Steps

Tunnels

Caldeirão do Inferno

ER-218

N

1580m ▪ ● Homem em Pé

Empenas

Achada do Teixeira

Refuge

Ⓢ Ⓢ 1862m

Pico Ruivo

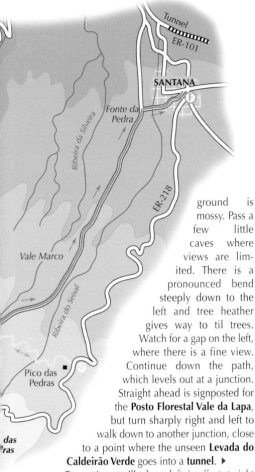

ground is
mossy. Pass a
few little
caves where
views are lim-
ited. There is a
pronounced bend
steeply down to the
left and tree heather
gives way to til trees.
Watch for a gap on the left,
where there is a fine view.
Continue down the path,
which levels out at a junction.
Straight ahead is signposted for
the **Posto Florestal Vale da Lapa**,
but turn sharply right and left to
walk down to another junction, close
to a point where the unseen **Levada do
Caldeirão Verde** goes into a **tunnel**. ▶

To continue to Ilha keep left, in effect straight
ahead as signposted from the junction. The course of
an old levada crosses a slope of laurel and heather,
where some rock outcrops are fenced, and hydrangeas
grow alongside. The water in the levada, if seen, is confined to a black plastic pipe. ▶ Follow the path downhill
and rejoin the path descending from the Posto Florestal.

The levada can be
followed for 4.5km
(2¾ miles) to
Queimadas,
see Walk 26.

Note a path leading
up to a spring and
small shrine.

141

Hundreds of log steps have been installed down through sunken paths in dense laurisilva forest

Continue down lots of log steps on the other side of the ridge, generally in mixed woods, to reach a turning point at the end of a track at **Poças**. Take care as the surface can be slippery, but follow the track until a right-hand bend is reached. Head left along a grassy path on a crest of gorse, heather and brambles. Drop down steps in a deep, dark cutting to reach the track again at a lower level. Cross over it and continue down more steps through another deep and dark cutting to land on the track yet again at **Lapinha**. Turn right along it then turn left along another track to reach a cultivated brow. A sign points to Garnal, but keep right to follow a path beside a narrow levada. This drops past a few sheds, with earth steps giving way to concrete steps, landing by a notice for the PR1.1 trail at a road junction.

Walk down the road and enjoy a view of the valley from the **Miradouro Cabeço do Resto**. ▶ Walk down the road, passing a small shop/bar on entering **Ilha**, but continue down to the church. There is a small shop, a bar and toilets. Only occasional bus services call here, so be absolutely sure of timetables.

A taxi may be available at a nearby house.

WALK 25
Pico Ruivo,
Queimadas and Santana

Start	Pico Ruivo – 184258
Finish	Santana – 243309
Distance	11.5km (7 miles)
Total Ascent	50m (165ft)
Total Descent	1490m (4890ft)
Time	3hrs 30mins
Maps	Carta Militar 3, 5 & 6
Terrain	The path down from Pico Ruivo is paved, but the forested descent to Queimadas can be steep and slippery. The last stretch is along a road.
Refreshments	Bar below Pico Ruivo. Plenty of choice at Santana.

Transport	Taxi from Santana to Achada do Teixeira or from Queimadas. Interurban bus 56, 103 & 138 serve Santana from Funchal and São Jorge.

See map on pages 140–141.

This descent may seem long, but it is quite direct and comes in three distinct stages. A paved path runs downhill from Pico Ruivo to Achada do Teixeira. A steep and rugged path zigzags down past heather trees and through *laurisilva* forest to Queimadas, where the walk could finish if a pick-up is arranged. The final stretch to Santana is along an easy minor road.

The statistics for this walk assume that the summit of Pico Ruivo has been reached by other means, such as Walks 20 or 23, leaving this route purely for the descent. However, the route can be restructured by starting from Achada do Teixeira, saving 3km (2 miles) by heading straight downhill.

Enjoy wide-ranging views of the mountains of Madeira from the summit of **Pico Ruivo**, at 1862m (6109ft). Walk down through the heather along a worn path, crunchy with red pumice, to reach a junction. Turn right to follow a well-worn path and crude steps down a heather-clad slope to reach a **refuge** (refreshments available, but it is almost impossible to get permission to stay overnight).

Right is for Pico do Areeiro, see Walk 23.

Walk down a flight of stone steps to leave the refuge, reaching another junction of paths. ◄ Keep straight ahead to follow the paved path across bare pumice then walk down stone steps to go through a gap in a wall. Pass ancient, gnarled tree heather, big boulders and rocky outcrops, reaching a stone shelter on a gap. Walk down to a signposted path junction and stay on the paved path, straight ahead. ◄

The path down to the left is used on Walk 24.

Climb along the paved path to pass another stone shelter and a water source. The path regains the ridge to pass yet another stone shelter. Views take in mountains, valleys and the sea, so enjoy them all before the path finally leads down to the road-end car park at **Achada do Teixeira**, around 1590m (5215ft). ▶

Pass in front of the 'government house' and turn left downhill to go though a gap in a wall and fence, entering a shallow valley near a few huts. Keep to the right of a peculiar, tall, blocky outcrop called **Homem em Pé**. Walk down a grassy path to a hut, then just below it turn left and roughly contour across a slope of tall heather. The path narrows and zigzags, needing care where it drops suddenly down onto a bend on the **ER-218 road**. Cross over the road to continue.

Walk down concrete steps and continue down eroded, steep, crudely-cut steps that can be slippery in wet weather. The path is often in a deep rut flanked by tree heather, and seems to zigzag forever. ▶ A steep paved track is reached, which leads down through dense *laurisilva* to a couple of houses. Continue down to a car park at **Queimadas** and look left to see lovely thatched houses. The **Levada do Caldeirão Verde** is crossed at this point, at 883m (2897ft) (see Walk 26).

The nearby 'government house' was once available for hire, but it is almost impossible to get permission to stay overnight.

Other tree species appear in due course, along with gorse and brambles.

Charming thatched houses at Queimadas

Arrange to be collected here if you wish to avoid the last 5km (3 miles) of road-walking.

◀ The road leaves the car park and turns right to descend steeply. It runs more gently around and across a bouldery stream and is flanked by laurels and hydrangeas. The road rises a little among eucalyptus then descends again in mixed woodlands. After a fairly level stretch above **Vale Marco** it descends more steeply, passing eucalyptus, pine and mimosa. Pass a junction at **Fonte da Pedra** and keep straight ahead, but turn right at another junction. Drop steeply into a valley and climb up the other side, then head for the middle of **Santana** (for facilities see page 102).

WALK 26

*Levada do Caldeirão Verde from
Pico das Pedras*

Start/Finish	Pico das Pedras – 229281, or Queimadas – 218285
Distance	17km or 21km (10½ or 13 miles) there-and-back
Total Ascent	100m (330ft)
Total Descent	100m (330ft)
Time	6hrs or 7hrs
Maps	Carta Militar 5 & 6
Terrain	The levada path is easy and well-wooded at the start. There are nine tunnels and some require a torch. Several narrow, rugged paths are followed, especially towards the end, with some being exposed and slippery
Refreshments	Snack bar at Pico das Pedras.
Transport	Taxi from Santana, to and from Pico das Pedras or Queimadas.

See map on pages 140–141.

Walking the Levada do Caldeirão Verde can be easy or difficult. Two starting points have easy paths in well-wooded surroundings. Tunnels and narrow paths feature further along. Either turn round after visiting a slender waterfall at Caldeirão Verde, or continue into a steep-sided, densely-wooded valley, climbing to Caldeirão do Inferno where waterfalls spill into a deep gorge.

The starting point for this walk can be Pico das Pedras or Queimadas. Neither place has a bus service, but both can be reached by car or taxi from Santana. Either place can serve as a finishing point, and the route also intersects with Walk 24 and Walk 25. The Levada do Caldeirão Verde is waymarked as the PR9 trail.

Leave the ER-218 road at **Pico das Pedras**, at 875m (2870ft), as if visiting the Bungalows do Rancho and its snack bar. Walk between the bar and the bungalows along a narrow road flanked by stone gateposts. A winding track runs through mixed woodlands dominated by eucalyptus, with the **Levada do Caldeirão Verde** alongside. Head upstream following the track through a rock cutting while the levada runs round the outside. Stone slabs cover the channel in places, then after turning round a couple of little valleys, cross the **Ribeira da Silveira** and follow the levada to **Queimadas**. ▸ The Parque das Queimadas is an alternative starting point with a small cobbled car park. A cobbled path leads past a couple of attractive thatched houses and is signposted for Caldeirão Verde and Caldeirão do Inferno. Pass through a picnic area among tall trees then cross a small duckpond. The levada has a broad and clear path with tall trees alongside. Cross over a track, the Caminho dos Folhadeiros. ▸ The broad path gives way to a narrow path, with views of wooded ridges and valleys.

The path has some fencing, but isn't particularly exposed. There are some drippy and slippery stretches then steps lead below a drippy hollow. There is more fencing alongside the path on the way round to the next valley. Cross a stone-arch bridge over the **Ribeira dos Cedros** at the head of the valley, but note how the levada once went further round the deep, green gorge. The path

Walk 25 crosses here.

Note the hydrangeas and oaks beside the levada, though the slopes are covered in *laurisilva* forest.

A walker emerges from a tall and narrow tunnel on the Levada do Caldeirão Verde near Vale da Lapa

continues with more fencing, making a pronounced turn into the next valley. Pass through a small rock cutting on a densely-wooded slope of *laurisilva*. There are views from time to time, taking in a slender waterfall and peaks high above. Cross a concrete bridge to face a waterfall on the **Ribeira da Fonte do Louro**, which cascades across the levada.

Leave the valley and continue along the fenced path. There are views for a while but also plenty of vegetation, with tree heather leaning low across the path. Watch out for rock cuttings with low headroom. The path winds across a slope and some parts are covered in landslip debris. Go through a low, bendy **tunnel** with an uneven path then continue across a slope of tree heather and laurel. A signpost for Caldeirão Verde points straight through another **tunnel**. ▶

Walk 24 crosses over the top of this tunnel.

The tunnel is high and the path is broad, while a fence separates the path from the water. Later the path becomes uneven, the roof lowers and a wall separates the path from the water. Exit with a fine view of a deep valley then enter the next **tunnel**. There is a high wall between the path and the water inside the tunnel, with low headroom and some constricted spaces. The path is narrow, uneven and wet, with a 'window' offering a view out to the valley of the **Ribeira Grande**. The tunnel is quite bendy and the exit is higher and drier.

The path is fenced, though not too exposed, but the parapet needs care. Part of the parapet is avoided by switching to a lower path. The way is partly fenced while winding across a steep slope to the next tunnel. Slabs cover part of the levada and the tunnel is short and curved. Continue across long, steep slopes and cliffs, well-vegetated in places, but quite exposed in other places. A pronounced turn leads into a huge green gully. This is **Caldeirão Verde**, where a path leads up to a fine slender waterfall spilling into a large pool. ▶

The waymarked trail ends at this point, but adventurous explorers with a head for heights can delve further into the valley to reach the Caldeirão do Inferno.

Note that the path gets rougher further along and the fencing isn't always in good order. Leave **Caldeirão Verde** to pick a way across a fenced slope to leave the green gully. Turn round beside a big stump of rock to re-enter the main valley. Continue across an unfenced slope, then pass some tattered fencing. When the levada channel narrows, go down a path and cross a stony slope, then head up on the other side. After passing tall til trees, watch for a badly-eroded flight of **steps** up to the left.

Climb around 200 steps, though there may have been twice that number at one time. Take care as the slope is steep and rugged, reaching a flat area beside a higher levada at a junction of three tunnels. Don't go through the tunnel on the left, except maybe for the view. The **tunnel** straight ahead has railway lines and leads under deep beneath Pico Ruivo to reach the generating station at Fajã da Nogueira (see Walk 14). Enter this tunnel, but immediately turn right through a very short **tunnel** and pass a wide, deep water tank to continue.

Walk along an uneven and exposed path to find a waterfall pouring down in front of another short **tunnel**. Go through this and immediately turn round into the next **tunnel**. This is long and bendy with a good path and good headroom. Later, there is plenty of headroom but the path is wet. Towards the end, the roof is rather lower and the path is stony. Walk along an even, but unfenced parapet and take care if it is wet and slippery. The final **tunnel** is bendy and rumbles ominously, featuring a stony path and low headroom. Although the exit can't be seen at first, there are a few 'windows' looking out into a deep, dark, narrow, green gorge. The rumbling noise becomes louder as you climb out of the tunnel to find two waterfalls thundering down into the gorge at **Caldeirão do Inferno**. Admire them, but obviously there is no way out of this place except by retracing your steps, negotiating all those tunnels a second time. Return to Queimadas or Pico das Pedras to finish, or end elsewhere by linking to Walk 24 or Walk 25.

WALK 27

Levada do Rei
from Quebradas

Start/Finish	Quebradas, above São Jorge – 201323
Distance	10km (6¼ miles) there-and-back
Total Ascent	150m (490ft)
Total Descent	150m (490ft
Time	3hrs 30mins
Maps	Carta Militar 2 & 3
Terrain	After an initial steep ascent, the levada path climbs gradually round increasingly forested slopes into a deep, steep-sided valley.
Refreshments	None closer than São Jorge.
Transport	Taxi from São Jorge to Quebradas. Interurban bus 103 & 138 serve São Jorge from Funchal and Santana.

The Levada do Rei is waymarked as the PR18 trail, following the watercourse upstream to its source, penetrating deep into the valley of the Ribeira Bonito. Lush *laurisilva* forest features tall til trees in an exceptionally steep-sided valley. When returning to São Jorge afterwards, it is worth visiting the nearby Moinho a Água, a working watermill powered by the Levada do Rei.

Either drive up through a maze of minor roads above São Jorge, or arrange for a taxi to take you and collect you later. The starting point is at **Quebradas**, where a track leads off a minor road. A notice explains about the PR18 trail and the track leads quickly to a **waterworks**. The **Levada do Rei** runs beside the track in a concrete channel and is fringed with agapanthus and eucalyptus. Pass the waterworks and a concrete dam, then turn right as signposted for Ribeiro Bonito, up concrete and earth steps

The Levada do Rei rushes downstream beside a waterworks near the start at Quebradas

parallel to the levada, where the water rushes furiously.

Turn left at a little water intake to follow the level levada path further upstream. It meanders, but swings noticeably to the right into a well-wooded little valley with limited views at **Achada do Milheiro**. Leaving the valley, cross an earth track. ◄ The path is good and isn't really exposed, but has short stretches of fencing as it slices across the side of a wooded valley. Longer fences feature where the levada is cut into rock, and in a couple of places the channel is covered. Turn round the head of a jungle-like valley and cross a river.

Enjoy views of Pico Ruivo, its forested northern ridges and valleys, with Ilha and Santana beyond.

Dense woodlands obscure views on the way round into the next little side-valley, where triangular stepping stones cross a stream. Leaving the valley, turn a wooded corner and go through a

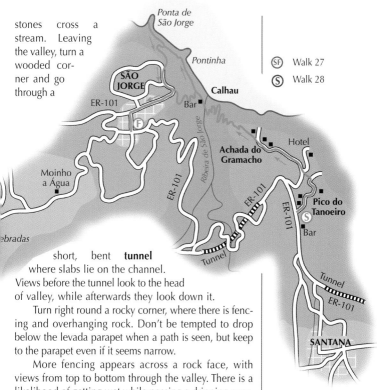

(SF) Walk 27
(S) Walk 28

short, bent **tunnel** where slabs lie on the channel. Views before the tunnel look to the head of valley, while afterwards they look down it.

Turn right round a rocky corner, where there is fencing and overhanging rock. Don't be tempted to drop below the levada parapet when a path is seen, but keep to the parapet even if it seems narrow.

More fencing appears across a rock face, with views from top to bottom through the valley. There is a likelihood of getting wet while passing a dripping overhang. After passing another fenced overhang, the steep and wooded valley sides draw in noticeably. The **Levada do Rei** drinks greedily from the mossy, bouldery, fern-hung **Ribero Bonito** in a deep gorge full of tall til trees.

To finish this walk, retrace steps back to the road at **Quebradas**. If a taxi was used for access and a pick-up wasn't arranged, it is possible to walk back to São Jorge by road in an hour or so. Find the time to visit the working watermill, Moinho a Água, which is powered by the Levada do Rei. Millstones can be seen grinding a variety of cereals.

153

WALK 28

Santana, Calhau and
São Jorge

Start	Pico de Tanoeiro, near Santana – 237323
Finish	São Jorge – 218334
Distance	6.5km or 7km (4 or 4½ miles)
Total Ascent	300m (985ft)
Total Descent	330m (1082ft)
Time	2hrs or 2hrs 30mins
Map	Carta Militar 3
Terrain	Mostly along winding cobbled tracks on steep slopes.
Refreshments	Restaurants at Quinta do Furão and Calhau. Bars and restaurants at São Jorge.
Transport	Interurban bus 103 & 138 link Santana and São Jorge with Funchal.

See map on
page 153.

The main road from Santana to São Jorge is anything but direct. In the past people followed a more direct cobbled road, which still exists and offers a fine short walking route. Leaving Santana, the old road zigzags down to the sea at Calhau, then zigzags up to São Jorge. Other coastal and cliff paths can also be explored, taking the walk out to the Ponta de São Jorge.

Travelling by bus between Santana and São Jorge, watch for a bus stop near Bragado's snack bar. This point, around 330m (1080ft), can be reached easily enough by walking down the main **ER-101 road** from **Santana**. Walk down the road a little further and turn right up an unmarked road for **Pico do Tanoeiro**. This levels out quickly with views from Achada do Teixeira to Pico Ruivo and onwards to Paúl da Serra. Pass a ruined pink building and follow the road downhill. Watch for steps

Traditional red-and-white thatched houses at Santana, part of a group containing the Tourist Information Office

on the left and a broken cobbled road leading down to another road. The splendid **hotel** at Quinta do Furão can be reached by turning right, but for today's walk turn left to reach a junction, then turn right to follow the road gently uphill.

Watch for a sign on the left at **Achada do Gramacho**, to follow the Caminho das Voltas past a couple of houses. A grassy, cobbled old road runs down past cultivated plots and terraces. It is broad and zigzags downhill on a well-engineered course, making light of what is almost a cliff face, with prickly pears growing on the lower slopes. ▶ Cross an arched bridge over the **Ribeira de São Jorge** and pass a swimming pool with a **bar**/restaurant. Keep right to walk through the little seaside settlement of **Calhau**, reaching a junction of cobbled tracks and a choice of routes.

For a short walk, turn left to follow a zigzag path up past a few plots and terraces. There are wild tangles of vegetation, as well as an undercut cliff where the track has been hacked from rock. Tall pines and eucalyptus grow at the top. Reach a cobbled car park and picnic site, where there is an old winch that used to serve Calhau.

Look inland to see the village of Ilha perched halfway up towards Pico Ruivo.

Beware of rock-falls as the cliff sheds huge boulders.

For a longer walk, keep straight ahead at **Calhau**, following a cobbled track and path across a cliff face. ◀ One stretch of path is well-buttressed and then stone steps cross an old landslip. Continue along the path and turn a corner to see the rocky **Ponta de São Jorge**, with a fisherman's path perched precariously over deep water. Walkers will probably not wish to go there so turn round and walk back along the cliff path, with a view along the coast to the distant Ponta de São Lourenço. Don't walk all the way back to Calhau, but turn right up another cobbled track, zigzagging up a slope covered in cane and malfurado. Turn left to follow a road to a cobbled car park and picnic site, where there is an old winch that used to serve Calhau.

The short and long walk join at the car park and all that remains is a road-walk up to São Jorge. Two roads leave the car park, so take the higher one and climb up a slope covered in pines to reach a walled cemetery. Follow the road called the Rua São Pedro to reach a junction with another road beside a chapel. Walk straight along the Rua Dr Leonel Mendonça to reach the church in **São Jorge**.

SÃO JORGE

Note the typical style of the little old houses in the area, which are wooden with thatched roofs. The church contains some extravagant gilded carvings and is worth visiting. There is a post office, a few shops, bars and restaurants. Interurban bus 103 & 138 link São Jorge with Santana and Funchal, and there are taxis.

WALK 29

Boca da Encumeada
and Pico Grande

Start/Finish	Boca da Encumeada – 112255
Distance	9km (5½ miles)
Total Ascent	1100m (3610ft)
Total Descent	1100m (3610ft)
Time	5hr
Map	Carta Militar 5
Terrain	Mountainous, with a well-wooded path, a paved path and the danger of rock-falls. Hands-on scrambling is required on Pico Grande. A very rough, rocky and overgrown path leads onwards, with an easier path to finish.
Refreshments	Snack Bar Restaurante Encumeada at the start/finish.
Transport	Rodoeste bus 6 & 139 serve Boca da Encumeada from Funchal, Ribeira Brava and São Vicente.

A rugged, circular mountain walk can be enjoyed from the Boca da Encumeada, reaching the summit of Pico Grande and passing close to other summits on the main mountain crest of Madeira. The outward and return paths are quite popular, while a rocky scramble leads onto Pico Grande. The path in the middle of this route is rough and rocky, needing care and attention.

Start on the **Boca da Encumeada** at 1007m (3304ft), where the Snack Bar Restaurante Encumeada is available. Follow the road downhill in the direction of Serra de Água, turning left round a bend to reach a junction with a track, where a notice indicates the start of the PR12 trail. ▶ Laurel, heather, broom and brambles grow on the slope, while the track narrows and at one bend features a fine view of Pico Grande. The path

Buses stop here if given due notice, but it is on an awkward bend.

passes a pipeline feeding the generating station at Serra de Água.

Walk down a slope dominated by eucalyptus and cross rocky stream-beds at **Poço**, the last one shaded by laurels. Cross a slope of bracken and brambles with open views. More woodland shade follows, then the path passes cultivation terraces and reaches a footbridge over a bouldery stream-bed.

Climb gently through pines, also passing eucalyptus, candleberry and bilberry. The shaded, stone-paved path leads to the head of the valley at **Curral Jangão**, where there are cultivated slopes and plenty of chestnuts. A stone-arched bridge spans a rocky gorge on the **Ribeiro do Poço**.

The path passes a small stone building and undulates, sometimes in dense woods and sometimes with views across the valley. Swing left through tall eucalyptus and pass beneath a frowning rock face, climbing along a stone-paved path to emerge at a corner where broom scrub grows. ◀ Climbing further, the path is flanked by bracken, broom and brambles, passing only a few trees. The route picks out a line of weakness between two cliff faces, working its way round a steep-sided hollow, then turning a prominent corner into another awesome hollow at **Fenda do Ferreiro** on the slopes of Pico Grande.

Pass round the base of a monstrous tower of rock, climbing through tree heather and passing some old til trees. There is rockfall debris on the slopes and some stretches are wet, muddy and slippery and, because of the water, well-vegetated. Follow a drier path across the

There are good views of the valley and mountains.

158

next cliff face, then after another wet patch the path levels out on a slope of gorse. There is a fine view ahead to Pico do Serradinho.

Turn left up a few stone steps onto the gorse-covered

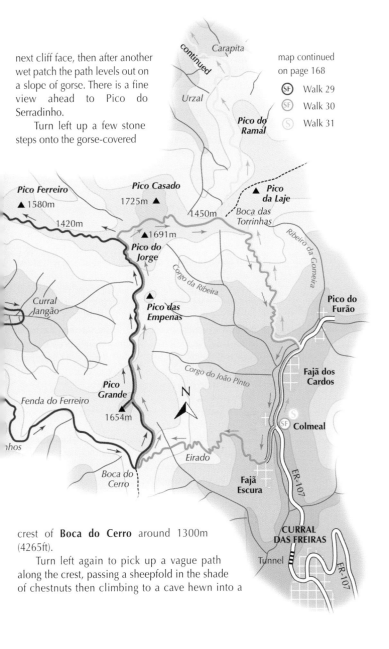

continued

Carapita

map continued on page 168

SF Walk 29

SF Walk 30

S Walk 31

Urzal

Pico do Ramal

Pico Ferreiro
▲ 1580m

Pico Casado
1725m ▲

1420m

▲1691m

Pico do Jorge

1450m

▲ Pico da Laje

Boca das Torrinhas

Ribeiro da Corneira

Corgo da Ribeira

Curral Jangão

▲ **Pico das Empenas**

Pico do Furão

Corgo do João Pinto

Fajã dos Cardos

Pico Grande
1654m

N

Fenda do Ferreiro

Eirado

SF Colmeal

nhos

Boca do Cerro

Fajã Escura

ER-107

CURRAL DAS FREIRAS

Tunnel

ER-107

crest of **Boca do Cerro** around 1300m (4265ft).

Turn left again to pick up a vague path along the crest, passing a sheepfold in the shade of chestnuts then climbing to a cave hewn into a cliff. A cable is fixed to the rock where exposed steps rise up a steep and rocky slope. A zigzag path climbs further, marked with paint and small cairns, passing occasional chestnuts on a steep and grassy slope, passing through a little valley full of broom. Keep climbing and swing well to the left to reach the rocky ridge, then scramble with the aid of a cable to the highest rocky peak of **Pico Grande**, at 1654m (5426ft). Views stretch from the plateau of Paúl da Serra, around the Curral valley to Pico Ruivo and Pico do Areeiro, with Funchal down by the sea.

Scramble down from the summit and retrace steps downhill, but watch for another path heading off to the left, crossing a gap where there is a dry-stone wall. Cross the wall and look carefully to the left to spot a vague path among rocks and boulders. A short flight of stone steps climbs uphill to confirm the route. On the other side, stone steps and broken steps drop steeply downhill and need care as there is so much loose rock. Watch very carefully for the line of the path, which passes beneath towering, overhanging cliffs. Get into the habit of looking ahead before making a move. Broom scrub obscures the path in places then there is a climb past some dead, blasted trees. Turn round a rocky corner for views of a rugged gap with Pico do Jorge beyond. Walk down past more blasted trees and short broom scrub to pass below a gap near **Pico das Empenas**. Go through a gate into a well-wooded area of tils and tree heather.

There are a couple of views as the path undulates across the slope. A towering peak of rock rises ahead as the path levels out. Climb up steps and steep, stony slopes, leaving the tils and tree heather behind to climb a well-buttressed flight of steps. The zigzag path climbing higher is very loose and worn, while the steps are crumbling, so there is a danger of rockfall. Stone steps and a zigzag path lead up through tree heather, which gives way to broom as the path gains a high crest around 1550m (5085ft) near **Pico do Jorge**. Turn left at a junction, along a clearer path which goes down fenced stone steps and eventually lands on a gap at 1420m (4660ft).

The path slips off to the left to avoid rocky pinnacles, zigzagging down a wooded slope to pass through a gateway. Pass along the base of a cliff on the southern flank of **Pico Ferreiro**, exploiting a thin, crumbling layer in the rock, passing through another gateway. ▶ Continue through tall tree heather, crossing a slope and going down steps. The path turns right then swings left to go down more steps. Pass a cave with a stone seat, then the path heads off to the left down buttressed, fenced steps, going through a gate to reach a narrow and well-vegetated gap.

▶ Climb gently while walking across the heathery dome of **Pico da Encumeada**, crossing a bare shoulder

Ancient til trees grow here and, at an open corner, there are views of the surrounding mountains, particularly Pico Grande.

Views on either side stretch to São Vicente and Ribeira Brava.

Mist drifts across the gap of Boca da Encumeada between some of Madeira's highest mountains

161

Views are lost among the dense vegetation, which is remarkably mixed and includes everything from *laurisilva* species to low-lying brambles.

offering good views. The path leads along the ridge past **Pico do Meio**, around 1250m (4100ft), then steep flights of stone steps follow, often fenced and buttressed. ◄ The final steps are rough and ready, with the narrow path reaching a stony track. Continue straight down to a road junction and turn left through a rocky cutting on the **Boca da Encumeada**, at 1007m (3304ft). Hopefully you reach the Snack Bar Restaurante Encumeada in good time for the last bus!

WALK 30
Colmeal and Pico Grande

Start/Finish	Colmeal, in the Curral valley – 158233
Distance	12km (7½ miles)
Total Ascent	1450m (4760ft)
Total Descent	1450m (4760ft)
Time	6hrs
Map	Carta Militar 5
Terrain	Mountainous, with a steep and stony climb giving way to hands-on scrambling on Pico Grande. A very rough, rocky and overgrown path leads onwards then a steep and well-wooded zigzag path leads downhill at the end.
Refreshments	Small bars at Fajã Escura, Fajã dos Cardos and Colmeal.
Transport	Interurban bus 81 serves Curral das Freiras from Funchal and some services run to Fajã Escura and Colmeal.

See map on page 159.

This is an arduous mountainous circuit, starting deep in the Curral valley, climbing steep and rocky slopes, including hands-on scrambling, to reach the summit of Pico Grande. The walk continues to Pico do Jorge then drops to the Boca das Torrinhas, which is a gap on the main mountain crest of Madeira. A steep and stony zigzag descent leads back into the Curral valley.

Start at **Colmeal**, where the Snack Bar Costa Verde is located, or if the bus is heading to nearby **Fajã Escura**, then stay on board to avoid a short road-walk. Climb from the last bus stop to pass the Snack Bar O Lagar. The road ends and a track climbs past cultivated plots, drifting right to enter a forest. Watch out for a path climbing to the right at a bend. Climb past pine, eucalyptus and tall chestnut, later climbing more open slopes to pass through a gate. Follow the zigzag path faithfully uphill, passing occasional chestnut and other trees. ▶ Climb past a steep spur at **Eirado** and zigzag up round a corner, brushing past broom and crossing a bouldery streambed. A few chestnuts offer shade on the slope and a pinnacle of rock lies to the left. The narrow path finally squeezes through broom and climbs to the gorse-covered crest of **Boca do Cerro** around 1300m (4265ft).

The ground is often stony underfoot, but the path is well-engineered, often stoutly buttressed or carved from rock.

Turn right to pick up a vague path along the crest, passing a sheepfold in the shade of chestnuts then climbing to a cave hewn into a cliff. A cable is fixed to the rock where exposed steps rise up a steep and rocky slope. A zigzag path climbs further, marked with paint and small cairns, passing occasional chestnuts on a steep and grassy slope, passing through a little valley full of broom. Keep climbing and swing well to the left to reach the rocky ridge then scramble with the aid of a cable to the highest rocky peak of **Pico Grande**, at 1654m (5426ft).
▶ Scramble down from the summit and retrace steps downhill, but watch for another path heading off to the left, crossing a gap where there is a dry-stone wall. Cross the wall and look carefully to the left to spot a vague path among rocks and boulders. A short flight of stone steps climbs uphill to confirm the route. On the other side, stone steps and broken steps drop steeply downhill and require care as there is so much loose rock. Watch very carefully for the line of the path, which passes beneath towering, overhanging cliffs. Get into the habit of looking ahead before making a move. Broom scrub obscures the path in places, then there is a climb past some dead, blasted trees. Turn round a rocky corner for views of a rugged gap with Pico do Jorge beyond. Walk

Views stretch from the plateau of Paúl da Serra, around the Curral valley to Pico Ruivo and Pico do Areeiro, with Funchal down by the sea.

Very rugged and complex terrain beyond Pico Grande needs careful attention to route-finding

down past more blasted trees and short broom scrub to pass below a gap near **Pico das Empenas**. Go through a gate into a well-wooded area of tils and tree heather.

There are a couple of views as the path undulates across the slope. A towering peak of rock rises ahead as the path levels out. Climb up steps and steep, stony slopes, leaving the tils and tree heather to climb a well-buttressed flight of steps. The zigzag path climbing higher is very loose and worn, while the steps are crumbling, so there is a danger of rockfall. Stone steps and a zigzag path lead up through tree heather, which gives way to broom as the path gains a high crest around 1550m (5085ft).

Turn right along a clearer path and climb steps on the northern flanks of **Pico do Jorge**, among dense tree heather and bilberry, reaching a shoulder where views take in Pico do Cedro, Pico Grande, Paúl da Serra and

Enjoy a stretch along the crest with good views, looking down from a stout stone buttress to São Vicente.

the north-west coast. ◄ Head downhill to reach a heathery shoulder with fine views. Continue up and along the crest, then cross a gritty gap around 1650m (5415ft) near **Pico Casado**.

Pass a blade-like outcrop of rock and zigzag downhill. Notice that some of the stones make musical chinking sounds underfoot. Pass a cave and head down steps on a slope of dense heather. The path levels out and squeezes through a rocky cleft full of ferns and exotic plants. The way ahead is more rugged, then a gentler path crosses the ridge. Walk down a fenced flight of stone steps to land on the **Boca das Torrinhas** at 1450m (4760ft). Big, faded sign-posts give destinations along all the paths that leave this point (see Walks 20, 31 & 32).

Follow the path signposted for Curral das Freiras, or the PR2 trail. This is narrow as it slices across a rocky slope. It can be grassy, stony or rocky underfoot, while some parts are buttressed and paved. ▶ Descend through tree heather then emerge on an open slope. Dense eucalyptus gives way to another open area. A few

There are views back to Pico Grande and its summit tor, and down through the Curral valley.

Looking down towards Fajã dos Cardos at the head of the Curral valley

165

chestnuts stand among the eucalyptus, along with charred and fallen pine trees. Zigzag downhill to find some pines still growing. Houses can be seen at the head of the valley with Pico Ruivo and other peaks high above. Take care on the lower zigzags and don't be tempted to short-cut. Emerge from the woods to follow the path down past cultivation terraces. It is still steep, rough and stony, but quickly leads down to a concrete bridge crossing a river. The Vereda de Fajã Capitão leads up a few steps to the road near **Pico do Furão**.

The Snack Bar Costa Verde is immediately available if waiting for a bus.

Turn right to walk down the road, passing a couple of small bars near a bridge and a few houses at **Fajã dos Cardos**. The road, the Estrada da Fajã dos Cardos, descends to a junction beside another bridge at **Colmeal**. ◄ If there is a long time to wait, follow the main ER-107 road to **Curral das Freiras**.

WALK 31
Curral das Freiras to Boaventura

Start	Colmeal, in the Curral valley – 158233
Finish	Bar A Fronteira near Boaventura – 162310
Distance	13km (8 miles)
Total Ascent	950m (3115ft)
Total Descent	1400m (4595ft)
Time	6hrs
Maps	Carta Militar 2 & 5
Terrain	Roads at the beginning and end of the walk, with zigzag mountain paths in between. Steep slopes are largely covered in dense woodland and paths are steep and stony in places.
Refreshments	Small bars at Colmeal and Fajã dos Cardos. Bar at the end of the walk near Boaventura.
Transport	Interurban bus 81 serves Curral das Freiras from Funchal and some services run to Colmeal. Rodoeste bus 6 passes the Bar A Fronteira near Boaventura, linking with São Vicente, Ribeira Brava and Funchal.

Roads are gradually advancing through the mountains of Madeira. For the most part they terminate at remote settlements, where old mountain paths and tracks can be followed further. This walk, which is designated as the PR2 trail, crosses from the Curral valley, over the Boca das Torrinhas, to descend through *laurisilva* forest to reach Lombo do Urzal, for Boaventura.

Start at **Colmeal**, where the Snack Bar Costa Verde is located. Follow the road steeply uphill to pass a couple of small bars and houses at **Fajã dos Cardos**. The road leads up to **Pico do Furão**, but before reaching that point watch for steps dropping down to the left. A path called the Vereda de Fajã Capitão leads down to a concrete bridge crossing a river. Rocky mountains rise on all sides, including Pico Grande, Pico do Jorge and the rugged flanks of Torres.

    Follow a steep, rough and stony path uphill, passing cultivation terraces. Zigzag up through tall eucalyptus

Signposts point back to the Curral valley and ahead to Lombo do Urzal on the Boca das Torrinhas

167

There are occasional views back down to houses at the head of the valley with Pico Ruivo and other peaks high above.

and don't be tempted to take a short cut on the steep slopes. ◄ Some pines grow among the eucalyptus, but many are charred and fallen. Chestnuts will also be noticed before an open area. Climb through dense eucalyptus to emerge on an open slope, then climb through tree heather. The path can be grassy, stony or rocky underfoot, while some parts are buttressed and paved. Enjoy views back to Pico Grande and its summit tor, as well as down through the Curral valley, before slicing across a rocky slope to reach the **Boca das Torrinhas** at 1450m (4760ft). Big, faded signposts give destinations along all the paths that leave this point (see Walks 20, 30 & 32).

Cross the gap at its lowest point as signposted for Lombo do Urzal, and note the immediate change in character of the route as it enters dense *laurisilva* forest. The path is narrow and may be overgrown as it is little-used. The path is well-engineered in places but look carefully ahead as it is not always possible to see far through dense tree heather, laurel, bilberry and flowery undergrowth. Watch for brambles and take care where the path crosses soft and crumbling earth.

Climb a little from time to time as the path negotiates a steep and densely wooded valley head below **Pico da Laje**. Contour across the steep slope, pass along the base of a cliff and turn a rocky corner where there may be a small waterfall. Later, the path runs along the base of another cliff, where there is a breach in the rock and steps zigzag uphill. Later, while turning a rocky corner, there is a view of the valley. The path rises and falls or uses mossy and uneven steps.

There are views down to the sea, but also huge til trees in dense woodland.

The zigzag descent is obvious when it starts and the path is less overgrown. ◄ The path cuts down across a cliff face where a rocky parapet ensures it doesn't feel exposed. Twin pinnacles stand below and mossy steps drop to a rocky cleft in the ridge. The path turns round the roots of a big til tree in this cleft and continues down more steps. Zigzag down through the undergrowth among tall tils to pass a shallow cave then follow a terrace path cut from the slope at **Carapita**. A few steps take the path through a small rocky gap. A road-end can be seen far below at Lombo do Urzal.

Keep zigzagging downhill and the path may be stony or gentle underfoot. Sometimes the path runs in a deeply worn groove and while there are short-cuts, it is easier to stay on the main path.   The path is more uneven among tall pines, brambles and rampant undergrowth then continues down through tree heather and laurels. At a small gateway below **Lapinha**, some walkers cut a corner and follow a rocky path steeply downhill. Going through the gate, the path is easier and swings round to pass another gate at a lower level. The rocky, grooved path has a few wooden steps then it lands beside a levada. ▶ Continue down from the levada, narrow and stony at first, but a broad paved path later. Pass willows before reaching the first house at **Lombo do Urzal**. Big concrete steps lead down past other houses to cross a concrete bridge over the bouldery **Ribeira do Porco**. Look round the densely-wooded mountains enclosing the valley then continue down what appears to be a concrete road, though it ends with another flight of big steps. Reach a tarmac road at a turning space and head uphill past a road junction to continue down through the valley. ▶ Keep right at a road junction to pass **Falca de Baixo** and its church (occasional bus). The road descends between a cliff and a river. Cross a bridge at the bottom and note the huge boulders in the river-bed. The road reaches a junction at a bend on the **ER-101 road**, and the Bar A Fronteira is just to the right. Buses stop here but, if there is time, continue walking to **Boaventura**.

Ⓕ Walk 31

map continued from page 159

The water flows through one of the longest tunnels in Madeira.

Steep terraces and red-roofed storage sheds are features of the valley, with plenty of vine trellises, while levadas can be seen on the slopes.

WALK 32
*Boca da Encumeada
to Colmeal*

Start	Boca da Encumeada – 112255
Finish	Colmeal, in the Curral valley – 158233
Distance	10km (6¼ miles)
Total Ascent	740m (2425ft)
Total Descent	1110m (3640ft)
Time	5hrs
Map	Carta Militar 5
Terrain	Mountainous, with paved paths and steps, as well as steep and stony stretches. A steep, forested zigzag path leads downhill at the end.
Refreshments	Snack Bar Restaurante Encumeada at the start. Small bars at Fajã dos Cardos and Colmeal.
Transport	Rodoeste Bus 6 & 139 serve Boca da Encumeada from Funchal, Ribeira Brava and São Vicente. Interurban bus 81 serves Curral das Freiras from Funchal and some services run to Colmeal.

One of the problems of walking through the mountains of Madeira is timing your arrival at a bus stop before the last bus leaves. On this walk, the main mountain crest is followed from the Boca da Encumeada to the Boca das Torrinhas. A descent is made into the Curral valley, where buses run quite late back to Funchal. This should allow plenty of time for slow walkers to finish.

Start at the Snack Bar Restaurante Encumeada and follow the road through a rock cutting on the **Boca da Encumeada** at 1007m (3304ft). Turn right to follow a stony track uphill, signposted as the PR1.3 trail. The track curves right towards some masts, but keep left to follow a narrow path further up rough and ready steps.

Mist creeps over the Boca da Encumeada, while the village of Serra de Água is seen down in the valley

▶ Climb steep flights of stone steps, often fenced and buttressed, to reach the crest of the mountain range around 1250m (4100ft) near **Pico do Meio**. Continue along the ridge and enjoy good views from a bare shoulder, looking directly down to Ribeira Brava. Cross the gentle, heathery dome of **Pico da Encumeada** to reach a narrow and well-vegetated gap, where São Vicente and Ribeira Brava can be seen.

The dense vegetation is remarkably mixed and includes everything from *laurisilva* species to low-lying brambles.

Go through a gate and climb stone steps, some of them buttressed and fenced, heading left then swinging right to pass a cave with a stone seat. Climb more steps, turning left and right while climbing through tall tree heather. ▶ Pass tall tree heather and ancient til trees and go through a gateway, then pass along the base of a cliff on the southern flank of **Pico Ferreiro**. The path exploits a thin, crumbling layer in the rock and reaches another gateway. Zigzag up a wooded slope to reach a gap on the ridge, around 1420m (4660ft), overlooked by rocky pinnacles.

At an open corner there are views of the surrounding mountains, particularly Pico Grande.

Climb again to reach fenced stone steps at a higher level. Enjoy the view, but take care not to be drawn along a path on the right, which is a very rugged route to

171

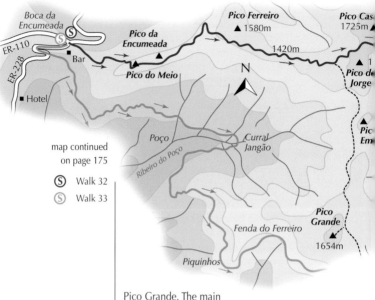

Boca da Encumeada
ER-110
ER-228
Bar
Hotel
Pico da Encumeada
Pico do Meio
Pico Ferreiro ▲ 1580m
1420m
Pico Cas 1725m
▲ 1
Pico d Jorge
Poço
Curral Jangão
Ribeiro do Poço
Pic Em
Pico Grande
1654m
Fenda do Ferreiro
Piquinhos

map continued
on page 175

Ⓢ Walk 32
Ⓢ Walk 33

Pico Grande. The main
path climbs more steps on the northern flanks of **Pico do Jorge**, among dense tree heather and bilberry, reaching a shoulder. ◀ Enjoy a stretch along the crest with good views, looking down from a stout stone buttress to São Vicente. Head downhill to reach a heathery shoulder, again with fine views. Continue up and along the crest, then cross a gritty gap around 1650m (5415ft) near **Pico Casado**.

Pass a blade-like outcrop of rock and zigzag down-hill, passing a cave and going down steps on a slope of dense heather. The path levels out and squeezes through a rocky cleft full of ferns and exotic plants. The way ahead is more rugged then a gentler path crosses the ridge. Walk down a fenced flight of stone steps to land on the **Boca das Torrinhas** at 1450m (4760ft). ◀ Follow the path signposted for Curral das Freiras, or the PR2 trail. This is narrow as it slices across a rocky slope. It can be grassy, stony or rocky underfoot, while some parts are buttressed and paved.

Views take in Pico do Cedro, Pico Grande, Paúl da Serra and the north-west coast.

Big, faded signposts give destinations along all the paths that leave this point (see Walks 20, 30 & 31).

▶ Descend through tree heather then emerge on an open slope. Dense eucalyptus gives way to another open area. A few chestnut stand among the eucalyptus, along with charred and fallen pine trees. Zigzag downhill to find some pines still growing. Houses can be seen at the head of the valley with Pico Ruivo and other peaks high above. Take care on the lower zigzags and don't be tempted to short-cut. Emerge from the woods to follow the path down past cultivation terraces. It is still steep, rough and stony, but quickly leads down to a concrete bridge crossing a river. The Vereda de Fajã Capitão leads up a few steps to the road near **Pico do Furão**.

Turn right to walk down the road through the Curral valley, passing a couple of small bars near a bridge and a few houses at **Fajã dos Cardos**. The road, the Estrada da Fajã dos Cardos, descends to a junction beside another bridge at **Colmeal**. The Snack Bar Costa Verde is immediately available if waiting for a bus. If there is a long time to wait, follow the main ER-107 road to **Curral das Freiras**.

Enjoy views back to Pico Grande and its summit tor, and down through the Curral valley.

Towering rocky buttresses catch the evening light high above the Curral valley

173

SECTION 4
Jardim da Serra

Jardim da Serra is literally the 'Garden of the Mountains'. The name refers to a loose conglomeration of little villages tucked into the mountains between Funchal and Ribeira Brava, and the name is also used for the Posto Florestal on the Boca da Corrida. Terreiros is the highest mountain in this region, and is also one of the easiest to climb on the Madeira. Its southern flanks are crisscrossed with paths and tracks. In fact, there are enough paths, tracks and acceptable gradients to allow for a couple of circular walks, which are rare in the mountains of Madeira.

The Levada do Norte wraps itself round most of this area and is something of a 'Jekyll and Hyde' route. The stretch between Serra de Água and Boa Morte is one of the most frightening levadas on the island, with a crumbling path cutting across sheer cliffs. The continuation from Boa Morte to Estreito de Câmara de Lobos, on the other hand, is relatively easy and quite popular.

This region is easily reached using Rodoeste buses from Funchal, but walkers who want to stay in quieter places will find good access by bus from Ribeira Brava. Take careful note of all the walking routes using the road to and from Boca da Corrida. This steep road becomes a bit wearing if you walk it too many times, and walkers who wish to arrive by taxi must hire one from Estreito de Câmara de Lobos.

Several walks in this region link with each other, and there are more opportunities to link with other rugged paths leading to the higher mountains. In fact, the longer the maps are studied, the greater the number of choices that present themselves, especially around the Boca da Encumeada and Curral das Freiras. However, few walkers would relish dropping deep into the Curral valley only to have to climb up the other side. Interurban buses link Curral das Freiras with Funchal.

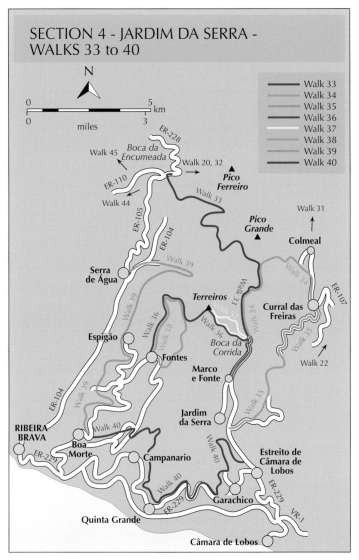

WALK 33
*Boca da Encumeada to
Marco e Fonte*

Start	Boca da Encumeada – 112255
Finish	Marco e Fonte – 137193
Distance	14km (8¾ miles)
Total Ascent	600m (1970ft)
Total Descent	700m (2300ft)
Time	6hrs
Map	Carta Militar 5
Terrain	Mountainous, with a well-wooded path at first, then a paved path, with the danger of rock-falls at a higher level. A good path leads from gap to gap, descending to link with a road leading further down a wooded slope.
Refreshments	Snack Bar Restaurante Encumeada at the start. Bar O Mário at Marco e Fonte.
Transport	Rodoeste bus 6 & 139 serve Boca da Encumeada from Funchal, Ribeira Brava and São Vicente. Rodoeste Bus 96 links Marco e Fonte with Funchal.

This route is waymarked as the Caminho Real da Encumeada, or PR12 trail. It links the Boca da Encumeada with the Boca da Corrida. Explore a wooded valley then follow a stone-paved path across the cliffs flanking Pico Grande. After passing the Boca da Cerro the path winds along a rugged crest to reach the Boca da Corrida, where a cobbled road leads down to Marco e Fonte.

Start on the **Boca da Encumeada** at 1007m (3304ft), where the Snack Bar Restaurante Encumeada is available. Follow the road downhill in the direction of Serra de Água, turning left round a bend to reach a junction with a track, where a notice indicates the start of the PR12 trail. Buses stop here if given due notice, but it is on an awkward bend.

Laurel, heather, broom and brambles grow on the slope, while the track narrows and at one bend features a fine view of Pico Grande. The path passes beneath a pipeline feeding the generating station at Serra de Água.

Walk down a slope dominated by eucalyptus and cross rocky stream-beds at **Poço**, the last one shaded by laurels. Cross a slope of bracken and brambles with open views. More woodland shade follows then the path passes cultivation terraces and reaches a footbridge over a bouldery stream-bed. Climb gently through pines, also passing eucalyptus, candleberry and bilberry. The shaded, stone-paved path leads to the head of the valley at **Curral Jangão**, where there are cultivated slopes and plenty of chestnuts. A stone-arched bridge spans a rocky gorge on the **Ribeiro do Poço**.

The path passes a small stone building and undulates, sometimes in dense woods and sometimes with views across the valley. Swing left through tall eucalyptus and pass beneath a frowning rock face, climbing along a stone-paved path to emerge at a corner where broom scrub grows. There are good views of the valley and mountains.

Climbing further, the path is flanked by bracken, broom and brambles, passing only a few trees. The route picks out a line of weakness between two cliff faces, working its way round a steep-sided hollow, then turning a prominent corner into another awesome hollow at **Fenda do Ferreiro** on the slopes of Pico Grande.

Pass round the base of a monstrous tower of rock, climbing through tree heather and passing some old til trees. There is rockfall debris on the slopes and some stretches are wet, muddy and slippery and, because of the water, well-vegetated. Follow a drier path across the next cliff face, then after another wet patch the path levels out on a slope of gorse. There is a fine view

map
continued
from page 172

Ⓕ   Walk 33

177

The 'Caminho Real' has been hacked from rock as it runs from one rugged gap to another

To climb Pico Grande, see Walk 29 or Walk 30.

ahead to Pico do Serradinho (see Walk 33). For today, turn left up a few stone steps and cross the gorse-covered crest of **Boca do Cerro**. ◄ There is a fine view ahead to **Pico do Serradinho**, but the path doesn't climb over it. Instead, it passes deep heather and chestnut, turning interesting corners with good views. The path later drops and levels out then passes through a gate on another gap, the **Passo de Ares**, around 1250m (4100ft). Climb and follow the path around and down the flank of Pico do Cavalo, where it is variously buttressed or cut from rock, with fine views of the mountains across the Curral valley. Reach yet another gap, the **Boca dos Corgos**, where there are chestnuts around 1230m (4035ft).

Climb steep zigzags and follow a broad path across a slope, levelling out among broom and chestnuts before descending. Drop steeply to a track and pass between chained pillars to reach the **Boca da Corrida**, around 1220m (4000ft). There is a small car park and picnic area beside the Posto Florestal Jardim da Serra, as well as a shrine to São Cristovão in the shade of a few trees. ▸ The walk can be ended here if a pick-up or a taxi can be arranged.

Splendid views take in mountains from Pico Grande to Pico Ruivo and Pico do Areeiro, while Curral das Freiras lies deep in the valley, with a glimpse of Funchal harbour far below.

To reach the nearest bus, walk down the attractively cobbled road, which bends sharply to the right and left, giving way to a steep tarmac road. Nearby slopes are dominated by chestnut, with some pine and eucalyptus, giving way to cultivated plots further downhill. Some buses turn round at a bus stop. ▸ If a bus isn't due for a while, keep walking downhill and wait at the Bar O Mário at a road junction at **Marco e Fonte**.

Rodoeste bus 96 marked 'Corrida'

WALK 34

*Boca da Corrida and
Curral das Freiras*

Start	Marco e Fonte – 137193
Finish	Curral das Freiras – 161216
Distance	10km (6¼ miles)
Total Ascent	660m (2165ft)
Total Descent	920m (3020ft)
Time	4hrs
Map	Carta Militar 5
Terrain	A steep road gives way to a good path leading from gap to gap. The descent is along a steep, stony, wooded path.
Refreshments	Bar O Mário at Marco e Fonte. Plenty of choice at Curral das Freiras.
Transport	Rodoeste bus 96 serves Marco e Fonte from Funchal, or taxi to Boca da Corrida. Interurban bus 81 links Fajã Escura and Curral das Freiras with Funchal.

Walkers who find themselves on the Boca da Corrida from time to time can enjoy splendid views of the Curral valley. Some may wonder if there is a way down there. There is, but first it involves following a path from gap to gap along a rugged ridge, then taking a very steep and rugged zigzag path into the Curral valley. There are options to shorten the walk at the start and finish, but plan in advance if you wish to do this. Buses marked 'Corrida' pass Marco e Fonte and run part-way up the steep Estrada da Corrida, but get off the bus early if the shop or Bar O Mário is needed. Walkers who wish to avoid the initial steep climb to Boca da Corrida should get off the bus at Estreito de Câmara de Lobos and hire a taxi. To finish early at Fajã Escura, arrive in time for one of the infrequent bus services.

Splendid views take in mountains from Pico Grande to Pico Ruivo and Pico do Areeiro, while Curral das Freiras lies deep in the valley, with a glimpse of Funchal harbour far below.

The bus marked 'Corrida' reaches a turning space above **Marco e Fonte**. The road continues to climb steeply past cultivated plots onto slopes dominated by chestnut, with some pine and eucalyptus. An attractively cobbled stretch bends right and left, leading to the **Boca da Corrida** around 1220m (4000ft). There is a small car park and picnic area beside the Posto Florestal Jardim da Serra, as well as a shrine to São Cristovão in the shade of a few trees. ◄

A track rises from the car park through chained pillars, where a steep path climbing to the right is marked as the PR12 trail to Boca da Encumeada, but also signposted for Curral das Freiras. The path levels out and crosses a slope covered in broom and a few chestnuts. Enjoy fine views around the Curral valley as the path descends, then steeper zigzags lead down to the **Boca dos Corgos**, where there are chestnuts around 1230m (4035ft).

The path slices across the rocky slopes of Pico do Cavalo, where the path is cut from rock or buttressed as it climbs. Cross the ridge and descend to a gap at **Passo de Ares**, around 1250m (4100ft). A level stretch goes

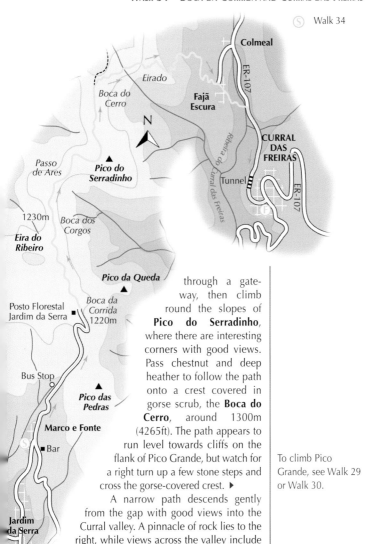

through a gateway, then climb round the slopes of **Pico do Serradinho**, where there are interesting corners with good views. Pass chestnut and deep heather to follow the path onto a crest covered in gorse scrub, the **Boca do Cerro**, around 1300m (4265ft). The path appears to run level towards cliffs on the flank of Pico Grande, but watch for a right turn up a few stone steps and cross the gorse-covered crest. ▶

A narrow path descends gently from the gap with good views into the Curral valley. A pinnacle of rock lies to the right, while views across the valley include Pico Ruivo and Pico do Areeiro.

To climb Pico Grande, see Walk 29 or Walk 30.

A few chestnuts offer shade on the slope, then the path goes through broom scrub and crosses a bouldery stream-bed. Brush past broom, turn round a corner and zigzag down a steep spur at **Eirado**. A well-engineered path, carved from rock or stoutly buttressed, is often stony underfoot. Chestnut and other trees clothe the slope as the zigzag path leads downhill. Go through a gateway on an open slope then pass tall chestnut, eucalyptus and pine. The path joins a forest track on a bend, and this track leads down past cultivated plots to a road-end at **Fajã Escura**. ◀

Snack Bar O Lagar

Catch a bus if one is due or walk to Curral das Freiras. Turn right to walk down the Caminho da Fajã Escura, following a concrete road, a steeper stone track

and steps down a wooded slope, with street lights alongside. Cross a bridge over the bouldery **Ribeira do Curral das Freiras**, where a path and steps lead up to the **ER-107 road**. There is a bus stop, otherwise turn right to keep walking. Cross a bridge over the Ribeira do Cidrão then follow the road up through a tunnel to reach **Curral das Freiras**. For facilities see page 111.

Curral das Freiras lies deep in a steep-sided valley below the Boca da Corrida

WALK 35

Boca dos Namorados and
Curral das Freiras

Start	Cabo Podão – 138177
Finish	Lombo Chão – 153200, or Curral das Freiras – 161216
Distance	4km or 8km (2½ or 5 miles)
Total Ascent	260m or 590m (855ft or 1935ft)
Total Descent	600m or 730m (1970ft or 2395ft)
Time	1hr 45mins or 3hrs 15mins
Maps	Carta Militar 5 & 8
Terrain	Wooded slopes. A clear track is used for the ascent and a steep and stony zigzag path is used on the descent, ending with a road walk.
Refreshments	Bars at Cabo Podão. Snack Bar Hostia in the Curral valley. Plenty of choice at Curral das Freiras.
Transport	Rodoeste Bus 96 serves Cabo Podão from Funchal. Interurban bus 81 links Lombo Chão and Curral das Freiras with Funchal.

No buses run to the Boca dos Namorados, overlooking the Curral valley, but cars can be driven there. An old cobbled track can be followed up there, climbing through forest from Cabo Podão then dropping down a steep and rugged zigzag path to Lombo Chão. There are buses at that point, or the road could be followed across the valley and up to Curral das Freiras. Not all buses heading for Jardim da Serra serve Cabo Podão. Getting the wrong bus means additional walking up steep roads from Corticeiras.

Start at a road junction at **Cabo Podão**, where the Bar Bilhares Pestana and Bar Bica stand opposite each other. A school, the Escola Básica Foro, is situated above, with a modern church dominating the area. Walk up a bendy

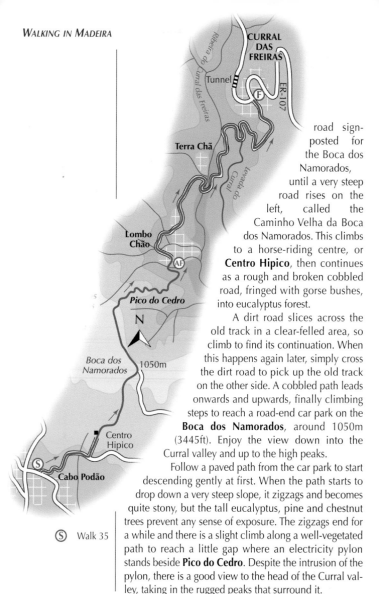

road sign-posted for the Boca dos Namorados, until a very steep road rises on the left, called the Caminho Velha da Boca dos Namorados. This climbs to a horse-riding centre, or **Centro Hipico**, then continues as a rough and broken cobbled road, fringed with gorse bushes, into eucalyptus forest.

A dirt road slices across the old track in a clear-felled area, so climb to find its continuation. When this happens again later, simply cross the dirt road to pick up the old track on the other side. A cobbled path leads onwards and upwards, finally climbing steps to reach a road-end car park on the **Boca dos Namorados**, around 1050m (3445ft). Enjoy the view down into the Curral valley and up to the high peaks.

Follow a paved path from the car park to start descending gently at first. When the path starts to drop down a very steep slope, it zigzags and becomes quite stony, but the tall eucalyptus, pine and chestnut trees prevent any sense of exposure. The zigzags end for a while and there is a slight climb along a well-vegetated path to reach a little gap where an electricity pylon stands beside **Pico do Cedro**. Despite the intrusion of the pylon, there is a good view to the head of the Curral valley, taking in the rugged peaks that surround it.

Ⓢ Walk 35

View of Curral das Freiras from the winding descent to the road at Lombo Chão

Descend more steep, rocky and stony zigzags, passing clumps of laurel, broom, gorse and brambles on an otherwise open slope with good views. The path levels out a little as it passes a little knoll where chestnuts grow. Zigzag further downhill among tall eucalyptus and pine, continuing down a densely-wooded slope of laurel and chestnut. The lower parts of the path have cobbled steps with mimosa alongside. Swing into a damp little valley to cross a stream-bed then follow a narrow concrete path uphill a short way. Prickly pears grow on a rocky slope and a few houses are reached at a road-end at **Lombo Chão**. Finish here for the short walk.

Either wait for a bus, or if one isn't due for a while, walk along the road to enjoy good views across to Curral das Freiras. There are sweeping loops along the road, but there are odd short-cuts down flights of steps with street lights alongside. The Snack Bar Hostia is reached near a bridge over the bouldery **Ribeira do Curral das Freiras**. Climb up the other side of the valley and the road rises in loops, crossing the **Levada do Curral**. The road levels out near the church in **Curral das Freiras**. ◄

For facilities see page 111.

WALK 36

Marco e Fonte to Fontes

Start	Marco e Fonte – 137193
Finish	Fontes – 109197
Distance	9.5km (6 miles)
Total Ascent	520m (1705ft)
Total Descent	480m (1575ft)
Time	3hrs 30mins
Map	Carta Militar 5
Terrain	A steep road gives way to good tracks on open slopes, but the ascent of Terreiros crosses rugged slopes where care is needed in mist.
Refreshments	Bar at Marco e Fonte. Bars at Fontes.

Transport	Rodoeste bus 96 serves Marco e Fonte from Funchal, or taxi to Boca da Corrida. Rodoeste bus 127 links Fontes with Ribeira Brava.

With careful reference to bus services, a fairly straightforward walk can be followed from Marco e Fonte to Boca da Corrida, over the summit of Terreiros to head down into Fontes. Good tracks are used most of the way and there are fine views of Madeira's highest mountains from Terreiros. Fontes is a very quiet little village with limited buses to Ribeira Brava.

Plan in advance if you wish to shorten this walk. Buses marked 'Corrida' pass Marco e Fonte and run part-way up the steep Estrada da Corrida, but get off the bus early if the shop or Bar O Mário is needed. Walkers who wish to avoid the initial steep climb to Boca da Corrida should get off the bus at Estreito de Câmara de Lobos and hire a taxi. Time your arrival at Fontes to pick up one of the infrequent buses to Ribeira Brava.

The bus marked 'Corrida' climbs part-way up the Estrada da Corrida from **Marco e Fonte** to reach a turning space. The road continues to climb steeply past cultivated plots onto slopes dominated by chestnut, with some pine and eucalyptus. An attractively cobbled stretch bends right and left, leading to the **Boca da Corrida** around 1220m (4000ft). There is a small car park and picnic area beside the **Posto Florestal Jardim da Serra**, as well as a shrine to São Cristovão in the shade of a few trees. ▶

Follow a track uphill from the car park through chained pillars, turning left to climb up and across a slope covered in broom and brambles. The track turns right and zigzags further uphill. Pass through an area of

Splendid views take in mountains from Pico Grande to Pico Ruivo and Pico do Areeiro, while Curral das Freiras lies deep in the valley, with a glimpse of Funchal harbour far below.

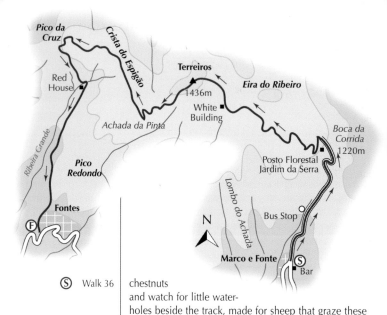

Ⓢ Walk 36

Views stretch from the sea near Ribeira Brava to the sloping plateau of Paúl da Serra, then along the rugged mountain crest of Madeira and down towards Funchal.

chestnuts and watch for little water-holes beside the track, made for sheep that graze these dry slopes. Keep walking to reach a junction of tracks. Take the track on the right, rising to an isolated **white building** close to a gap in a ridge near Terreiros.

Walk above the building to link vague sheep paths leading to the ridge. Bear left to follow the rugged ridge, crossing a gap and following a fence uphill. There is a short, steep, rocky stretch, then short grass and bracken on the higher parts. Cross a fence at a junction, then follow a path beside the fence to reach the summit of **Terreiros** at 1436m (4711ft), where a fence and wall meet. ◄

Cross the fence on the summit and walk down a narrow path. Swing right across a gentle grassy slope to follow a grassy track gently downhill. The track winds and goes through a gateway, then there is a broad zigzag on grass or stones before another gateway. Reach a junction with another track, where there is a rock cutting with a peculiar little cubbyhole alongside. Turn right here to follow the other broad track, which runs gently down and round the head of a valley. There is a gap in the ridge of

Crista do Espigão, offering a view across a deep, steep-sided valley to lofty Pico Grande and other high mountains. Much the same view is gained from the next gap. When the track zigzags downhill, there is a water-hole to the right and a fine view over a very steep slope to Serra de Água.

The track wriggles away from the edge and drops down into a valley, reaching an area of chestnut and eucalyptus, where there is a little **red house** beside the **Ribeira Grande**. Emerge from the trees to see old cultivation terraces and signs of former occupation. Continue down the stony track, and tangles of broom and brambles give way to cultivation terraces and small buildings. The track is rough and stony in places, but always clear to follow, with a narrow levada alongside. Pass more chestnut and eucalyptus then all of a sudden there are little houses and farms. A concrete road leads down to a tarmac road to the Bar Fontes, in the little village of **Fontes** at 936m (3071ft). ▶

Rodoeste bus 127 to Ribeira Brava

Looking downhill from Crista do Espigão, from grassy slopes to forests and finally the sea

WALK 37
Terreiros from Boca da Corrida

Start/Finish	Boca da Corrida – 142206
Distance	5km (3 miles)
Total Ascent	300m (985ft)
Total Descent	300m (985ft)
Time	2hrs
Map	Carta Militar 5
Terrain	Mostly easy tracks on open slopes, but Terreiros has rough and stony slopes, while Eira do Ribeiro has vague grassy paths.
Refreshments	None closer than the Bar O Mário at Marco e Fonte.
Transport	Taxi to Boca da Corrida.

Terreiros stands at the lofty height of 1436m (4711ft), but it can be approached using an easy track and a short, rugged path from the Boca da Corrida. This route would suit those who prefer to arrive by car, since it is possible to return to the start by another route, thereby enjoying a short, scenic mountain walk for relatively little effort. However, the route can be tricky in mist.

Cars can be driven up the Estrada da Corrida to Boca da Corrida. Walkers without cars who want to avoid the steep climb should get off the bus at Estreito de Câmara de Lobos and hire a taxi, arranging a pick-up for later.

Splendid views take in mountains from Pico Grande to Pico Ruivo and Pico do Areeiro, while Curral das Freiras lies deep in the valley, with a glimpse of Funchal harbour far below.

The **Boca da Corrida** stands around 1220m (4000ft), with a small car park and picnic area beside the Posto Florestal Jardim da Serra, as well as a shrine to São Cristovão in the shade of a few trees. ◄

Follow a track uphill from the car park through chained pillars, turning left to climb up and across a slope covered in broom and brambles. The track turns right and zigzags further uphill. Pass through an area of chestnuts and watch for little water-holes beside the track, made for sheep that graze these dry slopes. Keep walking to reach a junction of tracks. Take the track on the right, rising to an isolated **white building** close to a gap in a ridge near Terreiros.

Walk above the building to link vague sheep paths leading to the ridge. Bear left to follow the rugged ridge, crossing a gap and following a fence uphill. There is a short, steep, rocky stretch, then short grass and bracken on the higher parts. Cross a fence at a junction, then follow a path beside the fence to reach the summit of **Terreiros** at 1436m (4711ft), where a fence and wall meet. ▶ Retrace steps from the summit to the gap above the **white building**. Don't go down to the building, but aim to stay high instead. There is a narrow path along a grassy crest, very little rock, and the scant remains of an old fence can be followed along the undulating crest. Take great care in mist, as it would be easy to lose the path and there are cliffs to the north and east.

Cross the gently rounded summit of **Eira do Ribeiro** at 1410m (4626ft).

Stay faithful to the highest part of the crest, swinging right to enjoy views over the deep-cut Curral valley, with fine mountains beyond. Swing left downhill where the path is very vague, then right again further down the crest. Pick up the

Views stretch from the sea near Ribeira Brava to the sloping plateau of Paúl da Serra, then along the rugged mountain crest of Madeira and down towards Funchal.

Descending the grassy slopes of Eira do Ribeiro, with Pico do Cedro and Pico do Areeiro beyond

191

remains of the fence again on a more vegetated part of the crest and head down to a bend on a track. This track was followed on the outward journey, so turn left to follow it quickly back down to **Boca da Corrida**.

WALK 38
Crista do Espigão from Fontes

Start/Finish	Fontes – 109197
Distance	8.5km (5¼ miles)
Total Ascent	380m (1245ft)
Total Descent	380m (1245ft)
Time	3hrs
Map	Carta Militar 5
Terrain	Good tracks climb through forest onto open slopes, later descending through a valley.
Refreshments	Bars at Fontes.
Transport	Rodoeste bus 127 serves Fontes from Ribeira Brava.

A circular walk along broad and clear tracks is available above the little village of Fontes. An ascent through eucalyptus forest passes the Posto Florestal Trompica, then climbs onto more open broom-covered slopes. The highlight of the walk is the ridge of Crista do Espigão and the views that are available from the little gaps along it, especially looking down towards Serra de Água.

Start at the Bar Fontes in the little village of **Fontes** at 936m (3071ft). Follow the road signposted for Campanário, gently down round a valley and up past the Bar O Castanheiro, where there are a few chestnut trees. The road climbs past a few more houses, then there is a slight descent and a bend to the right. Watch for a concrete track rising sharply left, almost immediately swinging round to the right.

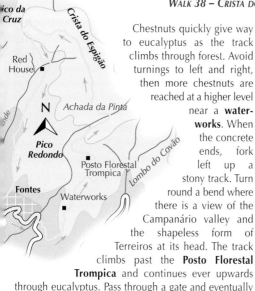

Walk 38

Chestnuts quickly give way to eucalyptus as the track climbs through forest. Avoid turnings to left and right, then more chestnuts are reached at a higher level near a **waterworks**. When the concrete ends, fork left up a stony track. Turn round a bend where there is a view of the Campanário valley and the shapeless form of Terreiros at its head. The track climbs past the **Posto Florestal Trompica** and continues ever upwards through eucalyptus. Pass through a gate and eventually reach a more open slope dotted with chestnut and covered in broom. ▸ Follow the winding track up through two more gateways to reach a track junction, around 1330m (4365ft), where a rock cutting has a peculiar little cubbyhole alongside.

Turn left to follow the track gently down and round the head of a valley. There is a gap in the ridge of **Crista do Espigão**, offering a view across a deep, steep-sided valley to lofty Pico Grande and other high mountains. Much the same view is gained from the next gap. When the track zigzags downhill, there is a water-hole to the right and a fine view over a very steep slope to Serra de Água.

The track wriggles away from the edge and drops down into a valley, reaching an area of chestnut and eucalyptus, where there is a little **red house** beside the **Ribeira Grande**. Emerge from the trees to see old cultivation terraces and signs of former occupation. Continue down the stony track, and tangles of broom and brambles give way to cultivation terraces and small buildings. The track is rough and stony in places, but always clear

Cattle, sheep and goats graze on this slope.

A walker passes the little red house down in the valley at the head of the Ribeira Grande

Rodoeste bus 127 to Ribeira Brava

to follow, with a narrow levada alongside. Pass more chestnut and eucalyptus then all of a sudden there are little houses and farms. A concrete road leads down to a tarmac road to the Bar Fontes, in the little village of **Fontes** at 936m (3071ft). ◄

WALK 39

Levada do Norte:
Serra de Água to Boa Morte

Start	Serra de Água – 103224
Finish	Boa Morte – 105235
Distance	14km (8¾ miles)
Total Ascent	240m (790ft)
Total Descent	30m (100ft)
Time	6hrs
Maps	Carta Militar 5 & 8
Terrain	A road leads up to the levada, then the path becomes very narrow and exposed, crossing sheer cliffs and passing through six tunnels. A torch is required. The path is wooded and much gentler later.
Refreshments	Bars at Serra de Água and Boa Morte.
Transport	Rodoeste bus 6, 100 & 139 serve Serra de Água from Funchal and/or Ribeira Brava. Rodoeste bus 127 & 148 link Boa Morte with Ribeira Brava and Funchal respectively.

The Levada do Norte comes in two halves. The stretch from Serra de Água to Boa Morte cuts across sheer cliffs at a general level of 550m (1805ft). It has six tunnels, a narrow and sometimes broken parapet, and a frightening amount of exposure. It is quite unsuitable for anyone who suffers from vertigo. Beyond Boa Morte the levada is much gentler and is described in Walk 40.

It used to be possible to start from the generating station near Serra de Água, but the Levada do Norte collapsed over the Ribeira do Poço. So, start in the village of **Serra de Água** at a road junction near the Snack Bar Conquilho. Follow a minor road across a river, passing a small bar, church and school. Cross over the main **ER-104 road**, which is an alternative starting point if arriving on a bus bypassing Serra de Água. Continue along a tarmac road, concrete road and dirt road, climbing parallel to the **Ribeira do Pico**, with a striking view across to Pico do Búzio, to reach a complex sluice system. ◄

The first 2.5km (1½ miles) could be covered by taxi from Serra de Água.

Turn right to pick up the **Levada do Norte** and follow it downstream. Agapanthus grows beside the path and it runs through dense chestnut woods. The path is very exposed as it turns round a corner on the cliff face of **Pico Frade**. Watch out for overhanging rock, then pass through a wooded patch. The parapet path continues to be very exposed as it turns round another cliff face. ◄ Chestnut, laurel and heather grow in places, helping to lessen the exposure, while agapanthus grows where there is enough soil beside the path. Reach a shady area of mixed woodland and prepare to enter a series of tunnels.

Enjoy fine mountain views beyond the main Serra de Água valley if you dare, otherwise keep an eye on the path and tread carefully.

This first **tunnel** has low head-room, a wall

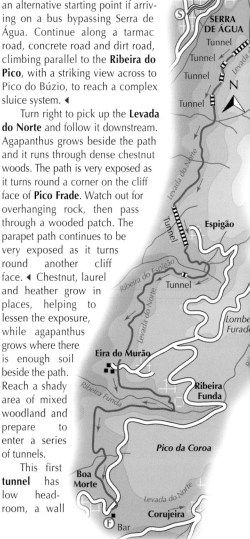

Ⓢ Walk 39

runs between the path and the channel, and it can be wet and muddy. Emerging, the path is flanked by bushes as it turns round the base of a rocky tower. Further along round a corner, beware of overhanging rock, while trees help it feel less exposed. Walk through a short **tunnel** that has a muddy path and low headroom. Pass chestnuts and turn a corner. ▸ Go through a short and curved **tunnel**, with a wall between the path and the channel, where again it can be very wet and muddy underfoot. Emerge on another very exposed stretch and walk with care. The next **tunnel** has good headroom, with a wall between the path and channel, but it is curved so the exit isn't immediately in view. A few slippery steps are climbed at the exit.

Continue round a hollow in the mountainside, where the channel is covered and a constant shower of drips make the way slippery. Cut across a very exposed sheer cliff, and there are other exposed stretches further along. ▸ The path runs in and out of little ravines and passes through a couple of small **rock cuttings** before turning a corner. A rather exposed overhang can be awkward to negotiate and some stretches of the channel are covered, before the path feels less exposed as it passes chestnuts. ▸ Take a good look back at the valley, with a view to the Boca da Encumeada, as the path suddenly reaches an exposed corner and enters the longest **tunnel**. There is a wall between the path and the channel, and good headroom, but the path can be muddy and wet. The exit is fringed by ferns. Take care following the path onwards beneath **Espigão**, as an overhanging stretch is covered in wet grass that drips onto the path, making it slippery.

Cross exposed and wooded stretches, following a convoluted course round a rugged side-valley drained by the **Ribeira do Espigão**. Swing round the valley head, passing chestnuts and going through a small **tunnel** with a cave carved above it. Go through a small rock cutting and turn a corner to overlook the main valley again.

Beware of rock-falls while negotiating a very exposed stretch.

The odd rocks, candleberry or agapanthus offer a slight feeling of security and less exposure.

Watch out for more overhanging rock and the path is flanked by agapanthus.

A short tunnel on the Levada do Norte, before Eira do Murão, with a cave-like room carved above it

Cross shrub-covered cliffs and take care where the path is narrow and uneven on a steep slope. The large 'Modela' supermarket can be seen below, while the path is narrow and grassy, with gentle loops. ◄ Cross a road where the little settlement of **Eira do Murão** sits on a knoll below the levada.

Turn a corner to enter a side-valley, passing a few houses and cultivation terraces at **Ribeira Funda**. Wild and mixed woods are passed while crossing a footbridge at the head of this valley, then the levada cuts across a slope of eucalyptus. Turn a corner to leave the side-valley and enjoy a view along the main valley from Ribeira Brava up to the Boca da Encumeada. ◄ The path loops and is attractively lined with agapanthus. Cross a road where there are signposts pointing back along the levada

The slopes are steep, but no longer vertical and not excessively rocky.

There are pines among the eucalyptus, but they have been burnt in the past.

for Serra de Água and ahead for Quinta Grande. Walk 40 continues along the **Levada do Norte**, but for the time being, the Snack Bar O Pinheiro and little village of **Boa Morte** lie just downhill. ▶

Buses to Ribeira Brava

WALK 40

Levada do Norte: Boa Morte to Estreito de Câmara de Lobos

Start	Boa Morte – 105235
Finish	Estreito de Câmara de Lobos – 146166
Distance	17km (10½ miles)
Total Ascent	30m (100ft)
Total Descent	20m (65ft)
Time	5hrs 30mins
Map	Carta Militar 8
Terrain	The levada path is level and either crosses well-cultivated slopes or goes through wooded valleys. Some short stretches are exposed and there is a tunnel.
Transport	Rodoeste bus 127 & 148 serve Boa Morte from Ribeira Brava and Funchal respectively. Rodoeste bus 96 links the end of the levada and Estreito de Câmara de Lobos with Funchal.
Refreshments	Bars at Boa Morte, Cruz de la Caldeira and Garachico. Plenty of choice at Estreito de Câmara de Lobos.

The Levada do Norte divides into two remarkably different halves. The first half (Walk 39), from Serra de Água to Boa Morte, is horribly exposed. The continuation to Estreito de Câmara de Lobos is much easier and very popular. Enjoy following it across well-cultivated and well-settled slopes, passing Campanário, Quinta Grande and Garachico at a general level of 550m (1805ft).

Stay on the bus to pass through **Boa Morte**, then get off either at the Snack Bar O Pinheiro or where the road crosses the **Levada do Norte**. Turn right to follow the flow downstream, passing a water intake where the path is planted with hydrangeas. Pass tall pines and cross a slope dotted with chestnuts. A couple of houses are passed above **Corujeira**, where the path loops round a couple of tucks in the valley side. Cross a tarmac road near a sports pitch and turn round the head of a valley drained by the Ribeiro dos Melões. Pass tall pines, a circular reservoir and chestnuts, passing the other side of the sports pitch along a path lined with agapanthus.

Turn sharply round to the left to cross a concrete road at a water intake and pass a few houses beside terraces covered in fruit and vegetables. There are street lights beside the levada which leads to another house. ◀ The path then makes a tight turn around a side-valley. As the levada swings round into the main Campanário valley, pines give way to eucalyptus, and a narrow parapet path picks its way across the top of a stout buttress. Cross the **Ribeira**

Cultivated slopes give way to mimosa and chestnut.

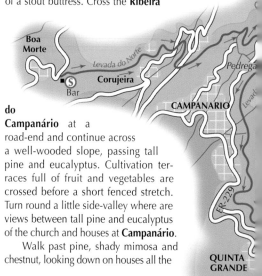

do Campanário at a road-end and continue across a well-wooded slope, passing tall pine and eucalyptus. Cultivation terraces full of fruit and vegetables are crossed before a short fenced stretch. Turn round a little side-valley where are views between tall pine and eucalyptus of the church and houses at **Campanário**.

Walk past pine, shady mimosa and chestnut, looking down on houses all the way across the side of the Campanário valley. The levada later crosses a couple of roads close together and follows concrete walkways. A slope above bears pine and eucalyptus, while the path passes cane and brambles, with some fencing alongside. Cross a steep cobbled track above a church at **Quinta Grande**, then a fence runs alongside the levada at a rock cutting. A curved stretch runs between pines and eucalyptus, passing houses and running just above the **ER-229 road**. The levada is later covered and the water runs beneath the main road, while walkers turn left after crossing the road to pick up its continuation by going down a flight of steps. Turn round the head of the valley to cross the **Ribeira da Quinta Grande**, then pass beneath **Cruz de Caldeira** by going through a short **tunnel** with an uneven path. ▶

The levada crosses rock-faces and has fences alongside, so it doesn't feel too exposed. Agapanthus and brambles grow on a steep slope and prickly pears are also seen. Turn round the head of the valley to cross the **Ribeiro da Caldeira**, after which the levada is covered. Go up steps and cross the main ER-229 road above Caldeira, noting that

A restaurant lies above the tunnel, but it is best to reach it via the main road.

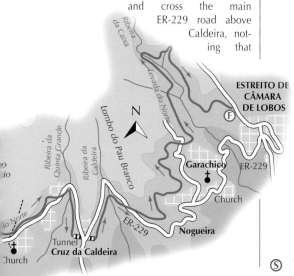

the levada is still covered. There is a landslip at **Nogueira**, where a building collapsed and destroyed the channel. The water flows through a buried pipe, so go down a slope of mimosa bushes, then head uphill to continue along another covered stretch. A house covers the levada, so walk downhill, then turn left up steps to pick up its course again.

The levada is again covered by slabs and has plenty of houses and street lights alongside as it swings round into a little valley. Leave the valley and turn round a spur where pines grow and the path is flanked by agapanthus, overlooking a hilltop church at **Garachico**. When a road is reached, the water flows beneath it, so walk uphill a short way (bar further uphill) then go down steps to continue. The channel is still covered in slabs as it passes houses. Leave the valley and turn round into the next long valley, catching a view beyond Estreito de Câmara de Lobos to distant Funchal.

Pass overhanging rock with care and walk across steep slopes and rock walls covered in mixed woodland. Cross a concrete footbridge over the **Ribeira da Caixa** at the wild and wooded head of the long valley, then cross one of its tributaries in a side-valley. Be careful of overhanging rock later, but don't worry when the parapet path narrows, as steps lead down to a lower path, climbing back to the levada shortly afterwards. Houses are reached on the way out of the long valley, as well as fruit and vegetable plots and vine trellises. The levada is sometimes open and sometimes covered on the way round a little valley then it is completely covered towards the end.

Follow a tarmac road and cross a concrete road, where the levada becomes a paved path leading round a little valley. Pass beneath vine trellises and reach a large sign announcing the **Levada do Norte** on a steep road. There are regular buses up and down this road, but it is also possible to walk down the road and finish at the prominent church in the middle of **Estreito de Câmara de Lobos**. ◀

Market, banks with ATMs, post office, shops, bars, restaurants, taxis, Rodoeste bus 96 to and from Funchal.

*Looking back towards Garachico before
the end of the Levada do Norte above
Estreito de Câmara de Lobos*

SECTION 5
Paúl da Serra

Paúl da Serra is a high plateau with fairly gentle gradients, which would appeal to those walkers who don't like steep and rugged slopes. However, not all the walking routes are gentle, especially those that run over the edge of the plateau, so be sure to read the route descriptions before launching into a route. When the mist descends, the plateau is rather featureless and good navigation is required.

Rodoeste buses serve the Boca da Encumeada and Porto Moniz from Ribeira Brava. There is no public transport onto Paúl da Serra, so walkers who want to explore the high plateau will have to arrive by car or taxi. There is a hotel at Pico da

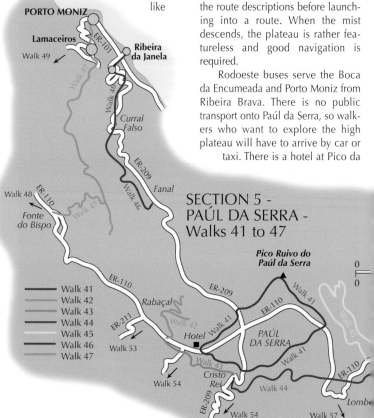

SECTION 5 -
PAÚL DA SERRA -
Walks 41 to 47

Walk 41
Walk 42
Walk 43
Walk 44
Walk 45
Walk 46
Walk 47

A moorland track between Estanquinhos and Bica da Cana goes on to pass several wind turbines (Walk 41)

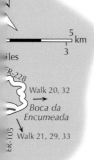

Walk 20, 32

Boca da Encumeada

Walk 21, 29, 33

Urze, the highest hotel in Madeira, and this is well-placed for exploring Pico Ruivo do Paúl da Serra, Rabaçal and the gentle Levada do Paúl. The last walk is easily linked with the Levada das Rabaças, but bear in mind that the levada runs through very long tunnels that would not be to everyone's liking. This in turn links with the Caminho do Pináculo e Folhadal, which includes even more tunnels. Neither of these walks would be suitable for anyone who suffers from claustrophobia.

Two long levadas are cut on either side of the deep, well-forested and well-watered Janela valley. The Levada dos Cedros has been completely restored and is quite delightful. The Levada da Janela, which is seldom shown correctly on maps, is altogether more of a challenge, running through several long tunnels.

Both levada walks can be extended down narrow, winding old roads to the sea. Careful planning is required to follow them. The simplest approach is to use Porto Moniz as a base and arrange for taxis to the start, then simply walk back 'home' during the day. Links with several mountain walks are available at the Boca da Encumeada, but roads off the plateau also link with long levada walks high above the west coast of Madeira.

205

WALK 41

*Pico Ruivo do Paúl da Serra
from Pico da Urze*

Start/Finish	Hotel Pico da Urze – 020251
Distance	16km (10 miles)
Total Ascent	360m (1180ft)
Total Descent	360m (1180ft)
Time	5hrs
Maps	Carta Militar 4 & 5
Terrain	Gently sloping moorland covered in bracken. Paths and tracks can be vague or stony underfoot. Care is needed with route-finding in mist.
Refreshments	Jungle Rain Café at the Hotel Pico da Urze.
Transport	None. The nearest taxis are at Calheta.

Paúl da Serra is a broad, gently sloping plateau around 1400 to 1600m (4600 to 5250ft), with the appearance of bleak, rolling moorland enclosed by rounded hills. Roads, tracks and paths criss-cross it in all directions. Either stay overnight at the remote Hotel Pico da Urze, or start early on a sunny day to make the most of this area, which is often blanketed by cloud in the afternoon.

Leave the **Hotel Pico da Urze** at 1350m (4430ft) and follow the **ER-110 road** gently uphill. Turn left along an old traffic-free road and follow it to a junction with the **ER-209 road**. Turn left along it, bending right and left to cross the bouldery bed of the **Ribeira do Lajeado**. Note the slight embankment to the right of the road. Turn right to go through a breach in this embankment before the next road bend and follow a vague grassy track liberally scattered with stones. Pass a fenced enclosure and rise gently up a slope of bracken. Trace a vague line used by wheeled vehicles, rising gently with bracken to the left and ochreous boulders to the right. There is a stony patch, then stones have been pushed to the right leaving the surface mostly grassy. Ahead, a patch of forest forms the skyline next to a rounded, bracken-covered hill. That hill is our objective.

A clear, stony, grassy track rises easily through the bracken towards the hill and forest. After a very slight descent, reach a point where a clearer grassy track slices in from right to left. Turn left to follow it, intersecting with another track. Turn right to walk towards the forest, entering it to find a picnic area. Turn left to follow a path out of the forest and climb a narrow path through bracken to reach the summit of **Pico Ruivo do Paúl da Serra**. A tall trig point at 1640m (5380ft) offers fine views round the plateau. ▶ Follow a signposted path downhill, heading south-east on a grass and bracken slope to reach a track junction on a gap. Keep straight ahead along a crunchy path flanked by gorse then take a rugged forest path to the **Posto Florestal Estanquinhos**. Walk down the access road, but immediately turn left to rise gently along a broad, stony forest track. When this starts to

Madeira's highest peaks are in view, and it is possible to look down to São Vicente, though sometimes an ocean of cloud laps against the edge of the plateau.

Rugged terrain on the higher slopes of Pico Ruivo do Paúl da Serra, with a view towards Fanal

If followed downhill far enough, it links with Walk 45.

descend ◀ turn right along a grassy track that runs gently downhill out of the forest. Turn left and later right to head towards prominent **wind turbines**.

Follow a stony access track from one turbine to another, but later fork left along a grassy track. Head downhill, then follow a rocky path and a narrow grassy path. A short walk through gorse reaches main ER-110 road at junction with an access road for Bica da Cana at 1546m (5072ft). The 'government house' was once available for hire, but it is almost impossible to get permission to use it. The access road and a track to the left of it offer a detour to a fine viewpoint.

Cross the main road and drop down to a bend on a rugged track. Follow the track down into a hollow of grass, bracken, gorse and broom, then head gently uphill. The track is roughly aligned to a fence as it crosses a rise, then it is stony as it descends into a shallow valley full of bracken. Cross a stony river-bed then enjoy a pleasant grassy stretch as the track drifts away from the fence to pass through bracken. ◀ Later the track is worn down to boulders and pumice bedrock, which proves awkward underfoot.

Wind turbines whirl on the brow to the right.

Always keep straight ahead along the most obvious track, but keep a fence running parallel far away to the left. By all means approach the fence, which guards a precipitous steep slope above **Cascalho** (see Walk 44). When a junction of tracks is reached, it hardly matters which one is taken, since both of them join later. So, either stay parallel to the fence, or follow the other track further away from the fence. The track later bends to the right and left and is anything but direct as it heads for the **ER-209 road** at a large 'Paúl da Serra' sign. Cross over the road and pick up another track, following it as it swings right, then left, to run further along the edge of the plateau at **Loiral**. ▶ Later, the track swings right and reaches a junction, so turn left to continue. The track swings round to the right again and descends across a rugged slope to land on the ER-110 road close to the **Hotel Pico da Urze**.

There are views down to the coast between Canhas and Calheta.

Ⓢ Walk 41

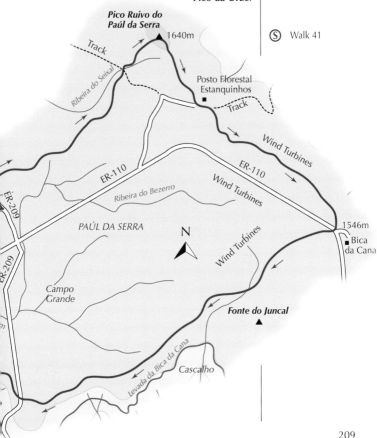

WALK 42

Rabaçal, Levada do Risco and 25 Fontes

Start/Finish	ER-110 above Rabaçal – 005256
Distance	11km (7 miles)
Total Ascent	300m (985ft)
Total Descent	300m (985ft)
Time	4hrs
Map	Carta Militar 4
Terrain	The levadas are level, while the paths vary from broad and easy to narrow and rugged. There are also flights of steps on steep and well-wooded slopes.
Refreshments	Jungle Rain Café off-route at the Hotel Pico da Urze.
Transport	None on the main road, but a minibus shuttle serves Rabaçal. The nearest taxis run from Calheta.

Most walkers who reach Rabaçal have their own cars, as there are no bus services to this part of Madeira. A steep-sided, well-forested valley bites into the flanks of Paúl da Serra, where copious quantities of water are collected to generate electricity at Calheta. This route enjoys short walks along a couple of levadas, admiring waterfalls that look spectacular after heavy rain.

Anyone using the minibus will save walking a total of 3.5km (2¼ miles). If walking late in the day, ask the driver what time he makes his last run.

Cars must be parked around 1290m (4230ft) beside the **ER-110 road** above Rabaçal, where a narrow road is closed by a barrier. Either walk down the road, or use the minibus shuttle. The road winds down round both sides of a steep-sided valley to reach isolated buildings around 1065m (3495ft) at **Rabaçal**. ◄

Leave the buildings to follow a clear and cobbled path downhill, signposted as the PR6 trail. When the path levels out, keep right to pass a junction, staying on the level as signposted for Risco. The path is broad, clear and easy to follow alongside the **Levada do Risco**. ▶ There are brief glimpses down into the valley, then a bouldery patch is crossed. The path appears to narrow, but actually remains broad as far as a viewpoint with stone seating at Risco. After heavy rain the last part of the path has a waterfall spilling onto it, so use waterproofs or an umbrella. From the viewpoint a slender waterfall is seen pouring in a rock-walled amphitheatre. Further access is forbidden as the rocks are dangerously wet and slippery, so retrace steps to the signposted path junction.

The steep slopes are covered in contorted ancient tree heather, laurel, bilberry and broom.

Turn right downhill as signposted for 25 Fontes. Winding steps lead down a steep and wooded slope. Turn right to follow the Levada das Vinte Cinco Fontes using a concrete path. Cross a bouldery gully and pass some pipework, then the path narrows. Walk down steps and cross a wide bridge over the bouldery Ribeira Grande, then climb up steps to pick up the levada again. The path loops round the valley side and is sometimes fenced. Where it runs along a buttressed wall, use the narrow levada parapet as a handrail. There are stony and uneven surfaces, so take care. ▶ Turn round a tight bend on a spur to enter a side valley. When a boulder stream-bed is reached, leave the levada and divert upstream for a few paces. A rock-walled amphitheatre at 25 Fontes drips and dribbles water, with a tall and slender waterfall pouring into a pool full of big boulders after heavy rain.There may not be as many as 25 springs here, but there are a lot!

The tree heather is often quite dense but there are some views of the Janela valley.

All that remains is to retrace steps back along the levada and climb back to the buildings at **Rabaçal**.

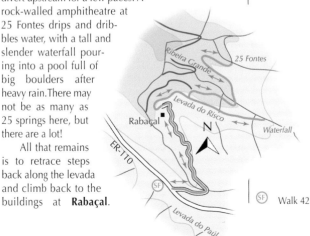

Looking down the steep and densely forested Janela valley from Rabaçal

Either walk back up to the main road or use the minibus shuttle.

WALK 43

*Levada do Paúl:
Rabaçal to Cristo Rei*

Start	ER-110 above Rabaçal – 005256
Finish	Cristo Rei statue on the ER-209 road – 035240
Distance	5.5km (3½ miles)
Total Ascent	50m (165ft)
Total Descent	10m (30ft)
Time	2hrs
Maps	Carta Militar 4 & 5
Terrain	The levada path is mostly level and easy, but narrow and stony in places.
Refreshments	Jungle Rain Café off-route at the Hotel Pico da Urze.
Transport	None. The nearest taxis run from Calheta.

The Levada do Paúl offers a short and easy walk on the south-western fringe of the Paúl da Serra plateau. The levada can be followed easily from Rabaçal to the ER-209 road below the prominent Cristo Rei statue. This short walk can be covered in addition to Walk 41 around Paúl da Serra, Walk 42 around Rabaçal, or extended using Walk 44 to Encumeada.

Cars must be parked around 1290m (4230ft) beside the **ER-110 road** above Rabaçal. The **Levada do Paúl** lies across the main road and a little way downhill, just to the left of a small shrine. Follow the levada upstream from a reservoir. The water runs in a small concrete channel across a steep slope of grass, heather and bracken. Cross a road that climbs all the way from the coast at Arco da Calheta, then as the ground becomes rockier there are masses of gorse bushes. The path is uneven as it passes some small caves then there is a tight loop across a small stream at the head of the **Ribeira do Pico da Urze**.

The slope is covered in bracken while turning round a corner, then turn round another corner and cross another little

stream at the head of the **Ribeira do Caldeirão**. The slope is still covered in bracken, though as it becomes more rugged it has more broom and brambles. Later, while passing a cave, there is tree heather and tall

Walk 43

Walkers enjoy a high-level stroll along the level and easy Levada do Paúl above Rabaçal

bilberry. The path swings into another little valley to cross the head of the **Ribeira do Covo Grande**, then cuts across a slope of broom and bracken, reaching the **ER-209 road**. There is a cottage across the road, and a short walk up the road reaches the **Cristo Rei** statue and a car park.

There are four options available at this point. Arrange to be collected by someone, retrace steps back to Rabaçal, extend the walk using Walk 44, or walk up the winding road to link with Walk 41 and turn left to reach the Hotel Pico da Urze.

WALK 44

*Levada das Rabaças and
Boca da Encumeada*

Start	Cristo Rei statue on the ER-209 road – 035240
Finish	Boca da Encumeada – 112255
Distance	12km (7½ miles)
Total Ascent	20m (65ft)
Total Descent	335m (1100ft)
Time	5hrs
Map	Carta Militar
Terrain	Easy at the start then a stony track down to Cascalho. An exposed levada goes through two long tunnels before an easy path towards the end.
Refreshments	Snack Bar Restaurante Encumeada at the end of the walk
Transport	None to the start. Rodoeste bus 6 & 139 serve Boca da Encumeada from Funchal, Ribeira Brava and São Vicente.

The gentle Levada da Bica da Cana is followed to the head of an amazingly rugged valley head at Cascalho, where water pours down rocky gullies and weeps from sheer cliffs. After dropping down to follow the exposed Levada das Rabaças, the longest tunnel in this guidebook has to be negotiated, and there is another tunnel before the walk ends at the Boca da Encumeada.

Start at the **Cristo Rei** statue high on the ER-209 road, walking down the road to find the **Levada do Paúl** crossing at 1310m (4300ft). Turn left and pass in front of a cottage to walk through a small cutting. Follow the **Levada da Bica da Cana** upstream through deep heather and broom, swinging left into a little valley. The levada crosses a bracken slope and passes a solitary pine tree. Cross a cobbled road then climb alongside an inclined channel. Cross a stile over a fence on a gentle gap, then turn left into a bigger valley.

The levada leads in easy loops across a steep and rugged slope, looking down on the **Levada Seca**. There is an exposed concrete parapet; be careful of rock leaning over the channel. The path continues as a grassy, stony or earthen line, with a few short exposed parts, crossing a steep slope covered in heather. Turn right down a broad track, passing a cave carved in the pumice bedrock. Descend in loops across the steep mountainside, passing a derelict building where there are fine views ahead. Go through a **tunnel** with an impressive amount of headroom, though it is curved and the exit isn't immediately seen. A levada channel crosses the

Ⓢ Walk 44 | floor so don't step in it!

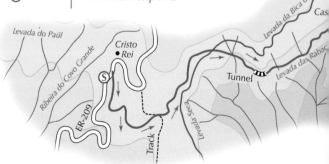

A waterfall drops from the Paúl da Serra plateau to the Levada das Rabaças at Cascalho

Walk down from the tunnel to pass a couple more tunnel mouths in the cliffs. Follow the **Levada das Rabaças** downstream on an

map continued on page 218

WALKING IN MADEIRA

Marvel at the
waterfalls – some
gushing and others
falling as misty
curtains.

This tunnel is 2.3km
(1½ miles) long and
takes an hour or so to
negotiate, so use
a torch and carry
a spare.

Bear in mind that
500m (1640ft) of
rock lies above you
on **Lombo do Mouro**.

inclined channel. It is a bit exposed but there is a fence alongside. ◄ Walk round a rocky amphitheatre at **Cascalho**. The levada path is narrow and exposed in places, but mostly fenced as leaves the valley. Follow the levada in loops round across steep and rugged slopes as it works its way into another rocky amphitheatre at Muros. There are a few tall trees and plenty of heather. The levada reaches a point where the Ribeira da Ponta do Sol drains the valley.

Peer into a **tunnel** mouth to observe a tiny pinprick of light at the distant exit. ◄ The roof is low at the entrance and the path is uneven, but there is more room and a better path further inside. A wall runs between the path and the channel for a while then one stretch of the tunnel is lined with concrete. The path becomes patchy for a while, and halfway through both tunnel mouths are mere pinpricks of light. ◄ Cross a concrete hump where the path drops, then a wall runs between the path and the channel again. The path is wet and muddy, and headroom limited, but things get better closer to the exit. Enjoy the light and open space at the end!

Turn left on leaving the tunnel to pass fine waterfalls. There is an isolated

building above the levada, but keep an eye on the exposed and unprotected path. There are fine views across the valley to Pico Grande. Some parts are fenced and there are trees at the mouth of another **tunnel**.

map continued from pages 216–217

Ⓕ Walk 44

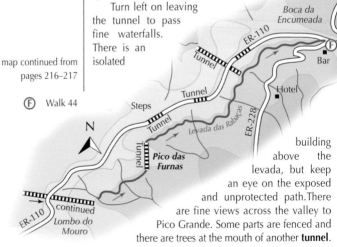

A walker emerges from the tunnel beneath Pico das Furnas.

This isn't too long, but it requires a torch, cutting straight beneath **Pico das Furnas**. It is rather drippy at both ends with puddles most of the way through, though the path is generally wide. There is good headroom, with a wall between the path and the channel. There are a few trees near the exit at a bouldery stream-bed.

Beware of overhanging rock further along the levada. The channel is covered in a number of places against rockfall and landslip debris. Pass a huge boulder sitting over the levada and go through a small gateway. Short stretches of the levada are covered as it loops across the steep mountainside. There are good views across the valley to the mountains beyond. There is more tree cover and a rectangular water intake is passed, then continue along a narrow concrete parapet. Note another **tunnel** off to the left. Don't go into it, but bear it in mind for another day (see Walk 45). Pass an overhanging rock cutting then easy loops lead past a cottage. Agapanthus grows alongside the path and there is a fine mixture of trees and shrubs along the way, including pine, oak, laurel, heather and malfurada. Go down a flight of steps to reach the road at the **Boca da Encumeada**. ◄

Snack bar and Rodoeste bus 6 & 139 to São Vicente, Ribeira Brava and Funchal

WALK 45
Caminho do Pináculo e Folhadal

Start/Finish	Boca da Encumeada – 112255
Distance	18km (11 miles)
Total Ascent	500m (1640ft)
Total Descent	500m (1640ft)
Time	8hrs
Map	Carta Militar 5
Terrain	Two level levadas prove to be quite difficult. The lower one has a series of six tunnels. A track and a rugged, densely-wooded mountain path climb to a

	higher levada then the descent is steep and rocky, giving way to a long road-walk.
Refreshments	Snack Bar Restaurante Encumeada is at the start/finish.
Transport	Rodoeste Bus 6 & 139 serve Boca da Encumeada from Funchal, Ribeira Brava and São Vicente.

Two remarkably different levadas can be linked on the steep north-eastern escarpment of Paúl da Serra. This route is waymarked as the PR17 trail and starts on the Boca da Encumeada. It follows the Levada do Norte through six tunnels, then climbs to the Levada da Serra, which slices across a cliff face. Even the final road-walk runs through three tunnels to return to Encumeada.

Start at the **Boca da Encumeada** beside the Snack Bar Restaurante Encumeada. Just across the road steps lead up to the **Levada do Norte** and a sign points upstream for Folhadal. The route is waymarked as the PR17 trail and the way is easy at first. Although well-wooded, there are breaks offering views down the valley. ▶ Pass a cottage and enjoy easy loops, with a view back to Encumeada from an overhanging rock cutting. Pico Grande and other mountains can be seen across the deep valley.

When a **tunnel** is seen to the right, reach for a torch. There is low headroom at the start, but the path is good. Later, there is more space to manoeuvre and plenty of headroom, but the path is uneven. There are drippy bits in the middle. Exit onto a good path flanked by agapanthus and hydrangea. The steep slopes are covered in ancient, dense *laurisilva* forest supporting mosses and ferns. The path is fenced in places, looping gently round a slope with little sense of exposure and few views between the trees.

Go through a short, tall **tunnel** cut through unstable boulders; there is a slender waterfall off to the left and

Agapanthus flanks the path and there is a fine mixture of trees and shrubs along the way, including pine, oak, laurel, heather and malfurada.

Ⓢ Walk 45

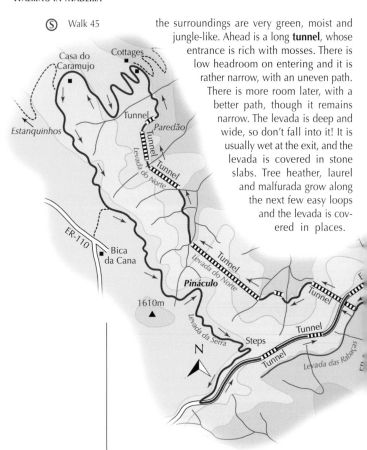

the surroundings are very green, moist and jungle-like. Ahead is a long **tunnel**, whose entrance is rich with mosses. There is low headroom on entering and it is rather narrow, with an uneven path. There is more room later, with a better path, though it remains narrow. The levada is deep and wide, so don't fall into it! It is usually wet at the exit, and the levada is covered in stone slabs. Tree heather, laurel and malfurada grow along the next few easy loops and the levada is covered in places.

The next **tunnel** has low entrance, with a narrow path, though the path is mostly even and there is more room in the middle. It narrows again towards the exit, then cross a well-wooded gully with a little waterfall to the left. Almost immediately walk into another **tunnel**. There is mostly good headroom and the path is even, but some parts are a bit narrow. Emerge on a wooded slope, then walk a short way and enter yet another **tunnel**, which is quite short and easy. There are views between the trees on the next steep slope, and although the path is unfenced, there is little feeling of exposure. The levada has been cut from a rocky slope and there is an overhang. An easy stretch loops round the slope and reaches a levada keeper's **cottage**.

Follow a broad and stony track uphill and gain views down to the sea. The track rises in easy zigzags and is flanked by deep heather and brambles with a few laurels. There is an old levada channel off to the left on one of the bends, then the track has some rough and stony stretches and rises past a crumbling cutting with large specimens of tree heather on top.

Watch to spot a log-step path signposted on the left at a bend. Step down from the track then walk up and along the narrow path through dense *laurisilva* forest. There is tall tree heather, laurel, tall bilberry and bracken. The path climbs gradually and is mossy and stony, but fairly clear despite being narrow. There are some level stretches and a couple of fallen trees, as well as a short bouldery stretch. Keep climbing along the foot of some cliffs. The path is usually good, but may be very narrow where it runs through bracken, heather and bilberry, and take care if there is a crumbling earth edge. ▸ If an exit is needed, watch for a path marked for **Bica da Cana** and the main **ER-110 road**. The path passes tall bilberry, crosses muddy patches, runs through heather and traverses beneath dripping cliffs.

Enjoy a view of Madeira's highest peaks from time to time.

Look ahead to spot the line of the **Levada da Serra**. Turn round a steep-sided hollow to find the narrow levada channel. Little streams and drips from the cliff are gathered and flow downstream. The path is often narrow and flanked by dense heather. There are some steep, but fenced drops, though little sense of exposure because of the vegetation. ▸ The path becomes easier and there is a wide stance where a break can be taken beside the big

Take care where the levada path is broken, usually because of rock-falls from the cliff above.

223

The Levada da Serra passes the prominent domed rock tower of Pináculo before dropping to a road

stump of rock called **Pináculo**. Again there is a view of the highest peaks on Madeira.

The levada suddenly runs down a steep chute. Don't follow it, but look for stone steps to descend. The flow remains vigorous and an easy path passes tall tree heather. There are a couple more steep chutes while turning a corner, then a splendid view of peaks and valleys beyond Encumeada. ▶ Follow a narrow, well-trodden path well to the left of the levada chute. Start zigzagging down a steep and rocky slope covered in broom and heather, crossing the levada chute twice. A terrace path and a flight of **steps** leads along and down a cliff into tree heather. There is wonderfully mixed vegetation while crossing the levada again, now seen as a lovely little waterfall. Walk beside the channel again using a good path through dense vegetation. Cross a drippy, slippery rock lip and continue past weeping walls, then the water runs through a pipe. Take care when stepping onto a blind bend on the **ER-110 road**.

Turn left to follow the road downhill from **Lombo do Mouro**. There is no way of avoiding the final road-walk, but maybe a motorist will offer a lift. The road runs down through three tunnels to return to the **Boca da Encumeada**.

The road seems far below and you may wonder how to reach it.

WALK 46
Levada dos Cedros:
Fanal to Ribeira da Janela

Start	Vão da Fanal – 002310
Finish	Central da Ribeira da Janela – 987368
Distance	13km (8 miles)
Total Ascent	Negligible
Total Descent	1200m (3940ft)
Time	4hrs 30mins
Map	Carta Militar 1
Terrain	A steep, forested descent and an easy levada walk, then another steep, forested descent followed by an old road down to the coast.
Refreshments	Bars at Ribeira da Janela.
Transport	None to Fanal. Rodoeste bus 150 links Ribeira da Janela with Porto Moniz and São Vicente. Rodoeste bus 139 offers an evening link to Porto Moniz, but other services pass through a tunnel.

Two recently waymarked paths can be joined together to provide a splendid route from high in the *laurisilva* forest at Fanal all the way down to the sea at Ribeira da Janela. Hundreds of steps lead down a steep, forested slope to the restored 17th century Levada dos Cedros. This offers easy walking to Curral Falso, where a continuation runs down to Ribeira da Janela and the coast.

This route starts very suddenly at 1200m (3940ft) beside the ER-209 road above the **Posto Florestal Fanal**. There are no bus services and only tiny parking spaces beside the road, so it is best to arrive by taxi, then walk down to the coast to intercept a bus. The starting point is at **Vão da Fanal**, where a prominent notice beside a bay tree explains about the waymarked PR14 trail, which forms the first half of the route.

Walk gently down a narrow path through forest dominated by heather trees, then drop more and more steeply down impressive flights of log steps. Cross a footbridge and walk down more steps close to a stream, crossing the course of an old levada. The path pulls away from the stream to continue its long descent, with tight zigzags appearing before the path lands beside the **Levada dos Cedros** around 1000m (3280ft). Turn left to walk a short way to see where the water is drawn from a river full of mossy boulders, with tall til trees blocking out the sunlight. Retrace steps to follow the levada downstream. ▸ The levada is very convoluted and the *laurisilva* forest is dense, so it is difficult to be certain of your location, but there are a few notable features along the way. The levada runs through a short curved cutting, then at another short cutting, a few stone steps lead up to the only real **viewpoint** along the way, overlooking the

The 17th-century levada channel has been completely restored and the path alongside has a firm earth surface, often supported on stone buttresses.

The Levada dos Cedros follows a very convoluted course round several ravines deep in the laurisilva

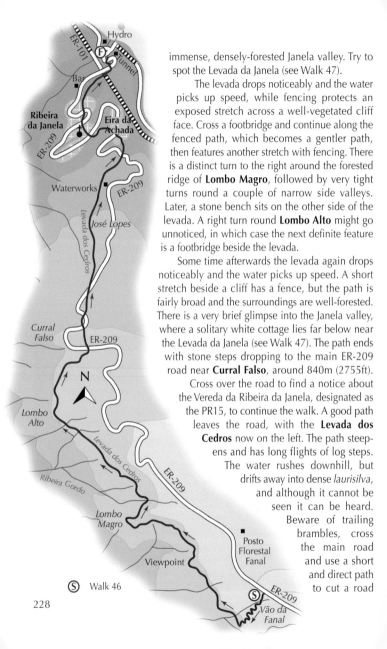

immense, densely-forested Janela valley. Try to spot the Levada da Janela (see Walk 47).

The levada drops noticeably and the water picks up speed, while fencing protects an exposed stretch across a well-vegetated cliff face. Cross a footbridge and continue along the fenced path, which becomes a gentler path, then features another stretch with fencing. There is a distinct turn to the right around the forested ridge of **Lombo Magro**, followed by very tight turns round a couple of narrow side valleys. Later, a stone bench sits on the other side of the levada. A right turn round **Lombo Alto** might go unnoticed, in which case the next definite feature is a footbridge beside the levada.

Some time afterwards the levada again drops noticeably and the water picks up speed. A short stretch beside a cliff has a fence, but the path is fairly broad and the surroundings are well-forested. There is a very brief glimpse into the Janela valley, where a solitary white cottage lies far below near the Levada da Janela (see Walk 47). The path ends with stone steps dropping to the main ER-209 road near **Curral Falso**, around 840m (2755ft).

Cross over the road to find a notice about the Vereda da Ribeira da Janela, designated as the PR15, to continue the walk. A good path leaves the road, with the **Levada dos Cedros** now on the left. The path steepens and has long flights of log steps. The water rushes downhill, but drifts away into dense *laurisilva*, and although it cannot be seen it can be heard. Beware of trailing brambles, cross the main road and use a short and direct path to cut a road bend. Cross the road again and follow a gentle track onwards. This becomes a steep path with more steps. When the road is reached yet again, turn right to walk down it, but watch for more log steps down to the left.

Follow a grassy path with rock poking through, while the levada crosses from left to right. When a track is reached at **José Lopes**, turn right, then immediately left to continue down a path. There are some log steps, but the path is mostly rugged and runs down through mixed forest dominated by tall pine and eucalyptus. Reach a gateway in a wall, but don't go through it. Turn right to follow a path downhill, which may be a bit muddy and brambly, but it gets better. Go through a small gateway and walk down a broadening path, then turn right at a track junction among tall eucalyptus.

Follow the track almost to the levada, where there is a picnic site and **waterworks**, but turn left beforehand to continue downhill. The path uses all kinds of steps, including log steps and rough-hewn steps. ▶ Cross a track and walk down log steps in a deep cutting through crumbling ancient beds of volcanic ash. Steps finally lead down to the main **ER-209 road** where there is a notice about the PR15 trail.

There is a glimpse of a village huddled on a hill, which will be reached in due course.

Cross the road and walk down a concrete road with steps down the middle, the Caminho da Terra da Fonte, leading into the hilltop village of **Eira da Achada**. Walk down round a bend on the main road to reach a bus stop, turning left down the Caminho Fundo. This road is concrete, cobbled and tarmac, leading down to the main road and another bus stop. Cross over to go down the Caminho da Voltinha, which is a steep, bendy tarmac road with steps down the middle. Cross a road halfway down it to pass a little shop/bar and reach the church in the village of **Ribeira da Janela**.

Walk down steps from the church, the Travessa da Igreja, then cross the main road to go down the Caminho do Ribeirinho, a steep concrete road with steps. Cross the main road again to walk down the Caminho dos Casais de Baixo, another steep concrete road with steps. The road becomes stone-paved and gentler, but misses

The striking forms of the Ilhéus da Ribeira da Janela, seen from a bouldery beach at the mouth of the river

Notice the heather windbreaks around tiny fruit and vegetable plots.

the shop and Bar O Negrinho just down on the main road. ◄ The stone-paved track ends where steps lead down to the main road.

Turn right down the road for a few paces then follow the Caminho do Piquinho, which has rough steps followed by cobbles. It bends left to reach steps dropping back down onto the main road again. Pick up the continuation of the path to avoid one last bend, reaching the main road near a bridge over the **Ribeira da Janela** (bar, campsite, Rodoeste bus 150 to Porto Moniz and São Vicente).

If time can be spared, follow the road to the cobbly beach to admire the towering rock pillars of the **Ilhéus da Ribeira da Janela**. Another point of interest is the Central da Ribeira da Janela hydro-electric station, fed by water collected from the deep and densely-forested Janela valley.

WALK 47

Levada da Janela:
Fonte do Bispo to Porto Moniz

Start	Fonte do Bispo – 958304
Finish	Lamaceiros – 973369, or Porto Moniz – 977383
Distance	16km, 18.5km or 23km (10, 11½ or 14¼ miles)
Total Ascent	15m (50ft)
Total Descent	1250m (4100ft)
Time	7hrs, 8hrs or 9hrs 30mins
Map	Carta Militar 1
Terrain	The descent is on a stony or grassy track and a steep and crumbling path. The levada goes through eight tunnels, including a very long and wet one, and a torch is required. Some parts of the path are exposed, but the slopes are mostly well-forested.
Refreshments	Small bars at Lamaceiros. Lots of choice at Porto Moniz.
Transport	Taxi to Fonte do Bispo. Rodoeste bus 80 from Porto Moniz to Ponta do Pargo, Ribeira Brava and Funchal. Rodoeste bus 139 from Porto Moniz to São Vicente, Ribeira Brava and Funchal. Rodoeste bus 150 from Porto Moniz to São Vicente.

This interesting and exciting levada is absent from many maps. It draws water from a deep, forested valley to feed a hydro-electric station. A taxi is required to Fonte do Bispo, where a steep track and path drop to the levada. There is an option to walk to the source, otherwise head downstream through eight tunnels to Lamaceiros. Another extension allows for a descent to Porto Moniz.

Start high on the ER-110 road at **Fonte do Bispo**, where there is a signpost at 1230m (4035ft) pointing along a grassy track for **Galhano**. The track rises slightly from a

There is good shade and occasional views across to Fanal on the far side of the valley (see Walk 46).

There is dense til woodland on a steep slope.

An optional detour is possible here, but consider the time.

There are constant showers from cracks in the roof, and a vicious 'power shower' from a crack in the rock wall to the right. Wear waterproofs or get very wet!

barrier gate then descends through chained gateposts and is stony as it winds downhill, with rough concrete strips. Cross a cattle grid and pass plenty of tree heather, laurel and tall bilberry, with some broom and candleberry. ◄ Pass a huddle of beehives at **Colmeias** and walk down past tall, dense til trees where it is quite dark at times. Emerge at a small rock cutting and a little wooden **hut**.

A narrow path runs behind the hut, dropping steeply and stonily, with an open stretch subject to landslips. Cross a small concrete footbridge over a rocky gorge then pick a way across the base of a cliff, rising gently. Walk downhill again on battered wooden steps. ◄ There are a few more substantial concrete and stone steps later, then a final series of steps lead down to the **Levada da Janela**, around 420m (1380ft). ◄ A sign reading 'Origem Levada 3km' is a bit misleading. It is actually 3km (2 miles) to the source of the levada and back to this point. To make the detour, head upstream round a corner to pass a levada keeper's **cottage**. The winding levada is occasionally fenced, then covered in slabs, reaching a **tunnel**. It is a bit drippy inside, but the path and headroom are mostly good. Emerge from the tunnel and later cross an exposed wall to reach the source of the levada in the broad and bouldery bed of the **Ribeira da Janela**. Retrace steps back through the **tunnel** and past the levada keeper's **cottage** to continue with the main route.

Enter a long **tunnel** that has good headroom and a good path, though the path slopes awkwardly towards the water. Exit into a deep, rocky, wooded gorge then enter the next **tunnel**. This is a longer one, measuring 1.2km (¾ mile). There is good headroom for the most part but the path is narrow at the start. The path widens but is uneven and bouldery in places. ◄ A much better path leads out in a wooded side-valley, where the levada goes through a rock arch and continues with an overhanging lip where it has been cut from a rock-face. Note the lovely ferns alongside on leaving the valley, and swing round into another side-valley. Cross the **Ribeira do Bonito** and notice the coverings over the levada to catch landslip debris. There is a tremendous view through the main, densely-forested Janela valley, taking in the river-bed, steep slopes and thick beds of volcanic boulders.

Go through a short **tunnel**. There are a couple of squeezes, but otherwise no problems. Curve round a rock wall and enter a longer **tunnel**, with low headroom in places and a narrow path. Exit and continue along a broad path, which narrows and leads into another little side-valley. A narrow levada path leads out of the valley and it is partly fenced as it crosses a wooded, rocky slope high above the Ribeira da Janela. There are splendid valley views and an easy stretch of path, then another short **tunnel**. This one has a low entry and exit, but good headroom in between. The path inside is good, but narrow. Walk a short way across a slope to reach

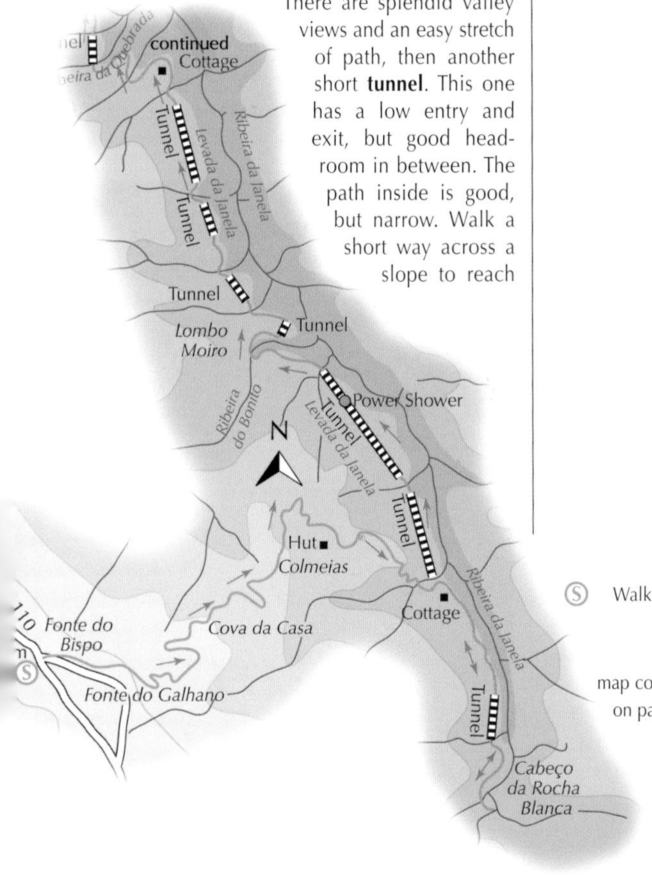

Tunnel
Ribeira da Quebrada
continued Cottage
Tunnel
Levada da Janela
Ribeira da Janela
Tunnel
Tunnel
Lombo Moiro
Tunnel
Ribeira do Bonito
Levada da Janela
Tunnel
Power Shower
N
Tunnel
Hut
Colmeias
110 m
Fonte do Bispo
Cova da Casa
Cottage
Ribeira da Janela
Fonte do Galhano
Tunnel
Cabeço da Rocha Blanca

Ⓢ Walk 47

map continued on page 235

233

The woodlands are *laurisilva* but the levada has a border of hydrangeas.

the next **tunnel**, which is longer. It has good headroom most of the time, but beware of projecting rock. The path can be narrow but is mostly good. Emerge in a tight little side-valley with plenty of ferns, and leave by following a narrow, fenced path. ◀ Swing round into the main Janela valley again and pass a levada keeper's **cottage**.

Walk round into another side-valley, passing a dripping cliff covered in ferns, mosses and liverworts. Leave this valley and turn round into the next little valley, where the levada is covered with concrete slabs.There are awesome rock walls on both sides and no room for a path beside the levada. Enter the penultimate **tunnel**, where there is good headroom and a good path, but puddles in the middle. Swing to the right to leave, ready for low headroom and lots of drips. There is a waterfall outside, so use stepping stones on the lev-

Emerge from a tunnel to pass beneath a tin shelter where a waterfall pours down before the final tunnel

234

ada and go through a shelter to avoid the water. The path is fenced round a sheer-sided valley head then goes through the final **tunnel**, which is a bit wet and muddy, has a good path, but is narrow and has low headroom in places. The levada swings left at the end while walkers exit separately. Enter a tight, ferny, wooded side-valley and follow the levada onwards.

The path is mostly fenced leaving the side-valley, then it swings round to overlook the main Janela valley. Enter a much more densely-wooded side-valley and, leaving this, walk round into a wet and dripping side-valley, crossing its bouldery head before leaving. There is a rock cutting to walk through while returning to the main valley, where a couple of small concrete **winch huts** are passed. The levada has no fencing, but isn't particularly exposed either. The levada widens into a deep trough and there is a sudden mixture of trees and shrubs, including hydrangeas and apples. Pass a concrete overspill and walk back among dense laurel, then pass another viewpoint with a picnic bench. Tall pine and eucalyptus stand above the levada, then there is a water intake before reaching a road.

Either follow the road straight away, or follow the levada as it turns a loop to enter a circular reservoir in an attractively-planted area. The road runs up to a junction where a right turn leads down into **Lamaceiros**. ▶

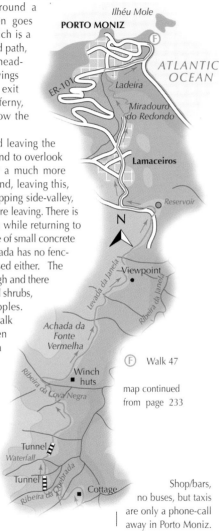

Ilhéu Mole

PORTO MONIZ

F

ATLANTIC OCEAN

ER-101

Ladeira

Miradouro do Redondo

Lamaceiros

Reservoir

N

Viewpoint

Levada da Janela

Ribeira da Janela

Achada da Fonte Vermelha

Ribeira da Cova Negra

Winch huts

F Walk 47

map continued from page 233

Tunnel
Waterfall

Tunnel

Ribeira da Quebrada

Cottage

Shop/bars, no buses, but taxis are only a phone-call away in Porto Moniz.

An easy stretch of the Levada da Janela is followed before a road is joined near Lamaceiros

Aerial view of Porto Moniz from the Miradouro do Redondo

To extend the walk a little further, it is possible to walk down to Porto Moniz. Simply head straight through a crossroads along the Caminho do Lombinho, then turn right along the Caminho da Assomada. Walk straight ahead and go steeply down the Caminho da Ladeira. This road is bendy as it passes the **Miradouro do Redondo**, where there are splendid aerial views of Porto Moniz. Continue the very steep descent to **Ladeira** ending on tarmac. Turn right down the main ER-101 road through the upper part of **Porto Moniz**. ▶

Banks with ATMs, shops and bars continuing down to the coastal resort.

PORTO MONIZ

This isolated resort is best explored by staying for a couple of nights. It is relatively modern, with the older parts of town clinging to a steep slope above. Signs for 'piscinas naturais' lead to rock-walled swimming pools kept topped-up with water when waves break over them. An aquarium allows the sea-life to be studied while the interesting Centro Ciência Vivo, www.ccvportomoniz.com, is themed around the *laurisilva* for which Madeira is famous. There are hotels, bars, restaurants, post office, buses, taxis and a Tourist Information Centre, tel. 291-852555.

Walk 47 → Tornadouro

Walk 48
Walk 49
Walk 50
Walk 51
Walk 52
Walk 53
Walk 54
Walk 55
Walk 56
Walk 57

Achadas
da Cruz

Cabo

Ponta
do Pargo

ER-101

Walk 49

Walk 50

Walk 48

Lombo

Walk 51

Fajã da
Ovelha

Raposeira

ER-223

Paúl do Mar

Walk 52

Prazéres

ER-210

Fonte do
Bispo

ER-110

Walk 47

N

0   5 km

0   miles   3

SECTION 6 -
WESTERN MADEIRA -
Walks 48 to 57

Walk 53

ER-211

Walk 42, 43

Walk 41, 42, 43

Estreito
da Calheta

Jardim do Mar

Lombo dos Faias

Walk 41, 4

Calheta

ER-222

Carva

Madalena
do Mar

PONTA DO SO

SECTION 6
Western Madeira

The western coast of Madeira is steep and rugged, though from time to time there is access to the shore, where a handful of little villages are located. At a higher level there are well-cultivated slopes and forested valleys, with small farmsteads dotted everywhere. Few tourists explored the area until recently, as the convoluted roads and sparse bus services meant that a lot of time was spent travelling. New roads have been built and the Rodoeste bus company has increased its services.

This well-cultivated area needs plenty of water, so there are lengthy levada walks available. Villages along the way have accommodation so there is an opportunity to enjoy long-distance levada walks, simply breaking the journey with minimal

fuss and continuing walking the following day. The Levada do Moinho above Porto Moniz is easily linked with the lengthy, looping Levada Calheta/ Ponta do Pargo, and once this has been followed all the way to Ponta do Sol, walkers can climb uphill to pick up the course of the Levada Nova, with a view to reaching Ribeira Brava.

Both Ribeira Brava and Ponta do Sol have a good range of services and provide a choice of accommodation options, while Rodoeste buses head westwards to other villages that lie on or near the walking routes. While there are no direct links with walking routes high above on Paúl da Serra, there are steep and winding roads that allow cars and taxis to reach the high plateau.

Adventurous long-distance walkers could proceed beyond Ribeira Brava and simply keep linking routes end-to-end to continue through the middle of Madeira, passing Funchal to reach the eastern parts of the island. Creating long-distance walks from simple day walks is simply a matter of studying the maps and looking for links, then checking whether there is accommodation, or buses off-route, along the way.

Walk 45

Lombo
do Mouro

Walk 55

Walk 57

Walk 56

Walk 57

BRAVA

WALK 48

Ponta do Pargo to Fonte do Bispo

Start	Farol at Ponta do Pargo – 885326
Finish	Fonte do Bispo – 959305
Distance	10km (6 miles)
Total Ascent	1210m (3970ft)
Total Descent	10m (30ft)
Time	3hrs 30mins
Map	Carta Militar 1
Terrain	Quiet roads and clear tracks climb from cultivated slopes to forested slopes, ending on a high moorland road.
Refreshments	Bars at Ponta do Pargo.
Transport	Rodoeste bus 142 serves Ponta da Pargo from Funchal and Ribeira Brava. Rodoeste bus 80 also serves Ponta do Pargo from Porto Moniz. No transport from Fonte do Bispo.

The red and white lighthouse, or 'farol', at **Ponta do Pargo** stands on 300m (1000ft) high cliffs at the extreme western end of Madeira. There is accommodation nearby at the Residencial O Farol. A fairly easy walk follows roads up through the village of Ponta do Pargo, where tracks continue up through forest to reach heathery heights around Fonte do Bispo. Of course, the walk finishes in the middle of nowhere and a pick-up needs to be arranged, but it is no hardship to walk back down.

Follow the cliff-top road signposted for the **Casa de Chá O Fío** teahouse. The Rua do Fío rises gently past the teahouse and its viewpoint. Enjoy coastal views then follow the road further uphill and inland, climbing to the church in the village of **Ponta do Pargo**. Banks with ATMs, post office, bars, shops and buses.

Either follow the road uphill from the church, or use the narrower Travessa da Eira Velha running parallel. Pass the Bar Girasol. Go straight through a crossroads on the main **ER-101 road**, around 500m (1640ft). ▶ Follow a road uphill, swinging right and left to climb past houses on the way out of the village. Pass the tall wall surrounding **Quinta da Serra** and continue uphill from a junction, on slope of tall pines, to reach a **waterworks**.

The road swings right and steps on the left reach the **Levada Calheta/Ponta do Pargo**. ▶ Turn right to follow it, crossing little cattle grids to enter and leave a field. Turn left up a concrete road, the Caminho da Corujeira, and continue up a clear, sunken track on a slope of pine and eucalyptus, where bracken and gorse form the undergrowth.

The Bar Garrido to the left is an alternative starting point.

The entire levada is followed on Walks 50, 51, 53 & 54.

Steep forested slopes give way to gentler high moorland slopes as the track passes Alto da Ponta do Pargo

Ⓢ Walk 48

Another track rises from the left, but keep climbing and avoid lesser tracks, sometimes passing through deep clay cuttings. One of the cuttings has hollowed-out caves to the left. There is a small levada to the left and a cattle grid is crossed at a fork. Keep right, climbing among tall pines with plenty of clearance between them. Other tracks converge on the main track, then cross a hump and descend a little. Keep left to climb again, always following the broadest and clearest track uphill. Tree cover is sparse and eventually peters out on extensive slopes of bracken. The summit to the left is the Alto da Ponta do Pargo, rising to 998m (3274ft).

Cattle and goats may be noticed grazing grass among the bracken. The track levels out and swings to the right onto the other side of a valley, even descending slightly. Tall heather, bilberry and gorse grow in places. The track makes a wide loop to the left as it climbs, and at least part of this can be short-cut if the opportunity to do so is spotted. Cross broken rock at a higher level where bracken gives way to clumps of heather. The track undulates gently, with tall heather alongside, then there is a final pull, keeping left at a fork, up a grassy track to the ER-110 road near Fonte do Bispo.

There is a road junction at 1233m (4045ft) signed for Fonte do Bispo, Prazéres, Paúl da Serra, Canhas and Porto Moniz. Arrange to be collected here or, if this is not possible, it is quick and easy to walk back down to Ponta do Pargo; just take care to reverse the route exactly and avoid being drawn down the wrong tracks. Very strong walkers could continue from this high road and walk down to Porto Moniz via the Levada da Janela (see Walk 47).

WALK 49
Levada do Moinho: Tornadouro to
Ribeira da Cruz

Start	Tornadouro – 965370
Finish	ER-101 at Ribeira da Cruz – 936342
Distance	9.5km or 11km (6 or 7 miles)
Total Ascent	400m (1310ft)
Total Descent	130m (425ft)
Time	3hrs 30mins or 4hrs
Map	Carta Militar 1
Terrain	The levada path can be narrow and overgrown initially, though good paths and tracks are used later. Cultivated slopes give way to forested slopes and areas of *laurisilva*.
Refreshments	Shop/bar off-route at Pinheiro.
Transport	Rodoeste bus 150 serves Levada Grande from Porto

Moniz and São Vicente. Rodoeste bus 80 serves Achadas da Cruz and Porto Moniz from Ribeira Brava and Ponta do Pargo. Rodoeste bus 67 serves Achadas da Cruz from Ponta do Pargo and Santa.

The Levada do Moinho is a rough and ready water-course. It wasn't a state-sponsored enterprise but was cut by people in the far north-west of Madeira. The name 'moinho' refers to watermills and some ruined examples can be seen as the water is followed upstream from Tornadouro to its source in the Ribeira da Cruz. Study bus timetables carefully to catch a bus at the end.

Tournadouro lies above the main ER-101 road at Levada Grande, reached by firstly following signposts for the Levada da Ribeira da Janela, then watching for a notice about the **Levada do Moinho** beside the road. ◀ The channel is quite narrow and leads across a road. A well-vegetated path leads onwards to a water store; turn left to continue upstream. Pass cultivated plots and reach a concrete road. Turn right to walk downhill a little, then left up another concrete road. Turn right to follow a concrete levada path, then left along a tarmac road for a short way with the levada running alongside.

The levada is waymarked as the PR7 trail and can be followed upstream from this point.

When the road falls turn left to continue along levada path. There is a steep climb beside the channel, or nearby steps could be used instead. Continue upstream and turn right at a junction of levadas, heading gradually up into eucalyptus. Cross ladder stiles to cross a rugged field. Cross a concrete road below a few houses while crossing small fields. Later, go up steps on a steeply inclined stretch of the levada, continuing a little less steeply upstream. The water emerges from a hole in some bushes and cannot be followed, so continue along the path to reach a grass and earth track. Turn left to follow this uphill and it levels out, broad and grassy, with the levada to the left and eucalyptus to the right. There are street lights beside the track at Moinho. The levada spouts from another hole and cannot be followed. Follow the track through a forest to reach an open area full of animal pens.

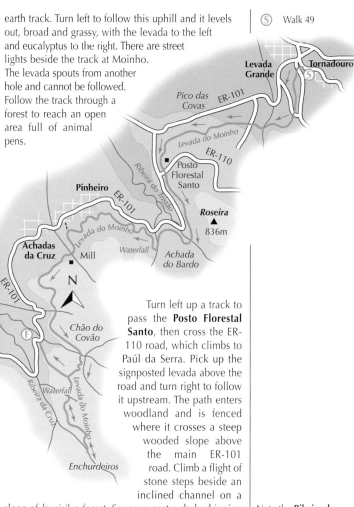

Turn left up a track to pass the **Posto Florestal Santo**, then cross the ER-110 road, which climbs to Paúl da Serra. Pick up the signposted levada above the road and turn right to follow it upstream. The path enters woodland and is fenced where it crosses a steep wooded slope above the main ER-101 road. Climb a flight of stone steps beside an inclined channel on a slope of *laurisilva* forest. Squeeze past a dark, dripping cliff and turn round the head of a fern-hung valley. ▶ The water channel is cut through rock in dark *laurisilva* forest, then is fenced where it makes a very

Note the **Ribeira do Tristão** feeding into the levada.

There is a brief glimpse down to **Pinheiro** (shop/bar and buses).

tight turn round a gully to pass a **waterfall** and pool. Walk gently up through the *laurisilva* and emerge on a slope where pine and eucalyptus have been felled. Climb log steps and continue through the remaining forest. Concrete steps are reached where bamboo grows beside the path. ◄

Head back into mixed woodland and turn round a side-valley. There is a small gate and a ruined levada-powered **mill**, with a rusting wheel in mud. Climb up some log steps and turn left, then go up more log steps on the left to follow the levada up a steep incline where the water flows fast and furious. A gentler path runs onwards from a concrete tank. Cross a slope of burnt gorse then cross a track and continue through a forest of pine and eucalyptus. The levada has a short concrete parapet, then it is lost in a bushy cutting so follow a path until the channel is found again. Continue through *laurisilva*, noting tall bilberry, and turn round the head of a valley where water enters the levada from a stream. Walk round to next valley, which features more *laurisilva*; here the levada draws water directly from a river at **Chão do Covão**.

Cross the dry river-bed and follow a path up lots of log steps on a steep, wooded slope. Pick up the course of the levada again and turn right to follow it upstream to a path junction. If time is pressing, turn right downhill to finish early. Otherwise, turn left to follow the levada to its source, bearing in mind that steps will be retraced later. ◄ A pleasant **waterfall** is seen in one little side-valley, with a smaller one in the next. Continue onwards to pass a dripping cliff, reaching a gorge deep in the *laurisilva* to find the source of the levada, where care needs to be taken on a narrow, mossy parapet. A little waterfall splashes into a pool in the **Ribeira da Cruz**.

There is a view across a forested valley, then eucalyptus, then dense *laurisilva*.

Retrace steps to the path junction and turn left downhill. Pass heather trees and other trees then go down log steps to a crest. There are more open views from the crest covered in devastated pines, which have been burnt or snapped in half and are now rotting and

The Levada do Moinho rushes down beside stone steps above the Posto Florestal Santo

A waterfall is passed before the source of the Levada do Moinho is reached in the Ribeira da Cruz

hoary with lichen. Log steps lead down to the right and reach a bend over a little river on the **ER-101 road**.

If catching a bus at this point (Rodoeste 67 & 80), be on the road in good time and find a place where the driver can see you. Alternatively, turn right to follow the road another 2km (1¼ miles) up to **Achadas da Cruz**, or turn left to follow the road downhill for another 3km (2 miles) to reach the start of Walk 50.

WALK 50

Levada Calheta/Ponta do
Pargo to Ponta do Pargo

Start	Rua da Capela, Cabo – 921341
Finish	Ponta do Pargo – 902323
Distance	11km (7 miles)
Total Ascent	Negligible
Total Descent	150m (490ft)
Time	4hrs
Map	Carta Militar 1
Terrain	The levada path runs level, mostly across steep forested slopes, but also open slopes. A road leads down through cultivated country at the end.
Refreshments	Restaurant off-route near the start. Bars at Ponta do Pargo.
Transport	Rodoeste bus 80 serves Ponta do Pargo from Funchal, Ribeira Brava and Porto Moniz. Rodoeste bus 142 serves Ponta do Pargo from Funchal and Ribeira Brava. Rodoeste bus 67 serves Ponta do Pargo from Raposeira and Santo.

The Levada Calheta / Ponta do Pargo is the longest continuous levada in Madeira. It can be followed on a very gradual gradient for over 60km (37 miles). This is more than most walkers cover in a day and facilities are often sparse, so it is best to walk the levada in stages. Starting above Cabo, a very convoluted route can be followed downstream towards Ponta do Pargo.

Start above the village of **Cabo** at the junction of the main ER-101 road and the minor Rua da Capela, around 650m (2130ft). Walk down the minor road and turn left opposite a rectangular concrete reservoir. The narrow

There is a lot of bracken on the slope, although the path is clear and easy.

concrete **Levada Calheta/Ponta do Pargo** is fringed with agapathus on a gentle slope of tall pine and eucalyptus that have suffered forest fires. ◄ The clear path winds gently and crosses the main **ER-101 road** soon after starting. The levada pulls gradually away from the road, turning as it crosses the **Ribeira da Veste** using a step-footbridge. A grassy track is crossed (restaurant down on the main road) as the levada swings round into another little valley and crosses another track above **Ribeira da Vaca**.

The first stage of the lengthy Levada Calheta/Ponta do Pargo is followed across a slope above Cabo

Curve round **Vale Seco** then head round into the next valley. The **Ribeira da Vaca** and a tributary are crossed by making tight turns at the valley head. Leave the valley and go through a little cutting on the way into the next valley, drained by the **Ribeiro do Pó Branco**.

▶ Swing round from the valley to cross a step-foot-bridge over a track in a deep cutting, passing a circular water store. The surroundings are well-wooded for a bit while crossing a track, then there is another slope of burnt pine. The levada runs beneath a track then continues across a gentle slope of tall burnt pines and bracken. Turn left into a large valley with steep slopes of grass and bracken and sparse burnt pines. Penetrate to a wooded head, passing a waterfall in one steep-sided ravine and crossing a river overspill in another.

There is plenty of forest below, but the higher slopes have been burnt and have fewer trees.

Head out of the ravine but soon swing left into another one, passing eucalyptus and crossing a step-footbridge over the ravine above a waterfall on the **Ribeira dos Moinhos**. Continue across a slope of pines, crossing two little cattle grids and turning left past a building. Head round into another little side-valley to cross another step-footbridge. Walk out of the valley at last to pass a levada keeper's cottage above a **water-works**. Turn right to walk down a road on a slope of pines, going straight through a junction and passing the tall wall surrounding **Quinta da Serra**.

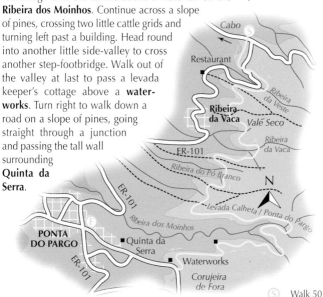

Several concrete step-footbridges carry the levada across narrow, steep-sided ravines

Walk down to the main ER-101 road near the Bar Garrido in **Ponta do Pargo**, around 500m (1640ft). ▶

Accommodation at Residencial O Farol, banks with ATMs, post office, bars, shops and buses.

WALK 51

*Levada Calheta/
Ponta do Pargo to Prazéres*

Start	Ponta do Pargo – 902323
Finish	Prazéres – 941260
Distance	20km (12½ miles)
Total Ascent	140m (460ft)
Total Descent	30m (100ft)
Time	6hrs 30mins
Maps	Carta Militar 1 & 4
Terrain	The initial ascent is by road, then the levada path is level and easy, crossing cultivated slopes, passing villages and turning round well-wooded valleys.
Refreshments	Bars and/or restaurants at Ponta do Pargo, Lombada dos Marinheiros, Lombada dos Cedros, Raposeira, Maloeira and Prazéres.
Transport	Rodoeste bus 80 serves Ponta do Pargo from Funchal, Ribeira Brava and Porto Moniz. Rodoeste bus 142 serves Ponta do Pargo from Funchal and Ribeira Brava. Rodoeste bus 67 serves Ponta do Pargo from Raposeira and Santo. Rodoeste bus 80, 142 & 107 serve Prazéres from Funchal and Ribeira Brava.

The Levada Calheta/Ponta do Pargo is incredibly convoluted as it contours at a general level of 640m (2100ft) between Ponta do Pargo and Prazéres. It passes through a number of charming little villages where occasional shops and bars are located. Bus services enable the walk to be broken into even shorter sections, while Ponta do Pargo and Prazéres offer accommodation.

Leave **Ponta do Pargo** from a crossroads near the Bar Garrido, around 500m (1640ft). Follow a minor road uphill, swinging right and left to climb past houses on the way out of the village. Pass the tall wall surrounding Quinta da Serra and continue uphill from a junction, on slope of tall pines, to reach a waterworks. The road swings right and steps on the left reach the **Levada Calheta/Ponta do Pargo** at 630m (2065ft). Turn right to follow it, crossing little cattle grids to enter and leave a field, then cross a concrete road. Walk through an earth cutting and cross a cultivated slope to go through a tiny rock cutting, reaching a slope of oak, pine and apple while turning round two little valley heads. Cross a slope of pines, while bracken, brambles and a few hydrangeas grow beside the levada. Cross a track when leaving the valley then cross a road above the village of **Amparo**.

Pass fruit and vegetable plots and cross another slope of pine, as well as oak, chestnut and apple. Turn round a valley drained by the **Ribeira dos Câmbios** and cross a grassy track. Turn round into the next little valley, which has a few charred pines and bracken on one side, while the other side bears eucalyptus. Pass a few chestnuts when leaving the valley. The levada is covered as it passes buildings at **Lombo** and crosses a narrow road. Go through a short, narrow cutting and pass a couple more houses as well as orange, chestnut and apple trees before crossing the **ER-101 road**. ◄

A grassy track crosses the levada where the path is flanked by agapanthus and apples. Cross another grassy track and note the view back to the lighthouse at Ponta do Pargo. The next slope has pine and chestnut dotted across it. Turn round a valley below a bend on the **ER-101 road**. There are mixed woods for a short way, then cross a track and swing round a cultivated spur. Go up a track and down a few steps to pass a house called Vivenda Andrade, then turn round a corner along a concrete path. Follow an earth path across a cultivated slope then the levada is partly covered until it reaches a narrow concrete road. Either walk up to the **Lombada dos**

Tall pine, eucalyptus and bracken grow on the slope.

The Levada Calheta/Ponta do Pargo runs through little fields high above Ponta do Pargo and Amparo

There is a viewpoint beside the road, looking down the deep Marinheiros valley.

Bracken and brambles grow beside the path.

Marinheiros (shop and Bar os Marinheiros) or walk straight across the **ER-101 road** below the village. ◄ The levada crosses a slope to reach higher, wooded parts of the valley to cross a step-footbridge over a waterfall on the **Ribeira dos Marinheiros**. Leave the valley and cross the **ER-101 road**, then the levada is stoutly buttressed. Little loops cross a slope, passing a few tall pines and odd chestnuts before crossing a narrow concrete track. ◄ A steep and narrow road is crossed at Casa da Levada, between São João and Fajã da Ovelha.

Cross a cultivated slope then climb steps up to a concrete road. Walk down a little, then walk up a narrow ramp to the right of a gateway at Colina da Fajã to regain the levada. Cultivated slopes give way to pines round a

Walkers follow an easy stretch of the Levada Calheta/Ponta do Pargo near São Lourenço

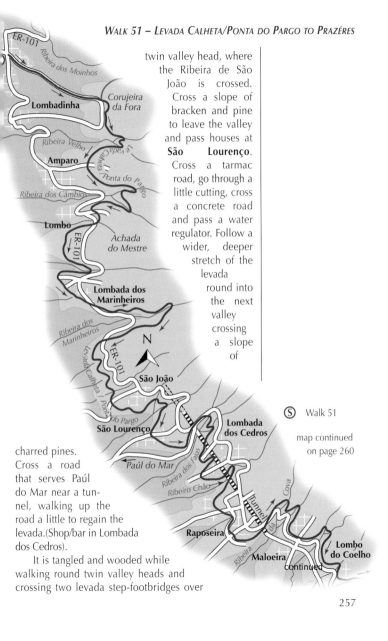

twin valley head, where the Ribeira de São João is crossed. Cross a slope of bracken and pine to leave the valley and pass houses at **São Lourenço**. Cross a tarmac road, go through a little cutting, cross a concrete road and pass a water regulator. Follow a wider, deeper stretch of the levada round into the next valley crossing a slope of charred pines. Cross a road that serves Paúl do Mar near a tunnel, walking up the road a little to regain the levada.(Shop/bar in Lombada dos Cedros).

It is tangled and wooded while walking round twin valley heads and crossing two levada step-footbridges over

(S) Walk 51

map continued on page 260

the **Ribeira das Faias**. The main ER-101 road lies just above while passing small vegetable plots and a few trees. Cross a concrete track and swing round into the next small valley. Pass a house and reach a tarmac road, turning left uphill then right down steps to regain the levada. Pass well-cultivated terraces and turn round the head of another valley, passing a few tall pines and crossing the **Ribeiro Chão**. Leave the valley and swing round a slope to follow a concrete path past fruit and vegetable plots. Cross a concrete road to follow a concrete path to a road and a bar, where the levada is signposted to the left. It is tightly enclosed to the next tarmac road and a school at **Raposeira**. ◀ The levada is covered where it leaves the road, then it flows over the top of a tunnel as it curves round a slope below the church. Agapanthus grows beside the path and mixed woods begin while crossing a road. A wonderful mixture of trees and shrubs are passed on the way round a little valley then on the way to the next little valley tall pines dominate. Cross the **Ribeira da Cova** using a step-footbridge and follow the path onwards. Cross a minor road above the main road and pass houses at **Maloeira**. ◀ Cross another road and walk past more buildings. Turn into the next valley at Poço Grande, where there are tall pines above. Cross another two step-footbridges then pass a few chestnut on the way out of the valley. ◀ Cross a tarmac road close to the main road at **Lombo do Coelho**. Make a tight turn around a little valley full of chestnut, laurel and brambles then follow the levada into another valley full of tall pine, chestnut and bay trees, crossing the **Ribeira Seca**. There is a greasy overspill, so cross the narrow river just upstream. The levada leads to a road and runs underground at **Lombo da Velha**.

Walk straight through a crossroads to continue along the road and the levada is seen heading off to the left. Pass vegetable plots and turn round a little valley full of tall pines. Leave the valley to follow the path past a water regulator where the levada is broader and deeper. Beyond is a road and the Posto Florestal Prazéres. Turn

Bar Gomes is up this road.

Restaurante Solar da Maloeira

Agapanthus lines the path the whole way round.

right down the road to reach a crossroads at the village of **Prazéres**. Accommodation, bars, restaurants, buses and link with Walk 52

WALK 52

Caminho Real:
Prazéres to Paúl do Mar

Start	Prazéres – 941260
Finish	Paúl do Mar – 920257
Distance	4km (2½ miles)
Total Ascent	Negligible
Total Descent	640m (2100ft)
Time	1hr 30mins
Map	Carta Militar 4
Terrain	A road-walk is followed by steep, cobbled, zigzag steps down into a canyon-like valley to reach the coast.
Refreshments	Bars and restaurants at Prazéres and Paúl do Mar.
Transport	Rodoeste bus 80 serves Prazéres from Funchal, Ribeira Brava and Porto Moniz. Rodoeste bus 142 serves Prazéres from Funchal and Ribeira Brava. Rodoeste 107 serves Prazéres from Funchal, Ribeira Brava and Raposeira. Rodoeste bus 107 & 115 link Paúl do Mar with Ribeira Brava and Funchal.

A *caminho real* is literally a 'royal road' and is generally used to describe a route built by the state or a municipal authority. The old cobbled road between Prazéres and Paúl do Mar links two remarkably different villages, one high up surrounded by agricultural acres, the other squeezed between cliffs and the sea. The route is one-way downhill. The challenge is to climb back up again!

Ⓕ Walk 51
Ⓢ Walk 52

map continued
from page 257

An interesting
additional experience
is available here,
known as the
'Barefoot Walk',
which involves
walking barefoot
across a variety of
textured materials.
Contact the hotel
reception for details.

Leave **Prazéres** and its striking church by following the Caminho Lombo da Rocha. This runs gently downhill and keeps to the right at junctions with other roads (bars, restaurants and an ATM along the way). The road leads to the **Hotel Jardim Atlantico** and its little supermarket. ◄ There is a notice for the Caminho Real do Paúl do Mar, or the PR19 trail. Follow a tarmac road downhill and turn right down a flight of concrete steps between apartments to reach a viewpoint overlooking Jardim do Mar and Paúl do Mar.

Walk down steep cobbled steps with a view across a deep-cut valley to Raposeira, passing an odd fig tree and prickly pears. The path curves left and an old 'danger' sign might be noticed at some stout pines. There is a danger of rockfall, but the path is often fenced where it crosses steep and rocky slopes. Zigzag down the 'rolled' cobbled steps to outflank cliff faces and avoid tangled undergrowth, noting spurges, malfurada and brambles. Cross a concrete bridge and continue down stone steps. Later, when the zigzags are steep and tightly convoluted, hacked from crumbling pumice, look for waterfalls spilling down through the valley, especially after heavy rain.

Cross a bridge spanning the **Ribeira Seca** in a gorge. The path is level then drops again, turning right and clinging to a crumbling cliff overlooking a concrete-walled harbour. The path swings left and drops steeply to

Long flights of steep, 'rolled', cobbled steps drop down to the coast at Paúl do Mar

Waterfalls spill into a precipitous gorge all the way down to the sea at Paúl do Mar

a notice about the PR19 trail. Visit the harbour and admire a waterfall spilling onto the beach, then walk into **Paúl do Mar**. ▶ If a bus isn't available, then either call for a taxi or climb back uphill to Prazéres, which could take twice as long as the descent!

Bars, restaurants and limited buses

WALK 53
Levada Calheta/Ponta do Pargo to Lombo dos Faias

Start	Prazéres – 941260
Finish	Lombo dos Faias, Calheta – 987233
Distance	19km (12 miles)
Total Ascent	15m (50ft)
Total Descent	190m (625ft)
Time	6hrs
Map	Carta Militar 4
Terrain	The levada path is level, easy and convoluted as it crosses open slopes and several wooded valleys. The final descent is by road.
Refreshments	Bars and restaurants at Prazéres.
Transport	Rodoeste bus 80 serves Prazéres from Funchal, Ribeira Brava and Porto Moniz. Rodoeste bus 142 serves Prazéres from Funchal and Ribeira Brava. Rodoeste 107 serves Prazéres from Funchal, Ribeira Brava and Raposeira. All the above are available at the end of the walk.

This stretch of the Levada Calheta/Ponta do Pargo is surprisingly distant from habitations. Very few buildings are passed but there are often views down onto well-settled slopes around Calheta. The levada crosses some open slopes and enters several well-wooded valleys. After passing the Central da Calheta generating station a road leads down to a bus route.

Start at a crossroads in the village of **Prazéres** and walk up the road signposted for Paúl da Serra to reach the Posto Florestal Prazéres. Turn right to follow the **Levada Calheta/ Ponta do Pargo**, at a general level of 640m (2100ft) away from the village. Agapanthus and hydrangeas line the path on a slope of pines. There is also oak, laurel and eucalyptus, with a brambly ground cover.

The Levada Calheta/ Ponta do Pargo crosses rugged slopes high above Calheta

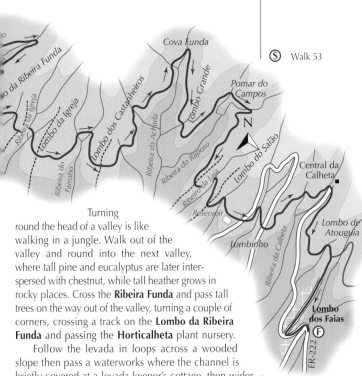

Turning round the head of a valley is like walking in a jungle. Walk out of the valley and round into the next valley, where tall pine and eucalyptus are later interspersed with chestnut, while tall heather grows in rocky places. Cross the **Ribeira Funda** and pass tall trees on the way out of the valley, turning a couple of corners, crossing a track on the **Lombo da Ribeira Funda** and passing the **Horticalheta** plant nursery.

Follow the levada in loops across a wooded slope then pass a waterworks where the channel is briefly covered at a levada keeper's cottage, then wider and deeper further upstream. Pass pine and eucalyptus and cross a track, then the levada is covered where it crosses a small ravine. Pass some fenced fruit plots followed by tall pine and eucalyptus. The levada continues making loops then there is a short, narrow cutting and another track to cross. ▶ Cross another track on the **Lombo das Castanheiros** and swing round into a big valley. Views down the lower slopes take in hundreds of houses sprawling around Calheta.

Go through a rickety gate to enter the valley and turn a corner to pass a small tin hut. ▶ The path narrows so take care, later passing another tin hut and crossing

Old terraces lie below the levada and the grass beneath the trees is used for grazing.

Watch for laurel among the eucalyptus and pine.

265

the head of the valley, where the **Ribeira da Achada** has a rocky bed and cobbled overspill. There is a mixture of laurel, tree heather and candleberry, giving way to eucalyptus and tall pine. The path narrows on a steep and rocky slope but isn't too exposed. There is a pronounced turn round the **Lombo Grande** into the next valley. Pass another tin hut among tall, burnt trees, including chestnut, while a little side-valley features tufts of heather. Continue past a fine variety of trees and shrubs, turning round the head of the valley to cross the **Ribeira do Raposo**. There is yet another tin hut beside the levada on the way out of the valley. ◄ The levada swings out of the valley and goes through a little cutting, staying among tall trees. Walk round a couple of smaller valleys, cross a track between them, then pass a concrete **reservoir**. Follow a concrete path to the left and the channel is wider, deeper and covered in big slabs. Pass a levada keeper's cottage then a very steep and patchy road offers a rapid descent to Calheta if needed.

Eucalyptus is dominant at first followed by tall pine.

The Levada Calheta/ Ponta do Pargo is broad and deep as it heads towards the Central da Calheta

Cross the road to find the levada flowing through a big concrete trough. Sometimes it is covered with slabs and sometimes it is open as it turns round a small,

wooded valley full of eucalyptus and pine. Steps lead up and down while crossing an old, grassy, cobbled road. Follow the concrete trough across the slope, sometimes on a concrete path or with fencing alongside. The slope is steep and grassy with a few trees. There is a tight little turn round a side valley then the levada runs into tall pines, with a few eucalyptus and mimosa.

Climb up a flight of steps and cross a dam on the **Ribeira da Calheta**, then walk past the **Central da Calheta** generating station and set off along its cobbled access road. ▶ The levada heads left with a wide and deep channel. Walk along the top of a wall between the levada and the road, then follow an earth path into mixed woods with agapanthus growing alongside. Cross an overgrown cobbled road and swing round into a little valley. Pass pines and a few cultivation terraces to reach buildings and a cobbled road. Unless continuing further, turn right to follow the cobbled road down to **Lombo dos Faias**, turning left to reach the main **ER-222 road** where it crosses a river, with buses available.

The Levada Calheta/ Ponta do Pargo finally approaches the Central da Calheta

Short-cut down to the main road is possible.

WALK 54
Levada Calheta/Ponta do Pargo to Ponta do Sol

Start	Lombo dos Faias, Calheta – 987233
Finish	Ponta do Sol – 030174
Distance	23km (14¼ miles)
Total Ascent	180m (590ft)
Total Descent	640m (2100ft)
Time	8hrs
Maps	Carta Militar 4, 5 & 8
Terrain	The levada path is mostly level and easy, crossing wooded valleys and cultivated slopes, but is exposed around the Madalena valley. A steep descent on roads at the end.
Refreshments	None along the way, but plenty of choice at Ponta do Sol.
Transport	Rodoeste bus 80, 107, 115 and 142 serve the main road above Calheta from Funchal and Ribeira Brava. All the above are available at the end of the walk, plus Rodoeste bus 4 to Ribeira Brava and Funchal. Taxis at Ponta do Sol.

The eastern part of the Levada Calheta/Ponta do Pargo runs to a point high above Ponta do Sol. It passes little farming communities but is well above the villages that sprawl along the main road. The levada loops in and out of several little valleys and also works its way round the magnificent Madalena valley. The final descent is along steep roads to the coast at Ponta do Sol.

Start on the ER-222 road above Calheta, where a road is signposted for the **Central da Calheta** generating station, around 460m (1510ft). Walk up the road, but turn right up another road to climb above **Lombo dos Faias**, continuing along a cobbled road onto a cultivated shoulder. Turn right along the Levada Calheta/Ponta do Pargo, around 640m (2100ft). Head into a little well-

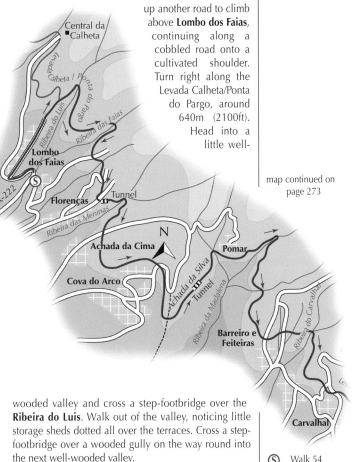

map continued on page 273

Ⓢ Walk 54

Views reveal well-settled slopes around Calheta while the road loops back round.

wooded valley and cross a step-footbridge over the **Ribeira do Luis**. Walk out of the valley, noticing little storage sheds dotted all over the terraces. Cross a step-footbridge over a wooded gully on the way round into the next well-wooded valley.

Cross a concrete slab footbridge over the **Ribeira das Faias**, then pass pine and chestnut on the way out of the valley. Walk through a shallow cutting lined with agapanthus, cross a concrete track and swing round into the next little valley at Faias, which is well cultivated. Cross a tarmac road and continue along the path. ▶ Cross a

The Levada Calheta/Ponta do Pargo crosses steep and rocky slopes as it runs round the Madalena valley

concrete road above **Florenças** and continue straight through a short and easy **tunnel** through the ridge to reach the next valley.

Cultivated slopes give way to a step-footbridge over the **Ribeira das Meninas** at the head of the valley. There are tall pines on leaving the valley, then pass circular water tanks and a levada keeper's cottage at **Achada de Cima**, where hydrangeas grow. Cross a road here and continue through tall pines, with agapanthus and hydrangeas beside the levada. ▶ Pass a water regulator and cross a steep, cobbled road, then continue along a slab-covered stretch of the levada as it passes through a small cutting. The channel crosses a cliff face and the parapet is narrow. Uneven slabs cover the levada and some are broken or missing. An easier path continues past tall eucalyptus and pine with charred trunks. Turn through a little cutting where the levada goes under a rough track and is covered with slabs; there is a glimpse down to Madalena do Mar before turning left at **Achada da Silva**.

Enter the Madalena valley, cross a slope of eucalyptus and mimosa, then follow a narrow parapet path. Rock overhangs the levada and there is a small, curved **tunnel** with a good path and good headroom. The channel is covered where the levada has cliffs above and below. Beware of gaps, holes and rockfalls. Turn round a rugged side-valley with rock walls, mixed woods, laurel and heather. Drop down a path with steps and cross a concrete slab footbridge, then climb steps to avoid a narrow, slippery parapet at the head of the valley.

Walk back into the main valley across slopes of fruit and vegetables, passing farm buildings at **Pomar** where the channel is again covered for short stretches. The head of the Madalena valley is wilder, with an undercut dripping cliff and narrow parapet in places, but it is not particularly exposed. There are plenty of laurels, then cross a step-footbridge over a bouldery gorge of the **Ribeira da Madalena**. ▶ Walk away from the head of the valley passing cliffs covered in pine and

Trees thin out to give a grand view over the well settled hollow of Arco da Calheta.

There are lovely ferns in this dark and damp recess.

eucalyptus. The path is exposed for a bit but some parts are fenced.

Turn into a side-valley full of eucalyptus and pine, and cross a step-footbridge over a deep, narrow, ferny gorge. Leave the side-valley and return to the main Madalena valley, where the levada is covered in slabs and earth. It is exposed for a bit, then less exposed as heather, agapanthus, broom and odd pines rise alongside. Turn left to walk among tall pines and the levada is open again on the way downstream. Gentle cultivated slopes are passed at **Barreiro e Feiteiras**. Cross a road, then a house sits on the levada, so keep to the garden wall on the downward side, climbing steps to rejoin the flow.

Walk round a large cultivated hollow and cross another road, passing houses and following a concrete path. A narrow earth path leads to a tight turn round the head of the valley. Cross a step-footbridge over the **Ribeira do Carvalhal**. ◄ Pass above a church, then at **Carvalhal**, in the next cultivated hollow, the levada runs beneath a vegetable plot, a concrete road and slabs to pass a house. Follow the path down to avoid a narrow parapet and climb up steps to continue. There is a step-footbridge over a concrete road, then other parts of the channel are under concrete. Cross the **ER-209 road** and continue past a circular water tank. A concrete path passes houses.

The levada swings into a little valley full of pine and eucalyptus. On leaving the valley there is a view for a while. Cross a road and another step-footbridge. Pass vegetable plots and cross another steep road, then walk into the Santiago valley, where a pipeline follows the levada. Pass eucalyptus, pine and mimosa to make a tight turn across the **Ribeira de Santiago**. The woods are quite dense on leaving the valley and many parts are dominated by eucalyptus. Cross a dirt track and a cobbled track on the **Lombo de São João**, still in tall eucalyptus. The next valley has a mixture of chestnut and eucalyptus. Turn round its head to cross the **Ribeiro de São João**. ◄ Greenhouses are seen below at **Pomar de Don João**. Cross a steep concrete road, the Caminho do Pomar de Don Joao, then pass a

The slope bears pines on leaving the valley, but there are other trees.

Pass pine, eucalyptus, chestnut and mimosa on the way out of the valley.

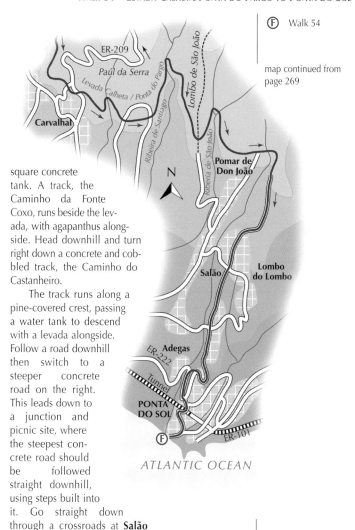

(F) Walk 54

map continued from page 269

square concrete tank. A track, the Caminho da Fonte Coxo, runs beside the levada, with agapanthus alongside. Head downhill and turn right down a concrete and cobbled track, the Caminho do Castanheiro.

The track runs along a pine-covered crest, passing a water tank to descend with a levada alongside. Follow a road downhill then switch to a steeper concrete road on the right. This leads down to a junction and picnic site, where the steepest concrete road should be followed straight downhill, using steps built into it. Go straight down through a crossroads at **Salão** and pass a church. Continue straight down the steepest tarmac road, the Estrada da Igreja de Cristo Rei, on a

The final descent from the Levada Calheta/Ponta do Pargo is on steep roads and steps to Ponta do Sol slope covered in bananas. It is usually possible to short-cut through sharp bends using concrete tracks and paths, watching for signs reading Caminho das Terças. Do this when the road makes really wide bends later. Land on the **ER-222 road** and continue down steep roads and flights of steps into **Ponta do Sol**.

PONTA DO SOL

Anyone who follows the whole of the Levada Calheta/Ponta do Pargo, detouring off-route for buses or accommodation, will walk 73km (45½ miles) to this bustling little town. Other levadas could be linked, albeit with gaps between them, to continue to Ribeira Brava, Funchal and even Caniçal. Ponta do Sol sits in a steep-sided, sun-trap valley. It offers hotels, banks with ATMs, post office, a shopping centre, bars, restaurants, buses and taxis. There is a tourist information office at nearby Lugar de Baixo, tel. 291-972850.

WALK 55
Levada Nova and Levada do Moinho from Ponta do Sol

Start	Ponta do Sol – 030174, or Jangão – 046190
Finish	Lombada – 043184, or Ponta do Sol – 030174
Distance	8km or 13km (5 or 8 miles)
Total Ascent	0m or 400m (0ft or 1310ft)
Total Descent	100m or 400m (330ft or 1310ft)
Time	3hrs or 4hrs 30mins
Maps	Carta Militar 5 & 8
Terrain	Steps and steep roads are used for the optional ascent and descent. The Levada Nova crosses cliffs, is often very exposed and has a tunnel. The Levada do Moinho crosses very steep slopes, but is often well-vegetated.
Refreshments	Plenty of choice at Ponta do Sol. Small bar at Lombada.
Transport	Rodoeste bus 4, 8, 107, 115 and 142 serve Ponta do Sol from Ribeira Brava and Funchal. Taxis at Ponta do Sol.

Two splendid levadas pick parallel courses across the steep and rocky flanks of a valley above Ponta do Sol. They run close together, but are separated by cliffs or excessively steep slopes, but there is an opportunity to link one with the other in the same walk. Either climb from Ponta do Sol to pick up the courses of these levadas or use a taxi to start as high as Jangão.

Leave **Ponta do Sol** by climbing steps behind the church, then follow the main road uphill as if for Funchal. Swing sharply right after passing a cliff lift to climb a steep road called the Caminho do Passo. Climb steps onto a headland for a fine view of the cliff coast beyond Ribeira Brava. Keep climbing a narrow concrete road up to a crossroads at a bend on the main **ER-222 road**. Cross with care to walk straight up the quiet Caminho do Pico do Melro. A little church stands to the right, but walk straight uphill past houses. The road levels out and descends gently to a junction.

Keep straight on along the road, climbing gently at first then turning left to climb the Caminho da Calçada, Turn left again to climb the steep concrete Caminho da Volta do Engenho, which has steps in the middle. Climb past houses and bananas to reach a shady square, church and school at **Lombada**. ◄ Walk towards a small bar and turn left up the steep concrete Travessa das Pedras. Continue up a tarmac road with fine views over the Ponta do Sol valley, trying to pick out the courses of the levadas that will be followed later. When the road drifts right, away from the edge, climb a concrete path and steps to reach a huddle of houses at **Jangão**. ◄

Turn left along the **Levada Nova**, which is covered with slabs until it leaves the houses and enters the awesome Ponta do Sol valley beyond. The path is exposed and crumbling, though other parts are safer and more vegetated. Watch your head when the levada curves to the left under a rocky cutting. ◄ After a drippy bit and a small waterfall where the path is slippery there is a more

The school building dates from the early settlement of Madeira.

Using a taxi saves all the distance and ascent so far.

Take in the view down the valley from the church at Lombada to the church at Ponta do Sol.

exposed curve to the left under another rock cutting. There are more exposed stretches then more tree cover, including laurel and candleberry. Turn round a corner into a rocky hollow full of chestnut.

Turn round another corner into a rocky hollow to find a **tunnel** where a torch is needed. The entrance is quite low but once inside there is good headroom and a good path. Exit into a rocky gorge with two waterfalls, then go through a rock arch and pass behind the falls, where slabs laid over the levada are slippery and there is a constant shower of drips. Wear waterproofs or use an umbrella. An exposed path leads out of the gorge then the way is more vegetated. Pass a water regulator and follow the levada to its source in the bouldery bed of the **Ribeira da Ponta do Sol**. This is an area of lush grass, heather and broom, with trees including laurel, chestnut, eucalyptus and pine.

Retrace steps along the **Levada Nova**, but watch for a steep, winding earth path dropping downhill. It starts after the water regulator and lands beside a fenced stretch of the **Levada do Moinho**. Turn right to follow the levada easily to its source in the bouldery bed of the **Ribeira da Ponta do Sol**. This area is well-wooded, with rampant undergrowth.

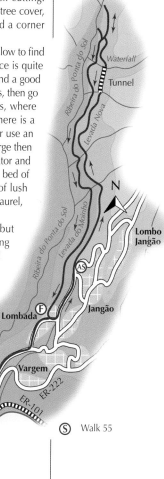

Double back downstream, passing bay trees and turning round into a dark side-valley. The levada crosses a river below the waterfalls on the Levada Nova.

The path is fenced where it crosses a rock-face, then the channel is obscured by flowery scrub, or the water passes beneath a couple of huge boulders. There are good views down a wooded part of the valley. Fencing

The Levada do Moinho traverses the steep and often well-wooded slopes of the Ponta do Sol valley

occurs from time to time and the path is fenced around a little side-valley. The path is fenced where it runs almost vertically above the **Ribeira da Ponta do Sol**, picking up speed as it turns a left-hand bend. This is generally a fast-flowing levada anyway, crossing a steep, wooded slope.

Avoid the parapet beneath a dripping cliff, going down concrete steps instead, then climb back to the levada. There is a view all the way to Ponta do Sol while crossing steep old terraces. The terraces are lost as the fenced path slices across steep slopes and cliff faces, though there is a splendid view back to the head of the valley. A concrete path runs beneath a chunky overhang, then there is a view from the church at Lombada all the way down to Ponta do Sol. The path cuts across steep, cultivated terraces and a tangled slope, reaching the church at **Lombada**. Either walk back down to Ponta do Sol, or retire to the bar and call for a taxi.

WALK 56

Levada Nova:
Jangão to Ribeira Brava

Start	Jangão – 046190
Finish	Ribeira Brava – 067162
Distance	11km (6½ miles)
Total Ascent	15m (50ft)
Total Descent	415m (1360ft)
Time	3hrs 30mins
Maps	Carta Militar 5 & 8
Terrain	The levada has a level, easy path across cultivated and wooded slopes. Steep roads and flights of steps run down to the coast.
Refreshments	Bar at Jangão. Café at Tábua. Plenty of choice at Ribeira Brava.
Transport	Plenty of Rodoeste bus services between Funchal, Ribeira Brava and Ponta do Sol. Some buses are termed 'Via Rapida', covering the distance much quicker than other buses. Taxis at Ponta do Sol and Ribeira Brava.

The Levada Nova loops through lovely valleys full of cultivation terraces high above Ponta do Sol and Ribeira Brava, running at a general level of 400m (1310ft). A lengthy traverse around a large valley passes the remote little village of Tábua. Towards the end, fine views are available from steep roads and flights of old steps, leading down to the coast at Ribeira Brava.

To start this walk, either climb from Ponta do Sol to Jangão (see Walk 55), or use a taxi to save a climb of 400m (1310ft) over 5km (3 miles). Make sure the taxi

The Ribeira da Caixa pours as a waterfall and can
be viewed from a metal footbridge

driver follows the **Levada Nova** signposts to where the road crosses the levada. Turn right to start walking, bearing in mind that the channel is covered as it passes houses in **Jangão**. Go down a flight of steps to reach the old part of the village where there is a shop/bar at a junction. Walk gently up the Caminho do Jangão, passing old and disused buildings. The levada is seen down on the right of the road, but don't try to reach it until a big flight of steps leads down to it, then follow it round the head of the valley.

Cross a cultivated slope and swing sharply into the next valley, crossing a narrow concrete path and finally leaving the village. The levada is covered in slabs where it passes a house then it goes through a short **tunnel** with low headroom and a narrow path. Emerge to see a rugged valley and follow the path across some rather overgrown cultivation terraces. Turn round the head of the valley, crossing a metal footbridge where the **Ribeira da Caixa** spills as a waterfall. Pass slender willow and cross overgrown and cultivated terraces. Walk along a short wall and cross a slope of tall pines where agapanthus and brambles flank the levada. Leave the valley and swing across a tarmac road. Continue along a concrete path then

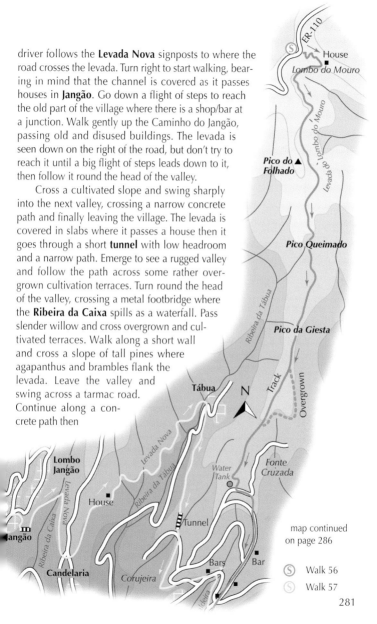

map continued
on page 286

Ⓢ Walk 56

Ⓢ Walk 57

281

leave the levada briefly where it flows under a house. Head up to the left to join a concrete road, then walk down a little and turn left to pick up the watercourse again.

The levada passes a couple of houses and enters the big Tábua valley, passing a few pine and mimosa. Walk along a short concrete wall and spot a cave cut into the hillside. Cross a gully full of rampant vegetation, then notice street lights following the levada, leading to a solitary **house** on the next spur. ◄ An open slope is followed by a small, shady wood in a side-valley. Swing round a rocky corner back into the main valley.

A few pines stand on a slope, with more round a rocky corner. Turn yet another rocky corner to enter a side-valley full of eucalyptus and continue across a cut in a rocky slope where there are brambles and malfurada bushes. Enter another little side-valley and cross a slippery river-bed at its head. Leave the valley and cross a few terraces, then there is a metal footbridge over a river. A short walk leads to the slippery bed of the **Ribeira da Tábua**, where it is better to cross using a road just upstream. Cross a tarmac road below the little church in the village of **Tábua**. ◄

Continue downstream beside the levada where tall pines and other trees limit views. There are some short, exposed stretches on the levada and big slabs cover the channel at a corner where there is a rock cutting. Brambles and agapanthus flank the path but there is another exposed stretch on the way to a short **tunnel**. The path inside is wide, but also uneven with low headroom. Emerge to walk along a concrete wall and cross a road.

A few exposed stretches are passed and a rocky edge is covered in mimosa, brambles and prickly pears. ◄ A little thatched building is seen on entering the next gentle valley while walking past terraces and vegetable plots. Climb a set of large steps rising to the left, walk up to a road and turn right to walk down it for a while. The levada is seen again to the left, so follow it onwards. Pass more vegetable plots and a house, then pass above the **Bar Bilhar a Volta**. Either walk down steps to the bar, or

Brambles and rampant vegetation engulf the old terraces.

There is a café above the church in Tábua.

Enjoy the view before leaving the Tábua valley by crossing a gentle ridge.

follow an exposed, fenced path along the top of a concrete wall. Either way, cross the road to continue and also cross the **Ribeira da Caldeira**.

The levada is narrow in its final stages with an earth or concrete path as it crosses terraces. A sign at a concrete road announces the end, so turn right downhill and continue down steep steps that wind to a road. Cross over and go down more steps, the Caminho do Lombo Cesteiro, turning left at the bottom down a concrete road to reach the edge of a huge valley. There is a safety rail alongside and splendid views over the edge. Briefly walk on tarmac further down, but keep straight onwards. The road bends right, away from the edge, but you should keep left at a junction along the Caminho da Cruz to get back to the edge of the valley. ▶

Right leads to the Hotel do Campo.

The concrete road zigzags and has steps built into it. In fact, the road becomes a flight of steps before landing on a hairpin bend on the **ER-222 road**. Walk down the road a short way then down another zigzag flight of steps. Cross the old road bridge at the bottom to reach bustling **Ribeira Brava**.

RIBEIRA BRAVA

The old part of Ribeira Brava, with its narrow cobbled streets, lies close to a cobbly beach. The centrepiece of the little town is its church and the square in front of it. In recent years the town has expanded well inland, limited by the narrowness of the canyon-like valley it occupies. There are hotels, banks with ATMs, post office, shops, bars and restaurants. Buses depart near the church and tickets can be bought from a kiosk. There are also taxis nearby and on the seafront. The Tourist Information Office is in a stout stone tower, tel. 291-951675.

WALK 57
Lombo do Mouro to Ribeira Brava

Start	Lombo do Mouro – 083236
Finish	Ribeira Brava – 067162
Distance	11km (6½ miles)
Total Ascent	Negligible
Total Descent	1300m (4265ft)
Time	3hrs 30mins
Maps	Carta Militar 5 & 8
Terrain	The levada path is rough and stony as it crosses steep slopes. Later it runs through forest and gives way to a broad track. Steep roads and steps lead down to the coast.
Refreshments	Two small bars are passed on high roads. Plenty of choice at Ribeira Brava.
Transport	Taxi to Lombo do Mouro. Plenty of Rodoeste bus services between Funchal, Ribeira Brava and Ponta do Sol. Some buses are termed 'Via Rapida', covering the distance much quicker than other buses. Taxis at Ribeira Brava.

There are no buses from the Boca da Encumeada to Lombo do Mouro, and as this is a linear walk, a taxi is needed for access. Starting on a high road, a rugged path follows a fast-flowing levada downstream, with a track continuing down through dense eucalyptus forest. The route drops down steep roads and winding flights of steps to reach the sea at Ribeira Brava.

Start at a parking space on the ER-110 road at **Lombo do Mouro**, around 1300m (4265ft). Just before this space, a path with steps and wooden fencing zigzags steeply downhill to land beside the narrow **Levada do Lombo do**

Looking down on the Residencial Encumeada complex from the road leading up to Lombo do Mouro

Mouro. The slope is rough and rocky, covered in bracken, broom and heather. Turn right to follow the path downstream from an isolated **house**. The levada runs more or less level, but can be overgrown as it cuts across the head of a steep-sided valley, susceptible to rockfalls.

Pass through a little gate and the path is easier as it continues gently downhill, flanked by bracken and the charred branches of former heather cover. Swing out of a valley head and cut across a rugged slope. As it picks up speed on an incline the water rushes downhill. ◄ Pass a cave cut from the rock, and enjoy fine views down the valley to Serra de Água as well as to the high mountains beyond. Walk down to a gate and turn a corner round **Pico do Folhado** to go through a small rock cutting on a ridge. Descend a grassy path on a slope of bracken past charred chestnuts.

The levada reaches a valley below **Pico Queimado** that is densely wooded with eucalyptus. After a fire in this valley eucalyptus colonised the slopes. Watch out for fallen tree trunks and take care where undergrowth obscures the path. Later, the trees step back a bit and bracken covers a gentle gap on the ridge near **Pico da Giesta**. Continue downstream and pass through a crumbling cutting. Exit left onto a track and turn right to follow it, noticing the levada on a couple of occasions on the left. Don't follow it if the surroundings look impenetrable. The track runs down to a road bend beside a large green **water tank**.

Turn left down the road then turn right down a steep concrete road. Walk straight along a tarmac road to pass the **Bar O Levadeiro**. The bar sits on an edge overlooking a steep-sided valley above Ribeira Brava. The road runs downhill, but when it swings to the right, leave it and head down a steep and narrow concrete road. A few houses stand on the top part of the road but the middle part is flanked by mimosa

Pumice and other stones rain down on the path from the cliff above, so take care.

map continued from page 281

Ⓕ Walk 56
Ⓕ Walk 57

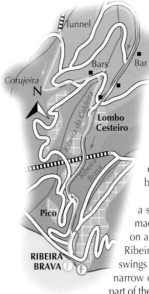

A sports complex deep in the rugged valley near Ribeira Brava

and pine. Cross a tarmac road at a bar and walk down another steep concrete road, crossing the **Levada Nova** (see Walk 36).

Steep steps wind down to a road. Cross over and go down more steps, the Caminho do Lombo Cesteiro, turning left at the bottom down a concrete road to reach the edge of a huge valley. There is a safety rail alongside and splendid views over the edge. Briefly walk on tarmac further down, but keep straight onwards. The road bends right, away from the edge, but keep left at a junction along the Caminho da Cruz to get back to the edge of the valley. ▶

Right leads to the Hotel do Campo.

The concrete road zigzags and has steps built into it. In fact, the road becomes a flight of steps before landing on a hairpin bend on the **ER-222 road**. Walk down the road a short way then down another zigzag flight of steps. Cross the old road bridge at the bottom to reach bustling **Ribeira Brava** (for facilities see page 265).

SECTION 7
Porto Santo

View from the flowery slopes of Pico do Facho to the rugged hill of Pico Branco (Wwalk 58)

The island of Porto Santo is remarkably different to Madeira, and while it has steep, rugged slopes and sheer cliffs, it also has plenty of gentle slopes and therefore offers easier walking. The size of the island naturally limits the amount of walking you can do, but while a keen walker could dash round it in a weekend, others might take up to a week. The things that strike immediately visitors as being different from Madeira include a rather arid and sparsely vegetated landscape, gentler contours, less hurried lifestyle, and an amazing, long, golden beach.

Walkers can either base themselves in the only real town, Vila Baleira, or in one of the hotels at Cabeço da Ponta. Bus services are limited, so if using them, be sure to study the timetables carefully. Taxis are also available and these can be used to get quickly and easily to the start of all the walks. The island is divided into three parts by two large-scale developments. The airport runs almost coast-to-coast, and so does a large golf course. As a result, three circular walks more or less suggest themselves in the east, middle and west of the island. Any or all of these

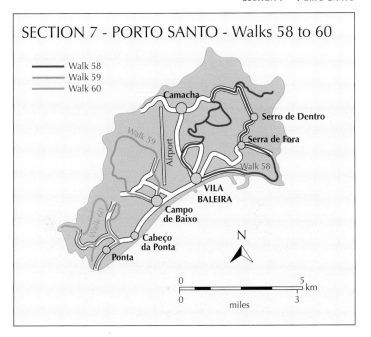

SECTION 7 - PORTO SANTO - Walks 58 to 60

—— Walk 58
▧▧▧ Walk 59
—— Walk 60

Camacha
Serro de Dentro
Serra de Fora
Walk 59
Airport
Walk 58
VILA BALEIRA
Campo de Baixo
Walk 60
Cabeço da Ponta
Ponta
N

0   5
|————| km
0   3
miles

walks can be extended along the sandy beach towards the end of each day.

Organising ferries or flights to Porto Santo is simple. Flights can be checked at the airport on Madeira, while ferries can be checked in Funchal. Either deal directly with the flight or ferry operators, or use any travel agent in Funchal. You can arrange your accommodation on Porto Santo at the same time as you book a ferry crossing, and this may work out cheaper than trying to book accommodation separately by yourself. Details are included in the main introduction to this guidebook.

WALK 58
*Pico do Castelo,
Pico do Facho and Pico Branco*

Start	Vila Baleira – 755586
Finish	Camacha – 751616, Serra de Fora – 775603, or Vila Baleira – 755586
Distance	10km, 18km or 25km (6¼, 11 or 15 miles)
Total Ascent	490m or 950m (1610ft or 3115ft)
Total Descent	390m or 950m (1280ft or 3115ft)
Time	3hrs 30mins, 6hrs or 8hrs
Map	None available
Terrain	Mostly good tracks and paths on forested slopes, open slopes and sea cliffs, as well as road-walking and a rough and rocky coastal track.
Refreshments	Bars at Camacha (off-route) and Serra de Fora. Plenty of choice at Vila Baleira.
Transport	Moinho bus 1 serves Camacha from Vila Baleira. Moinho bus 2 serves Serra de Fora from Vila Baleira.

The northern and eastern parts of Porto Santo include the highest hills, as well as impressive sea cliffs and headlands. Many slopes are dry and treeless, but there have been laudable attempts to reforest some parts. The full walk is long and takes all day, but it is possible to finish early at Camacha or Serra de Fora, if bus timetables suit, or with the aid of a taxi.

Leave **Vila Baleira** by following the main road straight inland. Turn left at the first roundabout and right at the second, then turn right up a cobbled road at **Dragoal** as signposted for Pico Castelo (shop/bar). Follow the road across an old levada and turn sharp left on a forested slope. Turn right at a junction to walk up to the **Miradouro Pico Castelo**, which is a viewpoint and picnic site.

Just before the viewpoint, turn left up a path signposted as the Vereda do Pico Castelo, or PR2 trail. Paths and stone steps zigzag uphill to pass a building and reach another signposted junction. Turn left to zigzag further up more than 300 stone steps on the steep forested slope, passing terraces full of interesting plants. A stone water tank is passed on the way to a fine viewpoint. ▶ A few more steps lead to the summit of **Pico Castelo** at 487m (1598ft).

Go down the only other stone steps off the summit, on steep forested slopes overlooking Camacha. Over 200 stone steps zigzag down to stone seats, benches and a hut at a picnic site. Just below is a forest track, which

There is a bust of the Regente Florestal António Schiappa de Azevedo who was responsible for reforesting Porto Santo's barren hills.

PICO CASTELO

From the 15th century, this steep-sided hill was a natural retreat. French and Algerian pirates raided Porto Santo and the top of Pico Castelo was fortified. There is a level summit platform and a building for shelter. In clear conditions views extend beyond Vila Baleira, Camacha and the airport to southernmost Porto Santo, with the Ilhas Desertas, Ponta de São Lourenço and the whaleback crest of Madeira prominent.

Looking back to Pico Castelo from a path around the flowery flanks of Pico do Facho

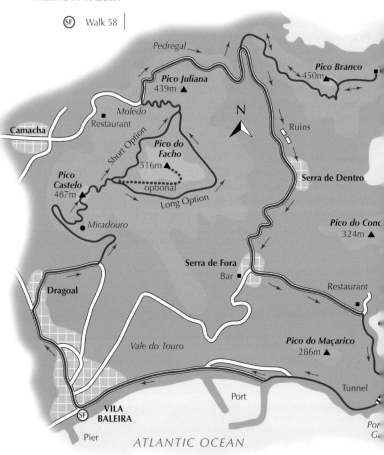

leads down to a broad, cobbled road. Turn right up this road to reach a gateway and another signpost for the PR2. The sign gives two options, but an ascent of Pico do Facho presents a third option.

Ascent of Pico do Facho

Follow the dirt road straight up through a cutting. The road is concrete as it bends left on the higher forested slopes. Watch for a few steps on the right, leading onto a path climbing between the trees to reach a small building and a tall communication mast. Go behind the building to scramble up bare rock to a trig point on **Pico do Facho** at 516m (1693ft). ▶ Walk back down to the gateway.

This is Porto Santo's highest point, offering views all round the island.

Long Option

Face the gateway, and this is signposted to the right for Moledo. A path climbs parallel to the dirt road but quickly drifts away from it, becoming a pleasant, grassy path contouring round the slopes of **Pico do Facho**. It stays just below the forest, undulates gently and zigzags up through a small gateway. Views include Pico Juliana, Pico Branco, Pico do Concelho and Pico do Maçarico. Flowers cover old terraces high above the deserted village of Serra de Dentro. The path enters the forest and winds round a slope to reach a gap between Pico do Facho and Pico Juliana.

Short Option

Face the gateway, and this is signposted to the left for Moledo. It starts as a narrow but obvious forest path zigzagging uphill a little, then undulating across the steep slopes of Pico do Facho. It occasionally crosses steep, grassy, flowery slopes and climbs a few log steps. A gap is reached between Pico do Facho and Pico Juliana, where both alternatives meet.

Follow a low stone wall along a forested crest towards Pico Juliana. Step down to the left to reach a stony track and follow it as it zigzags down to a road at **Moledo**. ▶ Those who wish to continue further should turn right to follow the road round the slopes of **Pico Juliana**.

Walkers who wish to finish early can turn left and follow the road to Camacha (bar/restaurants, museum and bus to Vila Baleira).

Cross bare and open slopes, passing a picnic site and viewpoint. There are ruined farms at **Pedregal**, then the road loops downhill in sight of a small quarry. A notice on the left announces the Vereda do Pico Branco e Terra Chã, or PR1 trail, one of the most dramatic on the island. Climb between short stretches of fencing, turning right as signposted at another stretch of fencing. The path climbs gradually across a steep and stony slope. There are wooden steps and splendid views back to Pico Juliana. Walk down fenced steps to turn round a rocky ravine below basalt columns. The path climbs gently across another rugged slope, crossing old terraces. There is plenty of fencing as the path zigzags steeply uphill, sometimes on bare rock. Cross a rocky ridge to reach a steep slope of pine and cypress where the path has been hacked from bare rock above an exceptionally rugged coast.

Turn left at a junction to climb stone steps and a zigzag path up a rocky, wooded slope to the summit of **Pico Branco**, crowned by a trig point at 450m (1476ft). Walk back downhill, then walk along the other path, down and up steps, then down and up again. Follow a crunchy red pumice path to a small building at **Terra Chã**. Enjoy splendid views of sea cliffs. ◄ Retrace steps back down to the road.

More distant views include the Ilhas Desertas and the Ponta de São Lourenço on Madeira.

Follow the road down past the deserted village of **Serra de Dentro** and notice gullies riven down hillsides.

The rough and rocky ridge of Pico Branco leads the eye to a small stone building at Terra Chã

Trees have been planted to stabilise the slopes and dams have been built across rivers. A few buildings at the bottom of the road are inhabited. Follow the road up a greener slope to pass a quarry on a gap then walk down to **Serra de Fora**. Snack Bar O Volante and bus to Vila Baleira

Follow a road signposted for Porto dos Frades, which leads down to a rugged cove at **Calhau** (bar/restaurant). Turn right and follow a track across a stream-bed where tamarisk bushes grow. ▶ Pass through an area of calcareous sandstone, then the track enters a big tunnel through **Ponta da Galé**, where the island of Ilhéu de Cima can be studied from both sides. Tread carefully beyond the tunnel as the cliffs are unstable, while in wet weather there is plenty of mud. ▶ Join a tarmac road beside a go-kart track and walk past the Marina. If you see a bus or taxi, use it to return to **Vila Baleira**, otherwise follow either the beach or the road back to town.

A sign warns of rockfalls and this is a constant problem along the coastal track.

A fine view along the coast takes in the Port, Vila Baleira and the long, sandy beach to Calheta.

WALK 59

*Campo de Baixo,
Bárbara Gomes and Eiras*

Start/Finish	Campo de Baixo – 739577
Distance	9km (5½ miles)
Total Ascent	300m (985ft)
Total Descent	300m (985ft)
Time	3hrs
Map	None available
Terrain	Road-walking at the start and finish, otherwise good tracks and paths on gentle scrubby slopes.
Refreshments	Bars and restaurants at Campo de Baixo.
Transport	Moinho bus 4 serves Campo de Baixo from Vila Baleira.

The middle part of Porto Santo contains only a few low, gently rolling hills, with a savage cliff coastline to one side and a glorious sandy beach to the other. The area is hemmed in by two large developments that run almost coast-to-coast across the island – the airport and Porto Santo Golf. A curious feature of this walk is the proximity of old windmills with modern wind turbines.

(SF)   Walk 59

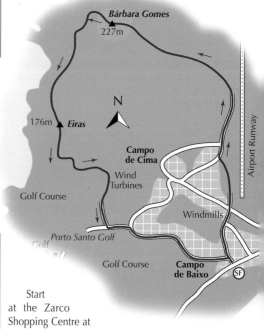

Bank with ATM, bars, restaurants, shops

Start at the Zarco Shopping Centre at **Campo de Baixo**. ◀ Walk inland by road and keep right, in effect straight ahead, along the Estrada José Joaquim Pestana Vasconcelos. Continue straight along the road signposted for Campo de Cima which has a limekiln *(forno da cal)* on the left. Cross a well-vegetated river then take the second turning uphill to the left, again signposted for Campo de Cima.

Old windmills can be visited by detouring
off-route by road into Campo da Cima

Bar Titanic, Quinta das Palmeiras mini-zoo and old windmills are all to the left.

Go straight past a roundabout ◀ and go straight up a dirt road to pass small fruit and vegetable plots. Turn right along a road at the top to reach a complex junction at the end of the Estrada Benvinda Ascensão Oliveira. Simply walk straight ahead along a broad, level dirt road to reach the **airport fence**.

Fork left at the fence to pass one last house and keep walking along the track to pass tiny walled plots. Keep left and also pass to the left of a quarry, studying a few tiny, stone-walled enclosures full of untended figs and vines. Climb straight uphill and ignore any tracks left or right, to reach masts and a dome on top of **Barbara Gomes**, at 227m (745ft). This stands in the middle of Porto Santo offering views all round the island. ◀ Walk straight down towards the cliff coast, crossing arid, stony scrub, landing on a track between a solitary farm and a quarry. Turn left to follow the track roughly parallel to the cliffs, keeping well away from the quarry. Climb to a building, a mast and a trig point on top of **Eiras**, at 176m (577ft). Continue along the track but don't go near the amazingly green golf course. Turn left at a track junction then keep right of an enclosure surrounded by concrete posts. Turn left round a lower corner of the enclosure, then right to walk away from it, as if approaching three **wind turbines** on a low hill.

Keep right of the turbines to follow a track downhill, which becomes a tarmac road, the Estrada das Eiras. Turn left at the bottom and walk to the end of the Estrada da Lapeira de Dentro. Keep straight ahead, walk downhill and go straight through a roundabout, then continue past the Bar O Viola. Keep straight ahead and walk gently downhill from the next junction, passing a couple of crumbling old farm buildings. At the bottom of the road, back in **Campo de Baixo**, is the Zarco Shopping Centre.

Those who want to extend the walk onto Porto Santo's wonderful sandy beach can go along the nearby Estrada do Forno da Cal. If staying at **Vila Baleira**, turn left along the beach. If staying at **Cabeço da Ponta**, turn right along the beach. Either way adds a pleasant and easy 2km (1¼ miles) to the walk.

Note the abundance of snail shells scattered everywhere, seldom seen on Madeira. Calcareous sandstone fills the middle of Porto Santo, providing snails with calcium for their shells.

WALK 60

Ponta, Pico de Ana Ferreira,
Espigão and Calheta

Start	Ponta – 721561
Finish	Calheta – 711549
Distance	14km (8¾ miles)
Total Ascent	450m (1475ft)
Total Descent	450m (1475ft)
Time	5hrs
Map	None available
Terrain	Road-walking at the start and finish, otherwise rugged slopes, vague paths and good tracks.
Refreshments	Bar at Calheta.
Transport	Moinho bus 4 serves Ponta and Calheta from Vila Baleira.

The south and western parts of Porto Santo include a couple of rugged hills, an impressive cliff coast and an amazing sandy beach unlike anything seen in Madeira. This walk includes spur routes to notable viewpoints and passes barren and eroded slopes that have been reforested. There is an option at Calheta to walk the entire golden sandy beach to Vila Baleira.

Start at a junction near **Ponta**, following a road signposted for Porto Santo Golf. When a **water treatment** station is reached, turn right up a steep and rugged forest track. Follow the track as it bends right and left, then walk straight across the slope to cross a low dry-stone wall. Leave the forest below the rocky summit of **Pico de Ana Ferreira**, at around 200m (655ft). Walk along a level track before heading downhill by keeping left at a couple of junctions. Land on a road near **Porto Santo Golf** and

Ⓢ Walk 60

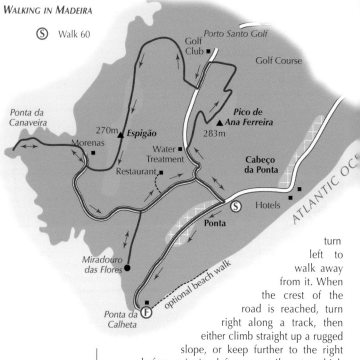

Porto Santo Golf

Golf Club ■

Golf Course

Ponta da Canaveira

270m ▲ *Espigão*

Morenas ■

Pico de
▲ **Ana Ferreira**

283m

Water
Treatment ■

Restaurant ■

**Cabeço
da Ponta**

Ⓢ

Hotels ■ ■

Ponta

ATLANTIC OCE

*Miradouro
das Flores* ●

optional beach walk

*Ponta da
Calheta* Ⓕ ■

Enjoy views all round
Porto Santo.

Pines and prickly
pears have been
planted to revegetate
the rugged, eroded
slopes.

turn left to walk away from it. When the crest of the road is reached, turn right along a track, then either climb straight up a rugged slope, or keep further to the right before swinging left more easily onto a high crest. A path runs beside a rocky ridge, a resistant basalt dyke, to reach a trig point at 270m (886ft) on **Espigão**.

◀ Follow the rocky crest further, with a fence accompanying it for a while, then the fence ends and the rock peters out at a concrete block. Either walk straight ahead to descend gradually to a dirt road, or start swinging right to pick a steeper way down to the dirt road. Either way, turn right to walk to an exotic picnic site at **Morenas**.

◀ Follow the track further to reach a parking space and fenced viewpoint at **Ponta da Canaveira** and study the offshore Ilhéu de Ferro. When heavy waves batter it, plumes of spray spout from a blowhole.

Retrace steps back to **Morenas** and continue gently up the dirt road. Pines grow on both sides of the road for a while during a descent then a prominent junction of

Looking down the slopes of Espigão, beyond Morenas, to the Ilhéu de Ferro

A bronze bust of the artist Francisco José Peile da Costa Maya stands at the viewpoint.

dirt roads is reached. Turn right as signposted for a *miradouro*. The dirt road reaches a car park and the **Miradouro das Flores**. ◀ Views embrace Porto Santo, the rugged Ilhéu de Baixo and the distant Madeira. Calheta is seen below, but the slopes are too dangerous to allow an approach.

Walk back to the junction and turn right to descend. A track on the left leads to a **restaurant**, otherwise keep walking down the road to reach the junction where the walk began near **Ponta**. Turning right, follow the road to its end at **Calheta** where there is a bar/restaurant. ◀

This is a fine place to enjoy food and drink while observing currents in conflict around Ilhéu de Baixo, but keep an eye on the time if hoping to catch a bus.

An excellent extension to the walk, up to 6km (3¾ miles), involves walking along the glorious golden beach. There is nothing like this on Madeira, so make the most of it! Calcareous sandstone outcrops on the shore at first, but this gives way to a wonderful strand. Walk either to the hotels at **Cabeço da Ponta** or come ashore at the pier at **Vila Baleira**.

The rocky and sandy beach stretching from Calheta to Vila Baleira is available as an extension to the walk

CRUISE TO THE ILHAS DESERTAS

Start/Finish	Funchal Harbour
Refreshments	Generous lunches are usually included on cruises. Food and drink are not available on Deserta Grande.
Transport	A handful of operators sail to the Ilhas Desertas. Check out the notices and ask at the kiosks at Funchal Harbour.

Those who wander round the harbour at Funchal will notice all kinds of sea-trips advertised, including day-trips to the Ilhas Desertas. The 'Desert Islands' feature in views from eastern Madeira, but seem distant and unapproachable. If you have an interest in marine wildlife and sea-birds, then a cruise will be most informative, but take one that includes a landing on Deserta Grande. Cruises to the Ilhas Desertas are of course weather-dependent and last all day, typically from 9am to 5pm, with most of the time spent sailing there and back. The journey is greatly enhanced if local wildlife experts are on board. Half-a-dozen species of dolphin frequent the region, plus even more species of whale, along with loggerhead turtles and a variety of birds. Sailings pass the Reserva Natural Parcial do Garajou on leaving Madeira and a local expert will be aware of any recent sightings.

Drawing close to the Ilhas Desertas, they appear impregnable, being flanked by cliffs on all approaches. They are, from north to south, little Ilhéu Chão, big Deserta Grande, and middle-sided Bugio. The islands were once frequented by pirates, but any attempts to

The landing place on Deserta Grande is a bouldery area formed by a landslip in 1894

establish settlements were thwarted by a lack of water. In 1894 a colossal landslip on the western flank of Deserta Grande formed a bouldery peninsula called **Fajã Grande**, creating a natural harbour suitable for landing. Usually lunch is served on board; swimming and snorkelling are popular, while a dinghy ferries people ashore for a brief visit. Anyone visiting with their own craft can moor for a period of 48hrs without special permission.

The islands and the nearby sea are designated as a Reserva Natural Parcial and Reserva Natural Integral, and access is strictly controlled. Day-trip landings rarely include more than an hour ashore, and access is limited to a short circular trail within sight of the warden's base. This offers an opportunity to see a few plants on arid, stony slopes, but little else. Stone steps climb up a cliff face, giving access to the high crest of the island, at 479m (1572ft), and the rolling plateau of **Pedregal**, but this is available only to visitors who book specific tours that include an overnight stop on the island. Information can be obtained from displays at the base. There are no real facilities for visitors, and even the water has to be delivered by the Portuguese navy.

Rare monk seals have a breeding colony and can occasionally be spotted. Apart from this local population, monk seals are found only in the Mediterranean. Rare Fea's petrels breed at the southern end of Bugio, while Zino's, Bulwer's and Madeiran storm petrels are also seen. Manx, Cory's and little shearwaters are present, along with roseate and common terns. Yellow-legged gulls are very likely to be seen. A herd of wild goats were introduced by humans, and the islands teem with little lizards. A rare spider lives on the top of Deserta Grande, along with a rare plant known as rock cabbage.

There are smaller members of the Madeira Islands group. The remote Ilhas Selvagens can't even be seen from Madeira and lie closer to Tenerife. Trips to these islands are not available from Madeira and, in any case, even among the scientific community there is apparently a long waiting-list for access.

N

▲ 444m
Pedregal

Deserta Grande

*ATLANTIC
OCEAN*

▲ 479m

Warden's Base ■

Fajã Grande

APPENDIX 1

Quick reference guide to routes

1. **Levada dos Tornos: Monte to Camacha** *16km (10 miles) – 5hrs*
   Apart from short ascents and descents at the start and finish, mostly level walking on wooded or cultivated slopes, with one avoidable tunnel.

2. **Levada dos Tornos: Camacha to Quatro Estradas** *18km (11 miles) – 5hrs 30mins* Apart from short descents and ascents at the start and finish, mostly level walking on wooded or cultivated slopes. Some short rugged stretches.

3. **Levada da Serra: Campo do Pomar to Camacha** *10km (6¼ miles) – 3hrs 15mins* The levada path is clear, level and easy to follow, generally well wooded with some cultivated areas.

4. **Levada da Serra: Camacha to Santo da Serra** *20km (12½ miles) – 6hrs 15mins* The levada path is clear, level and easy to follow; generally well-wooded with some cultivated areas.

5. **Levada Nova: Quatro Estradas to Santo da Serra** *13km (8 miles) – 4hrs* Steep roads and a difficult path down into a valley, then the levada is easy, level and well-wooded. The road-walk up to Santo da Serra starts steep and gradually levels out.

6. **Baia d'Abra and Ponta de São Lourenço** *7km (4½ miles) – 2hrs 30mins* Good paths and steps cross steep slopes and cliff edges. Several stretches have safety fencing.

7. **Levada do Caniçal: Maroços to Caniçal** *13km or 20km (8 or 12½ miles) – 4hrs or 6hrs 30mins* The level levada crosses steep wooded or cultivated slopes. The path is good, but narrow and more exposed above Caniçal.

8. **Levada da Portela: Santo da Serra to Portela** *8km (5 miles) – 2hrs 30mins* Paths and tracks are generally easy and clear. The higher parts are well-wooded. Some steep paths on the descent are slippery when wet.

9. **Vereda das Funduras: Portela to Maroços** *10km (6¼ miles) – 4hrs* A broad and easy forest road, followed by a narrow, convoluted forest path. A steep descent on paths and tracks ends on cultivated terraces.

10. **North Coast: Porto da Cruz to Ribeira Seca** *10km (6¼ miles) – 4hrs* Paths and roads climb uphill. A well-wooded path crosses a steep slope, becoming rocky and exposed, then wooded again. An easier valley path leads downhill at the end.

11. **Vereda da Penha d'Águia** *6km (3¼ miles) – 3hrs*
    Steep and narrow steps and paths may be rocky, crumbling or overgrown in places. Densely forested on top. The final stage is along a road.

12. **Levada do Furado: Portela to Ribeiro Frio** *11km (6¼ miles) – 4hrs*
    Paths, tracks and steps are used on the ascent. There are a few short tunnels and some parts are exposed, rocky, slippery. Most is well-wooded. The path towards the end is clear, level and easy.

13. **Caminho Velha: Poiso to Porto da Cruz** *13km (8 miles) – 4hrs*
    Intermittent paths give way to a good track on increasingly forested slopes. Steep and narrow paths later may be rocky, crumbling or overgrown. Road-walking towards the end.

14. **Fajã da Nogueira and Levada da Serra** *9km or 18km (5½ or 11 miles) – 4hrs or 7hrs* Broad and clear tracks at the start and finish, on steep and wooded slopes. A narrow and exposed levada walk includes ten small tunnels.

15. **Caminho Velha: Poiso to Santana** *20km (12½ miles) – 7hrs*
    Forested and cultivated ridges and valleys. Steep cobbled paths and tracks can be slippery when wet. Some road walking at intervals.

16. **Levada do Barreiro: Poço da Neve to Monte** *9km (5½ miles) – 3hrs*
    Paths are vague at first, becoming rugged and slippery. Wooded slopes can be overgrown. Old roads and tracks are used towards the end.

17. **Levada da Negra: Poço da Neve to Barreira** *8km (5 miles) – 2hrs 30mins*
    The path is narrow and stony in places, occasionally exposed, crossing steep and rocky mountain slopes. Woodland near the end gives way to a track and a steep road.

18. **Levada do Curral: Curral das Freiras to Funchal** *15km (9½ miles) – 5hrs*
    The levada path is uneven in places as it crosses steep, wooded slopes and sheer, exposed cliffs. Beware of rockfalls at first, then steep and slippery rock at Fajã. The final stretch into Funchal is without difficulties.

19. **Levada dos Piornais: Lombada to Funchal** *7km or 12km (4½ or 7½ miles) – 2hrs 15mins or 4hrs* The first stage crosses exposed cliffs and passes through tiny tunnels. The second stage is easier, crossing cultivated and urban slopes.

20. **Boca da Encumeada to Achada do Teixeira** *15km (9½ miles) – 7hrs*
    Mountainous, with paved paths and steps, as well as some steep and stony stretches. Paths are generally clear, but take care at junctions in mist. Dense vegetation hampers views on many stretches.

21. **Boca da Encumeada to Curral das Freiras** *13km (8 miles) – 5hrs*
Mountainous, with a well-wooded path at first, then a paved path, with the danger of rockfalls at a higher level. The descent is along a steep and stony path.

22. **Pico do Cedro and Pico do Areeiro** *6.5km (4 miles) – 4hrs*
A steep and rocky ascent with thorny scrub gives way to a grassy ridge with vague paths and a broad track.

23. **Pico do Areeiro to Pico Ruivo** *12km (7½ miles) – 6hrs*
Mountainous, with a narrow path, flights of steps and a tunnel. Steep, rocky and exposed slopes are often protected by fencing.

24. **Pico Ruivo, Vale da Lapa and Ilha** *10km (6 miles) – 3hrs 30mins*
The path down from Pico Ruivo is paved, but the spur to Ilha is vague and rugged at first, becoming clearer as it descends a forested ridge. An old levada, steep paths, steps, tracks and roads finally reach Ilha.

25. **Pico Ruivo, Queimadas and Santana** *11.5km (7 miles) – 3hrs 30mins*
The path down from Pico Ruivo is paved, but the forested descent to Queimadas can be steep and slippery. The last stretch is along a road.

26. **Levada do Caldeirão Verde from Pico das Pedras** *17km or 21km (10½ or 13 miles) – 6hrs or 7hrs* The levada path is easy and well-wooded at the start. There are nine tunnels and some require a torch. Several narrow, rugged paths are followed, especially towards the end, with some being exposed and slippery.

27. **Levada do Rei from Quebradas** *10km (6¼ miles) – 3hrs 30mins*
After an initial steep ascent, the levada path climbs gradually round increasingly forested slopes into a deep, steep-sided valley.

28. **Santana, Calhau and São Jorge** *6.5km or 7km (4 or 4½ miles) – 2hrs or 2hrs 30mins* Mostly along winding cobbled tracks on steep slopes.

29. **Boca da Encumeada and Pico Grande** *9km (5½ miles) – 5hrs*
Mountainous, with a well-wooded path, a paved path and the danger of rockfalls. Hands-on scrambling is required on Pico Grande. A very rough, rocky and overgrown path leads onwards, with an easier path to finish.

30. **Colmeal and Pico Grande** *12km (7½ miles) – 6hrs*
Mountainous, with a steep and stony climb giving way to hands-on scrambling on Pico Grande. A very rough, rocky and overgrown path leads onwards then a steep and well-wooded zigzag path leads downhill at the end.

31. **Curral das Freiras to Boaventura** *13km (8 miles) – 6hrs*
Roads at the beginning and end of the walk, with zigzag mountain paths in between. Steep slopes are largely covered in dense woodland and paths are steep and stony in places.

32. **Boca da Encumeada to Colmeal** *10km (6¼ miles) – 5hrs*
Mountainous, with paved paths and steps, as well as steep and stony stretches. A steep, forested zigzag path leads downhill at the end.

33. **Boca da Encumeada to Marco e Fonte** *14km (8¾ miles) – 6hrs*
Mountainous, with a well-wooded path at first, then a paved path, with the danger of rockfalls at a higher level. A good path leads from gap to gap, descending to link with a road leading further down a wooded slope.

34. **Boca da Corrida and Curral das Freiras** *10km (6¼ miles) – 4hrs*
A steep road gives way to a good path leading from gap to gap. The descent is along a steep, stony, wooded path

35. **Boca dos Namorados and Curral das Freiras** *4km or 8km (2½ or 5 miles) – 1* hour 45mins or 3hrs 15mins Wooded slopes. A clear track is used for the ascent and a steep and stony zigzag path is used on the descent, ending with a road walk.

36. **Marco e Fonte to Fontes** *9.5km (6 miles) – 3hrs 30mins*
A steep road gives way to good tracks on open slopes, but the ascent of Terreiros crosses rugged slopes where care is needed in mist.

37. **Terreiros from Boca da Corrida** *5km (3 miles) – 2hrs*
Mostly easy tracks on open slopes, but Terreiros has rough and stony slopes, while Eira do Ribeiro has vague grassy paths.

38. **Crista do Espigão from Fontes** *8.5km (5½ miles) – 3hrs*
Good tracks climb through forest onto open slopes, later descending through a valley.

39. **Levada do Norte: Serra de Água to Boa Morte** *14km (8¾ miles) – 6hrs*
A road leads up to the levada, then the path becomes very narrow and exposed, crossing sheer cliffs and passing through six tunnels. A torch is required. The path is wooded and much gentler later.

40. **Levada do Norte: Boa Morte to Estreito de Câmara de Lobos** *17km (10½ miles) – 5hrs 30mins* The levada path is level and either crosses well-cultivated slopes or goes through wooded valleys. Some short stretches are exposed and there is a tunnel.

41. **Pico Ruivo do Paúl da Serra from Pico da Urze** *16km (10 miles) – 5hrs*
Gently sloping moorland covered in bracken. Paths and tracks can be vague or stony underfoot. Care is needed with route-finding in mist.

42. **Rabaçal, Levada do Risco and 25 Fontes** *11km (7 miles) – 4hrs*
The levadas are level, while the paths vary from broad and easy to narrow and rugged. There are also flights of steps on steep and well-wooded slopes.

43. **Levada do Paúl: Rabaçal to Cristo Rei** *5.5km (3½ miles) – 2hrs*
    The levada path is mostly level and easy, but narrow and stony in places.

44. **Levada das Rabaças: Cristo Rei to Boca da Encumeada** *12km (7½ miles) – 5hrs*
    Easy at the start then a stony track down to Cascalho. An exposed levada goes through two long tunnels before an easy path towards the end.

45. **Caminho do Pináculo e Folhadal** *18km (11 miles) – 8hrs*
    Two level levadas prove to be quite difficult. The lower one has a series of six tunnels. A track and a rugged, densely-wooded mountain path climb to a higher levada then the descent is steep and rocky, giving way to a long road-walk.

46. **Levada dos Cedros: Fanal to Ribeira da Janela** *13km (8 miles) – 4hrs 30mins*
    A steep, forested descent and an easy levada walk, then another steep, forested descent followed by an old road down to the coast.

47. **Levada da Janela: Fonte do Bispo to Porto Moniz** *16km, 18.5km or 23km (10, 11½ or 14¼ miles) – 7hrs, 8hrs or 9hrs 30mins* The descent is on a stony or grassy track and a steep and crumbling path. The levada goes through eight tunnels, including a very long and wet one, and a torch is required. Some parts of the path are exposed, but the slopes are mostly well-forested.

48. **Ponta do Pargo to Fonte do Bispo** *10km (6 miles) – 3hrs 30mins*
    Quiet roads and clear tracks climb from cultivated slopes to forested slopes, ending on a high moorland road.

49. **Levada do Moinho: Tornadouro to Ribeira da Cruz** *9.5km or 11km (6 or 7 miles) – 3hrs 30mins or 4hrs* The levada path can be narrow and overgrown initially, though good paths and tracks are used later. Cultivated slopes give way to forested slopes and areas of laurisilva.

50. **Levada Calheta/Ponta do Pargo to Ponta do Pargo** *11km (7 miles) – 4hrs*
    The levada path runs level, mostly across steep forested slopes, but also open slopes. A road leads down through cultivated country at the end.

51. **Levada Calheta/Ponta do Pargo to Prazéres** *20km (12½ miles) – 6hrs 30mins*
    The initial ascent is by road, then the levada path is level and easy, crossing cultivated slopes, passing villages and turning round well-wooded valleys.

52. **Caminho Real: Prazéres to Paúl do Mar** *4km (2½ miles) – 1hr 30mins*
    A road-walk is followed by steep, cobbled, zigzag steps down into a canyon-like valley to reach the coast.

53. **Levada Calheta/Ponta do Pargo to Lombo dos Faias** *19km (12 miles) – 6hrs*
    The levada path is level, easy and convoluted as it crosses open slopes and several wooded valleys. The final descent is by road.

54. **Levada Calheta/Ponta do Pargo to Ponta do Sol** *23km (14¼ miles) – 8hrs*

The levada path is mostly level and easy, crossing wooded valleys and cultivated slopes, but is exposed around the Madalena valley. A steep descent on roads at the end.

55. **Levada Nova and Levada do Moinho from Ponta do Sol** *8m or 13km (5 or 8 miles) – 3hrs or 4hrs 30mins* Steps and steep roads are used for the optional ascent and descent. The Levada Nova crosses cliffs, is often very exposed and has a tunnel. The Levada do Moinho crosses very steep slopes, but is often well-vegetated.

56. **Levada Nova: Jangão to Ribeira Brava** *11km (6½ miles) – 3hrs 30mins* The levada has a level, easy path across cultivated and wooded slopes. Steep roads and flights of steps run down to the coast.

57. **Lombo do Mouro to Ribeira Brava** *11km (6½ miles) – 3hrs 30mins* The levada path is rough and stony as it crosses steep slopes. Later it runs through forest and gives way to a broad track. Steep roads and steps lead down to the coast.

58. **Porto Santo: Pico do Castelo, Pico do Facho and Pico Branco** *10km, 18km or 25km (6¼, 11 or 15 miles) – 3hrs 30mins, 6hrs or 8hrs* Mostly good tracks and paths on forested slopes, open slopes and sea cliffs, as well as road-walking and a rough and rocky coastal track.

59. **Porto Santo: Campo de Baixo, Bárbara Gomes and Eiras** *9km (5½ miles) – 3hrs* Road-walking at the start and finish, otherwise good tracks and paths on gentle scrubby slopes.

60. **Porto Santo: Ponta, Pico de Ana Ferreira, Espigão and Calheta** *14km (8¼ miles) – 5hrs* Road-walking at the start and finish, otherwise rugged slopes, vague paths and good tracks.

APPENDIX 2
Language notes

Days of the Week

Domingo	*Sunday*
Segunda-feira	*Monday*
Terça-feira	*Tuesday*
Quarta-feira	*Wednesday*
Quinta-feira	*Thursday*
Sexta-feira	*Friday*
Sábado	*Saturday*
2a–6a feira	*weekdays*

Transport and Timetables

Bus/Autocarro	*bus*
Paragem	*bus stop*
Carreira	*route number*
Chegadas	*arrivals*
Destino	*destination*
Duração da viagem	*journey time*
Feriados	*holidays*
Horários	*timetables*
Inicia no...	*departs from...*
Não se efectuam viagens no...	*doesn't run on...*
Não se realiza a...	*doesn't run on...*
Partidas	*departures*
Percurso	*route*
Regresso	*return*
Serviço	*service*
Só à 6a feira	*Fridays only*
Só no periodo escolar	*schooldays only*
Só no periodo não escolar	*school holidays only*
Todos os dias	*every day*

Food and Drink

Açorda	*bread soup*
Açúcar	*sugar*
Arroz	*rice*
Atum	*tuna*
Azeite	*olive oil*
Azeitonas	*olives*
Bacalhau	*salted cod*
Batata	*potato*
Batatas fritas	*chips*
Bebida	*drink*
Bolo do Caco	*bread (may contain meat!)*
Bolo do Mel	*honey (actually molasses) cake*
Café (com leite)	*black coffee (white)*
Caldeirada	*fish stew*
Caldo verde	*cabbage soup*
Carne	*meat*
Caseiro	*home-made*
Cebolla	*onion*
Cerveja	*beer*
Chã (com leite)	*black tea (white)*
Dourada	*golden bream*
Ensopada	*stew*
Espada	*black scabbard fish*
Espetada	*spicy skewered beef*
Farinha	*flour*
Frango	*chicken*
Gelado	*ice-cream*
Gelo	*ice*
Laranja	*orange*
Legumes	*vegetables*
Leite	*milk*

Maça	*apple*
Manteiga	*butter*
Maracúja	*passion fruit*
Marisco	*seafood*
Milho	*corn*
Ovos	*eggs*
Peixe	*fish*
Pequeno almoço	*breakfast*
Pimento	*pepper*
Porco	*pork*
Prato do dia	*dish of the day*
Queijo	*cheese*
Sal	*salt*
Salada	*salad*
Sobremesa	*dessert*
Sopa (de tomate e cebolla)	*soup (tomato and onion)*
Sumo	*juice*
Vino (branco/tinto)	*wine (white/red)*

Topographical Glossary

Achada	*Plateau*
Água	*Water*
Alto	*High*
Baia	*Bay*
Baixo	*Low*
Boca	*Col/Gap/Saddle*
Brava	*Wild*
Cabeço	*Head/Headland*
Cabo	*Cape/Headland*
Caldeirão	*Cauldron/Hollow*
Calheta	*Creek/Rivermouth*
Caminho	*Road/Path*
Campo	*Field/Plain*
Chão	*Flat area*
Cova	*Cave/Hollow*
Cruz	*Cross*
Cruzinhas	*Crossroads*
Curral	*Corral*
da/de/do/das/dos	*of the*

Eira	*Threshing floor*
Fajã	*Landslip*
Fonte	*Spring/Fountain*
Gordo	*Fat*
Grande	*Big/Large*
Igreja	*Church*
Levada	*Watercourse*
Lombada	*Long ridge*
Lombo	*Ridge/Crest*
Miradouro	*Viewpoint*
Monte	*Mountain*
Nova	*New*
Paúl	*Marsh*
Penha	*Cliff/Rocky*
Pequena	*Little/Small*
Pico	*Peak*
Ponta	*Point*
Porto	*Port/Harbour*
Posto Florestal	*Forestry Post*
Praia	*Beach*
Quebrada	*Steep slope*
Queimada	*Burnt*
Quinta	*Farm/Mansion*
Ribeira/Ribeiro	*River*
Rocha	*Rock*
Santo/São	*Saint*
Seixal	*Cobbly*
Serra	*Mountain range*
Torre	*Tower*
Vale	*Valley*
Velha	*Old*
Vereda	*Path*

APPENDIX 3

Useful contacts

Travel and Transport

Flights

Scheduled, charter and budget flights are available from many UK airports direct to Madeira. Direct flights to Porto Santo are rare, but the island can be reached by a 15-minute flight from Madeira.

Madeira Airports www.anam.pt
British Airways www.britishairways.com
Air Portugal www.flytap.com
Easyjet www.easyjet.com

Buses and Timetzables

A timetable summary booklet is available from tourist information offices, but it is not comprehensive. Either collect timetables from individual bus companies or check details of services online.

Horários do Funchal www.horariosdofunchal.pt
SAM www.sam.pt
Rodoeste www.rodoeste.pt

Porto Santo Line

The Porto Santo Line ferry, the Lobo Marinho, runs daily between Madeira and Porto Santo, taking about 2½hrs per crossing. The company can arrange accommodation for you, www.portosantoline.pt.

Madeira Islands Tourism

Tourist Information Office, Avenida Arriaga 16, Funchal, tel 291-211902. Open from 0900 to 2000 Monday to Friday and 0900 to 1800 at weekends, www.madeiraislands.travel. English-speaking staff can assist with queries about accommodation, transport, tours and visitor attractions. Smaller tourist information offices are found around Madeira.

Pontinha, Funchal, tel 291-281743.
Monumental Lido, Funchal, tel 291-775254.
Airport, Santa Catarina, tel 291-524933.
Caniço de Baixo, tel 291-932919.
Machico, tel 291-962289.
Ribeira Brava, tel 291-951675.
Lugar de Baixo, Ponta do Sol, tel 291-972850.
Câmara de Lobos, tel 291-943470.
Porto Moniz, tel 291-852555.
Santana, tel 291-572992.
Vila Baleira, Porto Santo, tel 291-982361.

Protected Areas

Much of the high mountainous area of Madeira is protected as the Parque Natural da Madeira. The rugged eastern end of the island is protected as the Reserva Natural da Ponta de São Lourenço. The native vegetation is being restored in an area north of Funchal, forming the Parque Ecológico do Funchal. A marine reserve is located east of Funchal: the Reserva Natural Parcial do Garajau. The whole of the Ilhas Desertas is protected by two reserves: the Reserva Natural Parcial and the Reserva Natural Integral. For details of protected areas around Madeira see www.pnm.pt. An interesting visitor centre at Porto Moniz, Centro Ciência Vivo, focuses on the *laurisilva*, www.ccvportomoniz.com.

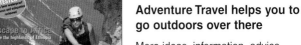

LISTING OF CICERONE GUIDES

BACKPACKING AND CHALLENGE WALKING
Backpacker's Britain:
  Vol 1 – Northern England
  Vol 2 – Wales
  Vol 3 – Northern Scotland
  Vol 4 – Central & Southern
           Scottish Highlands
Book of the Bivvy
End to End Trail
The National Trails
Three Peaks, Ten Tors

BRITISH CYCLING
Border Country Cycle Routes
Cumbria Cycle Way
Lancashire Cycle Way
Lands End to John O'Groats
Rural Rides:
  No 1 – West Surrey
  No 2 – East Surrey
South Lakeland Cycle Rides

PEAK DISTRICT AND DERBYSHIRE
High Peak Walks
Historic Walks in Derbyshire
The Star Family Walks – The Peak
  District & South Yorkshire
White Peak Walks:
  The Northern Dales
  The Southern Dales

MOUNTAINS OF ENGLAND AND WALES FOR COLLECTORS OF SUMMITS
Mountains of England & Wales:
  Vol 1 – Wales
  Vol 2 – England
Relative Hills of Britain

IRELAND
Irish Coast to Coast Walk
Irish Coastal Walks
Mountains of Ireland

THE ISLE OF MAN
Isle of Man Coastal Path
Walking on the Isle of Man

LAKE DISTRICT AND MORECAMBE BAY
Atlas of the English Lakes
Coniston Copper Mines
Cumbria Coastal Way
Cumbria Way and Allerdale Ramble
Great Mountain Days in the
  Lake District
Lake District Anglers' Guide
Lake District Winter Climbs
Lakeland Fellranger:
  The Central Fells
  The Mid-Western Fells
  The Near-Eastern Fells
  The Southern Fells
Roads and Tracks of the Lake District
Rocky Rambler's Wild Walks
Scrambles in the Lake District:
  North
  South

Short Walks in Lakeland:
  Book 1 – South Lakeland
  Book 2 – North Lakeland
  Book 3 – West Lakeland
Tarns of Lakeland:
  Vol 1 – West
  Vol 2 – East
Tour of the Lake District
Walks in Silverdale and Arnside

THE MIDLANDS
Cotswold Way

NORTHERN ENGLAND
LONG-DISTANCE TRAILS
Dales Way
Hadrian's Wall Path
Northern Coast to Coast Walk
Pennine Way
Teesdale Way

NORTH-WEST ENGLAND
OUTSIDE THE LAKE DISTRICT
Family Walks in the
  Forest of Bowland
Historic Walks in Cheshire
Ribble Way
Walking in the Forest of Bowland
  and Pendle
Walking in Lancashire
Walks in Lancashire Witch Country
Walks in Ribble Country

PENNINES AND NORTH-EAST ENGLAND
Cleveland Way and Yorkshire
  Wolds Way
Historic Walks in North Yorkshire
North York Moors
The Canoeist's Guide to the North-East
The Spirit of Hadrian's Wall
Yorkshire Dales – South and West
Walking in County Durham
Walking in Northumberland
Walking in the South Pennines
Walks in Dales Country
Walks in the Yorkshire Dales
Walks on the North York Moors:
  Books 1 and 2
Waterfall Walks – Teesdale and High
  Pennines
Yorkshire Dales Angler's Guide

SCOTLAND
Ben Nevis and Glen Coe
Border Country
Border Pubs and Inns
Central Highlands
Great Glen Way
Isle of Skye
North to the Cape
Lowther Hills
Pentland Hills
Scotland's Far North
Scotland's Far West
Scotland's Mountain Ridges

Scottish Glens:
  2 – Atholl Glens
  3 – Glens of Rannoch
  4 – Glens of Trossach
  5 – Glens of Argyll
  6 – The Great Glen
Scrambles in Lochaber
Southern Upland Way
Walking in the Cairngorms
Walking in the Hebrides
Walking in the Ochils, Campsie Fells
  and Lomond Hills
Walking on the Isle of Arran
Walking on the Orkney and Shetland
  Isles
Walking the Galloway Hills
Walking the Munros:
  Vol 1 – Southern, Central &
      Western
  Vol 2 – Northern and Cairngorms
West Highland Way
Winter Climbs – Ben Nevis and
  Glencoe
Winter Climbs in the Cairngorms

SOUTHERN ENGLAND
Channel Island Walks
Exmoor and the Quantocks
Greater Ridgeway
Lea Valley Walk
London – The Definitive Walking
  Guide
North Downs Way
South Downs Way
South West Coast Path
Thames Path
Walker's Guide to the Isle of Wight
Walking in Bedfordshire
Walking in Berkshire
Walking in Buckinghamshire
Walking in Kent
Walking in Somerset
Walking in Sussex
Walking in the Isles of Scilly
Walking on the Thames Valley
Walking on Dartmoor

WALES AND THE WELSH BORDERS
Ascent of Snowdon
Glyndwr's Way
Hillwalking in Snowdonia
Hillwalking in Wales:
  Vols 1 and 2
Lleyn Peninsula Coastal Path
Offa's Dyke Path
Pembrokeshire Coastal Path
Ridges of Snowdonia
Scrambles in Snowdonia
Shropshire Hills
Spirit Paths of Wales
Walking in Pembrokeshire
Welsh Winter Climbs

For full and up-to-date information on
our ever-expanding list of guides,
please visit our website:
www.cicerone.co.uk.

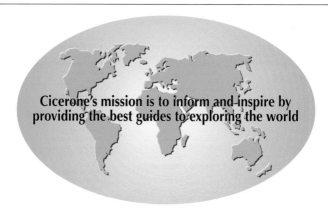

Cicerone's mission is to inform and inspire by providing the best guides to exploring the world

Since its foundation 40 years ago, Cicerone has specialised in publishing guidebooks and has built a reputation for quality and reliability. It now publishes nearly 300 guides to the major destinations for outdoor enthusiasts, including Europe, UK and the rest of the world.

Written by leading and committed specialists, Cicerone guides are recognised as the most authoritative. They are full of information, maps and illustrations so that the user can plan and complete a successful and safe trip or expedition – be it a long face climb, a walk over Lakeland fells, an alpine cycling tour, a Himalayan trek or a ramble in the countryside.

With a thorough introduction to assist planning, clear diagrams, maps and colour photographs to illustrate the terrain and route, and accurate and detailed text, Cicerone guides are designed for ease of use and access to the information.

If the facts on the ground change, or there is any aspect of a guide that you think we can improve, we are always delighted to hear from you.

Cicerone Press
2 Police Square Milnthorpe Cumbria LA7 7PY
Tel: 015395 62069 Fax: 015395 63417
info@cicerone.co.uk www.cicerone.co.uk

CICERONE